OUT OF THE DEPTHS

JOHN R. LAWSON
1942

OUT OF THE DEPTHS

The Story of John R. Lawson

a

Labor Leader

By

BARRON B. BESHOAR

THE COLORADO LABOR HISTORICAL COMMITTEE
OF THE
DENVER TRADES AND LABOR ASSEMBLY
1942

Printed in The United States of America
By
The World Press, Inc.
1837 Champa St., Denver, Colo.

"Out of the depths have I cried unto Thee, O Lord."

CONTENTS

CONTENTS

MAPS AND ILLUSTRATIONS

FOREWORD

Almost three decades have passed since the memorable Colorado coal strike of 1913-1914, an industrial struggle that left an indelible imprint on the civilized world. Labor and capital have come to grips on many occasions since those historic years, but, except for isolated instances which were little more than repeat performances, the differences have not been so broad in scope or so far reaching in their consequences. It was on the field of Ludlow, where the blood of strikers, their women and children, was shed by a subsidized soldiery, that labor finally established its right to share in such basic American principles as those of religious and political liberty, free speech and free assembly, and economic freedom. The 1913-1914 strike was not a purely Colorado matter as the state was merely the testing ground for two divergent principles of life. On the one hand, firmly entrenched and in full power and strength, were those who hold to the theory that all benefits properly trickle down from above, and on the other were those who devotedly maintain the democratic proposition that men and women who toil with their backs and hands are entitled to share in the fruits of their productive labor.

Colorado was the testing ground for several reasons. The great corporations of the East seized control of the natural resources of the state during its early, formative years. They invested their surpluses in the isolated holdings as business conditions warranted and they sought through crafty political arts a perpetuation of their absentee landlordism without regard for the desires of the people or the welfare of their own employes. That their policies and methods, which reached such full flower in Colorado, were both unbusinesslike and unmoral, has been demonstrated time and again in the years since 1913. It is a sad commentary on human intelligence and decency to record that it took a bloody war to expose the errors in all of their hideous implications and institute corrective measures, just as it required a war between the states to settle the slavery and federal questions.

Any story of the 1913-1914 strike must, of necessity, be the story of John R. Lawson who was the outstanding labor leader of the day. There were others who outranked him in the United Mine Workers of America, but none who equalled him in strike leadership or in the love and respect of the Colorado coal miners. He stood for the best in the union movement and has remained through the years a personification of honest, intelligent and capable leadership. While many of his colleagues, who held positions of trust and importance, sold themselves to the enemy or sought glory and personal power at the expense of the miners, John Lawson remained faithful to an ideal and devoted himself exclusively to the welfare of those who placed themselves under his care. His story and that of the strike are inseparably interwoven, so much so that the one cannot be told without the other. Much credit is due the United Mine Workers of America as an organization for the work it did in Colorado in 1913-1914. It spent much treasure, effort and blood in a glorious crusade, but John Lawson remains the outstanding figure. To him, both as a representative of the United Mine Workers and as an individual, the coal miners and labor generally owe the greatest measure of gratitude, respect and honor.

The record shows that the 1913-1914 strike was lost by the United Mine Workers, but in reality it was won. It is true that the great strike was brought to an end by the organization before its objectives were achieved, but public opinion, which had been aroused as never before or since in an industrial dispute, battered down the gates of the coal operators and in the end the miners and citizens of Colorado were the victors. It is fair to say that the citizens of the state shared in the victory because through it they were freed from a political domination that was as close to absolutism as anything ever attempted in a nation founded on such documents as the U. S. Constitution and the Bill of Rights.

To those who may feel the account is biased and prejudiced in favor of the coal miners and labor, the author must frankly admit his pro-union inclinations and beliefs. They are based, not upon sentiment, but upon the record in Colorado, a record that is clear and sustaining, and substantiated not once but many times by courts of record and the reports of impartial investigators.

The material contained herein is not fiction. It is factual. Perhaps at times the coal operators and their henchmen will appear too devilish and the coal miners too angelic. If this proves to be the case, the reader is asked to remember that there were honest, moral men on both sides, and that each camp had its share of the evil and criminally-minded. However, the opposing principles that motivated the coal operators and the miners give an implication to the story of 1913-1914 that is inescapable in any honest presentation.

Many of the coal operators believed their system was fundamental and necessary. They were sincere in their fear that union organization would spell the end of business enterprise and industrial freedom of the type cherished by boards of directors. Their psychology was not unlike that of the ruling class of a monarchy or a kingdom of a century ago. They had appropriated or inherited their wealth and believed it well within the realm of possibility for any deserving man to do likewise. It is charitable to believe that few of those who sat on the boards of the powerful coal corporations had any understanding of the lives and problems of their workers.

If the mine guards and detectives, those cruel mercenaries who served as the Gestapo of the coal districts, appear villainous, the author will be pleased. If they appear to be vile scoundrels without a trace of human decency, who sold themselves and their fellowmen for a few corporation dollars, he will consider them adequately presented.

This book was conceived by the Denver Trades and Labor Assembly in a praiseworthy desire to preserve an important chapter in United States and Colorado Labor history. The members of an historical committee have been patient and kind. They have not allowed their own intense unionism to override a sense of justice or prevent the giving of a word of praise to the opponents of the coal miners of 1913-1914 where due. They have not held that unionists are perfect or that industrial managers are invariably wicked. They have seen the motes in union eyes as well as those in the eyes of employers. They have given freely of their time and efforts, and have provided many of the records necessary for the preparation of this volume.

Thanks are due, too, to John R. Lawson for his assistance though his innate sense of modesty made him a reluctant and oftentimes unwilling witness to the events of 1913-1914 where John R. Lawson was directly concerned. However, his colleagues and the record have supplied details of incidents that he waved aside as unworthy of mention because he was involved.

The author would also like to express appreciation to John Van Male of Denver, a member of the staffs of the Denver Public Library and the University of Denver library, whose clear conception of Colorado's industrial history and its significance has been of invaluable assistance. Appreciation is also due Edward Keating, editor of the newspaper *Labor* in Washington, D. C., who served as a congressman from Colorado in 1913-1914; to Edward Doyle, a member of a railway brotherhood and secretary-treasurer of the United Mine Workers in strike days; to Miss Mary Van Kleeck and Edward A. Wieck of the Russell Sage Foundation, and to Lee Taylor Casey, associate editor of the Rocky Mountain News of Denver, whose knowledge of the subject was gained from personal observations as a reporter during the coal wars and from a close study of Colorado history in the years that followed. A number of former coal operators and men who served in the Colorado militia have also aided, but, for obvious reasons, have asked that their names not be mentioned.

And lastly, the author would like to stress that the work was undertaken, not with the intention of rubbing salt in old wounds, but in the hope that it may contribute something toward a better understanding of unionism, of the differences that have resulted in strife in the past, and of the errors on both sides to the end that more amicable relations may exist in the future between the men who sign the payroll and those who cash the checks.

BARRON B. BESHOAR,
Denver, Colorado.

Oct. 30, 1941

AN INTRODUCTION

BY EDWARD KEATING
(Editor of Labor, Washington, D. C.)

In preparing the story of John Lawson, the labor movement of Denver and Colorado, is rendering not only a unique, but also a very valuable service. Strong, capable, self-sacrificing and self-effacing—a noble character—Lawson symbolizes thousands of leaders of the labor movement, in this and other countries, who organized and directed great struggles for economic justice.

Most of them lie in unmarked graves. A few have been privileged to help reap the harvest and to receive the plaudits of those whom they served.

Arraigned before a crooked judge and packed jury, John Lawson narrowly missed the hangman's noose. Powerful interests, backed by untold wealth, sought to put him away and would have succeeded had a free and just Supreme Court not intervened. In the quarter of a century that has elapsed since Lawson was freed, he has been an honored citizen of the commonwealth which sought to take his life for crimes he had never committed.

In selecting Mr. Beshoar to prepare this volume, the labor movement made a happy choice. Mr. Beshoar comes from pioneer stock. His grandfather, Dr. Michael Beshoar, is almost a legendary character in Southern Colorado. A man of means, he could, with Robert Emmet, have boasted, "I might have been among the proudest of my country's oppressors," but, like

Emmet, Dr. Michael and the members of his family, for three generations, have been on the workers' side in all those grim struggles which have stained with blood the hills and valleys of the coal counties.

With such a background, Mr. Beshoar brings to his task the all-essential elements of sympathy and understanding.

There are in this country groups which very fervently defend what might be described as the cycle theory. The weather, business depressions, wars, almost every event which seriously affects the inhabitants of this mundane sphere is a part of some cycle, according to these earnest people.

I neither affirm nor deny that they have discovered something worth knowing, but with my own eyes I have seen a curious sort of cycle in Colorado.

In 1893-94, Colorado had strikes of the most serious character throughout the mining towns. The most spectacular development was in Cripple Creek, then a comparatively new camp.

The mine owners brought in an army of gunmen. The miners threw up intrenchments on Bull Hill. Gov. Davis H. Waite, a Populist, sent in the militia to save the miners and restore industrial peace.

A group of vigilantes, organized by the mine owners, invaded the Antlers Hotel, in the heart of Colorado Springs, seized T. J. Tarsney, adjutant general of state militia, and treated him to a coat of tar and feathers.

This grievous assault on a high official of the state, who was performing a duty assigned him by the chief executive, was never punished. With the exception of the old Rocky Mountain News, then owned by Senator Tom Patterson, practically all the newspapers in Colorado condoned the crime. There wasn't a murmur of protest from the press outside the state.

I have often wondered what those same newspapers would have said if a group of trade unionists had seized and tarred and feathered an adjutant general of a state while he was on active duty in the field.

Ten years later, in 1903-04, Colorado had another convulsion. This time Gov. James H. Peabody, a Republican, was in the Statehouse, and Sherman Bell, wearing a $1,000 uniform, commanded the state militia. All the mining camps were tied up by strikes. The governor placed the militia at the disposal of the mine owners. Miners were rounded up, loaded in box cars, taken to the border of Kansas in some instances and to the border of New Mexico in others, dumped out on the prairie and, after a volley had been fired over their heads, warned never to return to the state.

Finally, at the end of another 10-year cycle, came the Rockefeller strike of 1913-14, in which John Lawson played such a conspicuous part and which culminated in the Massacre of Ludlow.

I believe more lives were sacrificed on both sides in that struggle than in any other industrial struggle in the history of this country. It is difficult to sustain that claim with precise figures, because no one knows just how many lives were lost.

At the outset, this struggle appeared hopeless. It would have been hopeless if it hadn't been for John Lawson and his devoted associates—men like Edward Doyle and Frank Hayes, once president of the United Mine Workers of America and more recently lieutenant governor of Colorado.

The record shows the strike was lost. As a matter of fact, it was won.

When the United Mine Workers called off the strike in the Spring of 1915, the Rockefellers were badly battered. Public sentiment was emphatically against them. Word went out from No. 26 Broadway that for the present there must be no more labor disturbances on Rockefeller properties. In Colorado, especially, that mandate was rigidly enforced.

Taking advantage of the situation, Rockefeller's miners flocked into the union, and for the first time in its history, the Rockefeller steel plant in Pueblo was organized.

John D. Jr., accompanied by William Lyon Mackenzie King, now premier of Canada, visited his Colorado coal properties and, with the assistance of Mr. King, set up the first of America's company unions. However, he did not dare force his men to join this fake organization and, for all practical purposes, the regular unions were in control.

The strike produced an equally significant triumph in the political field. For a quarter of a century, the coal magnates, including the Rockefellers, dominated the politics of the coal counties. They owned all public officials, from the judge on the bench, through the various county and city offices, to the humblest worker on a public payroll. Anyone who dared defy them was in constant danger of physical reprisal. More than one man was murdered, and scores were beaten and driven out of the country.

Elections were farcical performances. The coal company employees were voted like sheep. They were counted even if they didn't go to the polls. In state and national elections, the coal counties could be depended upon to turn in such majorities as the coal moguls directed. The strike of 1913-14 changed all this.

What I have written has to do only with one episode in John Lawson's life, but it was perhaps his greatest fight and his greatest victory. If he had done no more, that one achievement would be sufficient to entitle him to a place in Labor's Hall of Fame, but he has done much more, as Mr. Beshoar will tell you.

"It is the command of Ludlow's living dead."
                                —George Creel

Denver, Colo., April 27, 1914.

CHAPTER I
THE COAL FIELDS

Hatred and despair gripped the polyglot peoples of the Colorado coal districts as the violent Winter of 1907 gave way to a mountain excuse for Spring. Far underground, in labyrinths of gaseous shafts, thousands of men toiled long hours each day with a sullenness matched only in the squatty mules that tugged at overladen coal cars and watched with wicked eyes for a chance to crush a skull or rip a shoulder. The miners hated the mules, and they hated each other, but most of all they hated their employers with all the intensity of simple men who rankle under abuses which they feel powerless either to correct or escape. The Scotch, the Welsh and the Irish miners, who had seen thousands of their blood brothers driven from the coal fields after the strike of 1903, loathed the hordes of foreigners gathered by enterprising labor agents of the coal barons from the Mediterranean countries and the far corners of Europe and Asia to take the places of the rebels of 1903. The newcomers, in turn, despised each other, according to race. The Italians looked down on the Greeks, the Greeks scorned the Poles as social inferiors, and the latter had only contempt for the skinny-armed Mexicans. They were united only in their hatred for their employers and their belief that Japanese were scum of the worst sort.

They lived in wretched, isolated camps strung along the slopes

1

of twisting canons on either side of the coal mine with its unpainted shafthouse, breaker buildings and powerhouse. The single men lived in company-owned boarding houses and those with families in company-owned houses and shanties, barren little homes that reared their weather-beaten boards above piles of ashes and tin cans. Public roads ran through the canons, but at the approach to each camp a gate and a sign, "Private Property—Keep Out." barred the way. Armed guards, employed by the coal company and deputized by the sheriff of the county, watched over the gates and kept order in the camps. The term "to keep order" had an interpretation all its own in the coal camps. Men could get as drunk as they pleased in a company saloon, carouse about with daughters of joy, and brawl with fists or knives without undue interference from the camp marshal or his deputies. It was only when strangers made their way into camp on business that the superintendent in his great wisdom considered inimical to the company, or when the miners found fault with their way of life that the marshal's brand of order was rigidly enforced. Fault-finders, individually or collectively, were not tolerated in these closed camps. Intruders and malcontents were ferreted out by an intricate espionage system and treated by heavily-armed guards to the kangaroo, the coal district term for a professional beating. Along with the kangaroo went the dread sentence of "Down the canon." And to go "down the canon" meant blacklisting and starvation—or exile.

Each marshal was responsible only to the company superintendent, the all-powerful local agent of men who were little more than names to the coal miners, the executive officers and directors of such wealthy, far-flung corporations as The Victor-American Fuel Company, The Rocky Mountain Fuel Company, and the Rockefellers' own Colorado Fuel & Iron Company which was the largest and most influential in the Colorado coal fields. Both superintendents and mashals encouraged racial dislikes and animosities on the theory that the more the men were divided the less likely they were to exchange ideas and discuss possible grievances.

Below the closed or privately owned camps, where the canons emptied out into broad valleys and rolling prairie country, lay the so-called open towns that were the business centers of the coal fields. In the southern part of the state, where most of the coal was mined, these towns, with their railroad spurs reaching up to the camps, were theoretically free from corporation control, but in actual practice they, too, were subject to the wishes and whims of the powerful coal operators and their agents.

Such a town was Walsenburg, a city of 4,000 in the heart of the southern field, when John R. Lawson, international organizer for the United Mine Workers of America and a member of the union's international board, arrived there in the late Spring of 1907 to establish headquarters for an organization campaign. A man of thirty, Lawson gave an immediate impression of great strength. His broad shoulders, slim waist, and springy step gave evidence of his years in the amateur prize ring. Although his face was free from ring marks and as smooth and serene as that of any well-situated Episcopal clergyman, it was saved from any suggestion of complacency by a strong, well-set jaw and a pair of steady blue eyes that could chill an adversary as quickly as they could win the confidence of a child. John Lawson had moved west from his native Mt. Carmel, Pa., where he had started work in a coal mine as a breaker boy at the age of eight, to find steadier work and better pay. He had found neither and the disappointments, coupled with the lessons he had learned from his big Scotch father, who had been a member of the Knights of Labor, led him to the United Mine Workers of America. His first job in Colorado had been in the C. F. & I. Company's big Walsen Mine on the western outskirts of Walsenburg. He had worked there as a coal digger for several months and then, sickened by the brutality and tyranny of the mine management, had moved across the

COLORADO

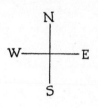

Northern Coal Fields

BOULDER
LOUISVILLE
LAFAYETTE
FREDERICK
ERIE
Columbine Mine
Hecla Mine

DENVER

COLORADO SPRINGS

CAÑON CITY   FLORENCE

PUEBLO
(C.F.+I Steel Mill)

Southern Coal Fields

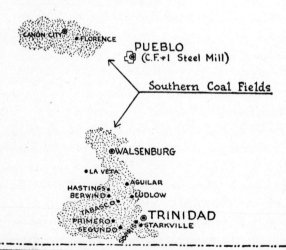

WALSENBURG

LA VETA

HASTINGS
BERWIND
AGUILAR
LUDLOW

TABASCO
PRIMERO
SEGUNDO
SOPRIS
TRINIDAD
STARKVILLE

〰️〰️ Miners' Tent
〰️ Colony
◎ WALSENBURG

To LA VETA

N
W —┼— E
S

Miners Tent
〰️〰️ Colony
◎ AGUILAR

Black Hills.
Where miners
reorganized after
Ludlow massacre.

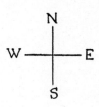

PRYOR ●
ROUSE ●

〰️〰️ Miners' Tent
〰️〰️ Colony
Union
● Headquarters

DELAGUA ●   Militia
HASTINGS ◎   Camp 〰️〰️   ◎ LUDLOW
                          Depot, Saloon
                          and Post office

BERWIND ●   ● FORBES
TABASCO ●   〰️〰️ Miners' Tent Colony

            ● SUFFIELD
            〰️〰️ Tent Colony

         ◎ TRINIDAD
           ● Camp Beshoar

PRIMERO ●
SEGUNDO ●
VALDEZ ●
COKEDALE ●
SOPRIS ●
           ● STARKVILLE
           〰️〰️ Tent Colony

           ● MORLEY

mountains to Colorado's Western Slope and the coal mines of the New Castle district.

Although the big corporations did not operate in this district, he had found conditions little better. In desperation, he had led an impromptu strike that was local in character. It had failed, but the experience had made him a leader in the unsuccessful strike of 1903, a strike in which he had suffered as had few other United Mine Worker leaders. His home had been dynamited along with those of three other strikers. His wife, Olive, and their baby daughter, Fern, had barely escaped from the wreckage. The miners blamed Perry C. Coryell, a mine owner, for the explosions, but were unable to bring him to trial. When the investigations ended, Lawson worked in a number of small mines, but he was unable to keep a job. Each time he obtained work, the mine was sabotaged.

"Sorry, John," the owners had told him. "You're a good miner, but we can't afford to keep you. Somebody, maybe it is Coryell, wants you."

Lawson had gone to Nevada and then returned to New Castle when Coryell bragged in his newspaper, the New Castle Non Pariel, that he had driven John Lawson from the district. They met in a barbershop. That meeting, in a way, was responsible for Lawson's presence in Walsenburg for it had brought him to the attention of every miner in Colorado and the nation. Unarmed and defenseless, he had been shot down by the mine owner. A blast from Coryell's shotgun left John Lawson crippled for months, but it had raised him to prominence and driven Coryell from the state.

The New Castle struggles had led Lawson naturally into union organization work and back to Walsenburg, the county seat of Huerfano County. The town was similar in appearance to many other small towns in the United States. The business section consisted of a long thoroughfare, appropriately named Main Street, lined with the usual mercantile stores, blacksmith shops, livery stables, hardware stores, and a generous number of saloons and cafes. The doctors and other professional men had their offices upstairs in the two-story buildings, structures that sported tawdry fronts that protruded over the sidewalks in a brazen manner remindful of the ample bosoms of the town's many ladies of the night. The people were typical of those in mining and industrial sections of Ohio, Pennsylvania and West Virginia, a hard lot, warped by poverty, ignorance and unending toil in the gaseous, dust-filled mines. Walsenburg's distinction, and it was one shared by Trinidad and other towns in the Southern Colorado coal district, was to be found in its politics. The Huerfano County courthouse, an ugly, gray stone building of uncertain architecture, was considered by many as little more than a branch office of the C. F. & I. Co. though citizens who held such opinions seldom voiced them in more than a whisper. The political boss and majordomo for the C. F. & I. Co. was Sheriff Jefferson Farr, a squinty-eyed, red-faced Texan who was, perhaps, best described by a fellow citizen as "that animated beer barrel."

According to his own lights, Jeff Farr was a pretty decent citizen. He had the 100 per cent American's contempt for the uneducated foreigners who toiled in the mines, and a respect that was akin to reverence for the mine owners. Jeff saw, too, the vices of the workers, their brutality and baseness. He never bothered about their redeeming qualities nor wondered if the operating methods of the coal barons might be in some measure responsible for the condition of the miners and their families. Jeff's philosophy was built around the belief that "coal has got to be dug and by God somebody has got to dig it." It cannot be denied that Jeff had his admirers. Many Colorado residents, and some of them were the very best people, saw in him a stalwart personification of law and order, a Horatius who could be counted on to stand fast when the status quo in the coal fields was subjected to assault.

Jeff's enemies, and they were more numerous than his friends, saw nothing but evil in him. The more charitable ones called him Czar Farr and his county the "Kingdom of Huerfano." They pointed to his control of saloons, to property holdings that were hardly in keeping with his visible income as sheriff, to his political methods, and to his complete subservience to the coal operators whose wishes were obviously more sacred to Jeff than the statutes he was sworn to uphold. If a butcher, grocer, or dairyman questioned Sheriff Farr's authority in matters political or sought to vote other than a straight Republican ticket, the offender went to jail on a trumped up charge of violating some food or sanitation law. Doctors and lawyers who failed to follow Jeff's lead found themselves without a practice. The coal company's control of moneys and credits enabled Jeff to keep the businessmen well in hand. When a man was tried in District Court, Jeff sat near the jury box and signalled its occupants in much the same way that the ancient Romans signalled the fate of a Christian—thumb up for freedom, thumb down for conviction and woe to the juryman who failed to understand or obey.

One Walsenburg physician, who dared raise his voice against Jeff, was promptly arrested on a charge of immoral practice, and held many weeks without trial. The intervention of the Eagles, a powerful fraternal order that provided some measure of democracy and fellowship in Huerfano County, was all that saved the man of medicine from complete ruin. Common laborers who rebelled against Jeff received less consideration. They were beaten by gunmen or shot down. There was no prosecution for such attacks or murders, as the attackers wore silver stars and were the agents of the law.

With the efficient Jeff Farr on the job, Lawson faced a difficult task in Walsenburg. It was his job to organize the miners into union locals as quickly and as quietly as possible. Others had tried and failed, not because the miners didn't want organization, but because of the vigilance of coal company watchdogs. Some of Lawson's predecessors had been broken in body and spirit before being driven from the county and state; still others had been murdered by persons unknown to the coroner's jury.

Sheriff Farr and his deputies worked in close cooperation with the camp marshals and the special agents of W. H. Reno, chief detective for the C. F. & I. Co. Spies and informers kept Sheriff Farr and Detective Reno advised of the movements of every stranger. Despite a close watch, Lawson managed to arrange for meetings with the miners through union sympathizers whose names were furnished him by the Denver office of the union. The first meeting was held on a mountain side, far above a C. F. & I. camp. The miners came in groups of two or three and seated themselves about a pinon fire in a sheltered cleft. They were silent and grim, like so many brigands gathered to plot a secret foray. They knew they would receive no protection from a 10-year-old statute that made it illegal for an employer to discourage or prevent an employe from joining or belonging to a lawful labor organization.

Before he spoke, Lawson studied the men gathered about him. They were a confused lot, he knew. They didn't know who or what to believe. They had heard as many unfavorable stories about union leaders as about coal operators. Impromptu rebellions had been put down by the coal operators with an iron hand, and the United Mine Workers had not come to their aid. They didn't know that organization had to be on a large scale to stand any chance of success. Time and again they had been sold out by corrupt leaders. They were afraid even to discuss their problems. The sunken-cheeked Greek across the circle had a wild eye, but he might be gloating over the silver he would receive for a report to the marshal instead of exulting in an organization drive and a promise of economic freedom. When Lawson spoke to the men, he was brief and to the point:

"Brothers, the time is near at hand. The Constitution of the United States guarantees your personal and political freedom. You are entitled to an eight-hour day, and you have the right to bargain collectively with your employers for a living wage, for decent housing, for honest weights on the coal you dig, and for the right to trade where you please."

He named a few of the abuses—the system that compelled miners to accept coal company scrip and buy in company-owned stores at exorbitant prices, the requirement that they buy their powder from the company at high prices, and the manipulation of coroner's juries to avoid payment of death awards to widows and orphans. The juries almost invariably found the luckless miner came to his death through his own negligence regardless of the fact that most deaths resulted from poor timbering or explosions of gases and coal dust.

"You all know that safety precautions are not taken," Lawson told the men. "All of you have seen fathers, brothers and friends die horrible deaths because the coal companies will not even obey the inadequate laws on the books of the state. You know and I know they find it cheaper to get more men than to make their mines reasonably safe. You know and I know they value a mule more highly than a human being."

He reminded them of company restrictions on personal liberty. The mails were watched. Those who received letters, magazines or newspapers from sources considered inimical to the management were liable to instant discharge and a trip down the canon. The regular Protestant minister was employed by the company and held his post as long as his teachings did not conflict with the practices of the camp overlords. The teacher was as shackled in the classroom as the preacher in the pulpit.

When the brief meeting ended, a number of miners filled out union applications and then slipped off into the darkness. When the last one had left, Lawson put out the fire and picked his way carefully along the mountain side to avoid the camp below. He had made a start. Much could be accomplished if he could only have a little time. There was a small, hidden union nucleus in each camp to work with, and the rest of the miners were chafing under company oppression. When he reached Walsenburg, Lawson made his way through vacant lots and little-used streets to the comparative safety of his room.

Early the next morning, Lawson learned from union sources that Detective Reno had advised Jeff Farr by telegraph to get Lawson out of Walsenburg and the county. Jeff Farr moved promptly. That same night, as Lawson walked up Main Street from a restaurant, he passed Sheriff Farr and a man known as Johnson. The two men were sitting in front of a saloon. Lawson walked by them without so much as a glance in their direction. Before he had gone a dozen yards, he heard swift footsteps behind him. Lawson kept walking until the pursuer was close behind him, then he whirled. The stalker proved to be Sheriff Farr's companion. A large man, plainly dressed, Johnson did not look like a Huerfano County official. His pink cheeks betrayed the fact that he was new to this sun-baked country.

"I want to speak to you a minute," Johnson said.

"Certainly, go ahead," Lawson replied.

"I've been appointed by a committee of citizens to tell you it is time for you to leave Huerfano County," Johnson said menacingly.

"Is that so? Who are you, anyway?"

"My name is Johnson."

"Who appointed you to look after me, Mr. Johnson?"

"A committee of businessmen."

"Are you an officer of the law?"

"No, I'm not," Johnson replied, a little nervously. "I am a businessman, from Hastings."

"I see," Lawson said with a short laugh. "You don't know this section of the country very well, do you Mr. Johnson? Let me help you. Hastings, where you are in business, is in Las Animas County, the next county to the south."

Johnson scowled, but before he could reply, two men came lurching down the street. They appeared to be very drunk. Lawson backed against the window of a store so they would have to pass in front of him. The two men asked Johnson where they could find a room and when he growled, "Go on around the corner," they stalked off, walking straight and soberly.

"Well, Mr. Johnson," Lawson said politely. "I am an American citizen, and I have just as much right in Walsenburg as you or any other man. When and if I violate a law here the proper officers can attend to it, not some Hastings businessman. Goodnight."

He walked across the sidewalk and into the deserted street. The two thugs were probably still waiting around the corner. Johnson followed as far as the curb.

"A word to the wise, Lawson. I've warned you."

"Again I'll bid you goodnight," Lawson replied.

He went straight to his hotel room where he found a fellow organizer who had arrived from Trinidad during the afternoon. Pale and frightened, the man told Lawson he had received a warning from a Hastings businessman.

"It was in a saloon," the organizer said excitedly. "I appealed to Ed Steele, the bartender, and do you know what he told me?"

"No, what did he say?"

"He said, 'Well, brother, when they hang the Indian sign on a man in this country he gets out.' I think maybe that is good advice. Hell, all we're getting out of this is wages anyway."

"Any man who is in this business for wages is a fool," Lawson said angrily. "You'd better get out right away."

He saw the organizer off in the morning and then made a tour of the business houses to check up on Johnson's story. When he related the experience, the businessmen stared at him dumbly and then turned away though one little shopkeeper managed to summon up enough courage to whisper, "This committee is made up of Jeff Farr and his deputies. You'd better leave town."

Lawson left the store and turned toward the courthouse. He found Jeff Farr in his office.

"I've violated no law here and I claim the same protection as any other citizen," Lawson said after he had made his complaint about Johnson.

Farr leaned back in his swivel chair. His pig-like eyes nar-
rowed, and his upper lip curled into a sneer as he folded his
hands over his protruding stomach.

"Never heard of this Johnson, and besides your story sounds
like a lot of bull," he said. "You know, Lawson, sometimes citizens of a town find it advisable to urge a stranger to move on."

"I've never been run out of a town yet," Lawson replied
evenly. "I don't intend to begin here."

"You've been organizing around here, and we don't go for
that sort of thing in these parts. It's time you moved on."

Lawson grinned at Jeff and at half a dozen deputies who were
lounging about the room: "I know you don't worry much about
laws, but nonetheless citizens do have certain rights—even in
Huerfano County."

He had not walked three blocks from the courthouse when he
again heard swift footsteps behind him. He turned and saw
Severio Martinez, the town marshal, and his assistant, Vigil,
running toward him and calling to him to stop.

Severio Martinez, a Farr man, was known as Shorty to his
intimates. He was six feet six and appeared even taller in his
high-heeled boots and Texas hat. His huge, black mustache
gave him a comic opera appearance, but in reality he was deadly.

"Well," Lawson said as they caught up with him. "What is
the matter this time?"

"You're under arrest." Martinez placed a heavy hand on
Lawson's shoulder, a hand that trembled slightly.

"All right," Lawson said calmly. "What for?"

"You've been going around looking into people's doors and
going into their houses."

Lawson laughed. His natural good humor was restored. He
had been looking for sudden violence, or even subtlety, but this
was child's play.

"I have a right to go into a man's house if I am invited,
haven't I?" he asked with a chuckle.

Martinez was disconcerted.

"Anyway you are under arrest."

"Yes, I know. You told me that before."

"Haven't you got a gun?"

Lawson laughed again. "What would a man want with a gun in a lovely town like this?" he asked.

The marshal reached into his own capacious pocket and pulled out an absurd little nickel-plated revolver. He laid it against Lawson's coat and asked, "What have you got there?"

"That trick was a chestnut when I was a small boy." Lawson's voice was teasing, contemptuous.

"Just the same you're under arrest for carrying concealed weapons," Martinez muttered.

Lawson was taken to the little jail behind the courthouse and the nickel-plated revolver was returned to its place in Jeff Farr's office.[1]

Lawson's request for permission to telephone a lawyer was denied, and the next morning he was taken before Justice of the Peace Hunt and sentenced to 30 days in jail and fined $50 for carrying concealed weapons. A union lawyer from Trinidad, Jack Hendricks, got him out of the filthy jail a week later by appealing the justice case to County Court. The case was then dropped. That same day, the corporations ordered the arrest of union organizers in Trinidad. The Las Animas County sheriff did not bother with a frameup. Deputy Sheriff Thatcher rounded up Joseph Sharp, a member of the UMWA international board from Iowa, who was in charge of the Trinidad office, and his assistants, Tom Fenolio, Harry Douthwaite, and John Mc-Lennan. Lawson went to Trinidad to take care of the mine workers' office. When the organizers were released a few days later, Deputy Thatcher gave them a lecture.

"You boys had better high tail it out of this country if you know what is good for you. We can jail you twice a year and hold you six months each time. That goes for Lawson, too."

[1] U. S. Commission on Industrial Relations, Report on Colorado Strike, 1915. P. 60.

Lawson stayed on in Trinidad, aiding with the organization work in Las Animas County as he had done about all that could be done in Huerfano County for the present. By December it had become almost impossible for an organizer to appear on a street in a Southern Colorado town without being subjected to a sudden assault. They traveled in pairs after one of their number, Alex Oberlinsky, a skilled organizer, was attacked and killed by a Mexican gunman in near-by Rugby. A coal company official, posing as a deputy U. S. marshal, saved the murderer from an angry crowd and promptly disappeared with him.

The next attack was made on Sharp, who was slugged in the Trinidad office by a Negro. The next day, while walking along Commercial Street in Trinidad with John Lawson, Sharp was attacked a second time. A thug known as Warford crept up behind the two organizers on a crowded sidewalk and cracked Sharp over the head with the butt of a heavy pistol. Sharp staggered and cried out. Lawson turned just in time to see Warford on tiptoe, gun upraised for a second blow. Lawson hit straight from the shoulder and saw the thug go down. A half dozen gunmen came running from doorways as Lawson grabbed Sharp's arm and forced the injured man to run. No effort was made by the Trinidad authorities to arrest or punish Warford. He was saved for a violent death in a subsequent strike in Cripple Creek.

Lawson went to Denver and, after a conference with other union leaders, led a delegation to the State Capitol to obtain the aid of Rev. Henry Augustus Buchtel, governor of Colorado and chancellor of the University of Denver, a Methodist institution. The members of the committee hoped to appeal to Governor Buchtel's sense of fair play although they believed him to be a coal company tool. They knew that coal company money had gone into his campaign chest in sizeable amounts, and that he had the reputation of doing the bidding of the coal barons and the Denver corporations.

After some delay, the delegation was ushered into the governor's office. The Reverend Buchtel sat behind his desk, ear trumpet cocked in their direction.

"I don't have much time for you," he said abruptly. "Please state your case as briefly as possible."

The opening was inauspicious, but the union men took turns relating company abuses and reciting deeds of terrorism in the southern coal fields.

"We want assurances of protection from . . ." Lawson got no further as Buchtel broke in on him impatiently.

"You men can stay away from the southern fields," he said peevishly. "It is my understanding the miners in that section of the state have no grievances. John Mitchell tried to organize those men in 1903 and failed because they didn't want to join the United Mine Workers. Those miners down there are well paid. They have a snap of it. They don't want to join your union, and you are not going to use me as a club to make them join."

The union leaders pointed out the failure of the coal companies to observe a state law requiring semi-monthly payment of wages.

"I have reason to believe the coal companies are obeying all of the laws," Governor Buchtel said. "They pay only once a month because the miners' wives petitioned them to pay only once a month. They think one drunk a month is enough for their husbands."

"I never heard of such a petition, and I don't think any one else has," Lawson said. "What about their paying in scrip? That practice is contrary to the laws of this state."

"It is done," the governor replied, "for the convenience of the miners."

"But the miners can draw their pay in scrip and get drunk every night if they want to—in a company saloon," Lawson objected.

Governor Buchtel was argued into a number of contradictions. When he saw he had no case, he lost his temper.

"I want you to understand," he cried, "that this is not a court of justice."

His face crimson with anger, George Halley, president of the State Federation of Labor, arose and, leaning across the desk, yelled into the governor's ear trumpet: "It's plain that it isn't."

The members of the committee left the State Capitol, angry and at the same time amused. The solution of their problem did not lie with this irascible creature. They knew that much, and they knew, too, that they had no further hope of compelling enforcement of state laws. The statutes were dead letters. A strike would have been the path of desperation and one the union could not follow. The financial panic of 1907 was paralyzing industry. The coal operators would welcome a strike under such circumstances as it would provide an excuse to shut down and lay the blame on union shoulders. At a secret conference in Denver, the union chieftans agreed the coal companies were trying to force a strike. The union had no money with which to wage a battle. Union headquarters in Trinidad were ordered closed and all organizers who were known to the gunmen and law enforcement officers in the coal fields were ordered back to Denver. To all appearances, the union organization had simply collapsed. No representatives of the United Mine Workers remained in the field or the coal towns except secret agents. Branch organizations were no longer formed. As new men were enrolled, they were given special cards as members of the international union. The recruits were not affiliated with a union local nor did they know each other as union members. In this manner, the company spy system was frustrated.

Deceived by this strategy, the C. F. & I. and the Victor-American Fuel companies became more confident of their power than ever before. Abuses of long standing, which had been tempered somewhat while the organizers were in Southern Colorado, were revived and intensified. Oppressive tactics were employed everywhere, but they merely served to aid the work of secret organization. Revolt was in the air.

CHAPTER II
STRIKE OF 1910

While the secret organization work in the south was carried on into 1908, John Lawson craftily diverted the attention of the operators by a drive to completely unionize the mines in the northern part of the state. The mines of Jefferson, Boulder and Weld counties, west and north of Denver, were not as important as those in the south either in production or number of men employed, but they were more accessible and offered better prospects for an organization campaign. There were no closed camps or easily guarded canons as the mines were located in the midst of a rich farming area, and the miners lived away from company-owned property. Many owned their own homes in such towns as Lafayette, Louisville, Superior, Erie and Frederick. During the slack seasons, they worked their own little patches of land or hired out to neighboring farmers. There was little opportunity for mine superintendents to control elections and, as a result, few public officials found it worth their while to ape Jefferson Farr or his methods. There were sheriffs in the northern part of the state who were impartial or even friendly to coal miners. There was comparatively little danger of the kangaroo or the split head.

The field was similar, however, to the southern in mine abuses if not in political control. The Rocky Mountain Fuel Co., the Consolidated Coal and Coke Co., were neither better nor worse than the C. F. & I. and Victor-American as far as methods were concerned. They took every possible advantage of their miners and sternly repressed crude attempts at collective bargaining. There were several union locals in the field, but they lacked numerical strength and morale. Their position was weakened by the open shop policy of the southern field. Coal operators might quarrel with each other over business and indulge in unsound price wars, but they usually presented a united front when they faced labor.

Lawson found a familiar undertone of discontent and rebellion in the district. Checkweighmen were tolerated in a number of mines, but there was constant trouble about weights. A ton of coal might weigh a theoretical 2,000 pounds in school textbooks, but in actual practice a miner had to dig from 2,500 to 2,800 pounds of coal to get credit for a ton on the operator's scales. On his first trip through the northern mining areas, Lawson learned that at several mines the scale hand weights had been loaded with lead. Edward Doyle, an official of the Lafayette union local and a mine checkweighman, supplied him with specific instances of such frauds. Lawson found a strong ally in Doyle, a strapping young Irishman with an infectious grin and a spontaneity that belied his cunning and resourcefulness. He, too, had started in the mines as a small boy.

"I guess I was raised a union man," he told Lawson. "My mother always said I was still nursing when I joined the Knights of Labor and that my voice hadn't changed when I went into the United Mine Workers."

Lawson and his associates quickly organized the entire field and in June, 1908, moved to obtain a contract for the miners in the Louisville-Lafayette area. After first refusing to meet with them, the coal operators finally agreed to a conference. The negotiations, if such they could be called, quickly bogged down, and on the morning of June 19, James McCune, president of the Lafayette local, and P. M. Brillhart, its secretary, issued a notice to the miners, threatening strike. The threat, coupled with the bold confidence of the union leaders, caught the northern operators off guard and they signed a contract with the United Mine Workers July 14, 1908.[1] The agreement provided for a closed shop and the eight-hour day, a work day that had long been on the statute books of the state. The operators agreed to keep their mines reasonably dry; to provide proper ventilation; to permit the miners to knock off for the day when one of their number was killed on the job; to limit blacksmith charges for loaders to 20 cents a month and for pick men to 40 cents a month, and not to charge employes more than $2 a ton for coal for their own use. Other provisions called for improved safety measures in the mines, and the settlement of disputes through grievance committees. The right to hire and fire remained with the coal operator.

The agreement was signed by the executive officers of 17 coal companies, and by T. L. Lewis, president of the United Mine Workers of America; Thomas Kirby, president of the union's District No. 15, which embraced all of Colorado and part of New Mexico, and by John R. Lawson. Although the contract assurances to the miners were insignificant, the agreement was of major importance in that it constituted recognition of the UMWA as a bargaining agency and gave the organization a foothold in the state. It gave impetus to the organization work in the southern field and had an important effect in the Fall political campaign when the miners united behind Congressman John Shafroth, a Democrat, for the governorship.

Shafroth defeated Jesse F. McDonald, the Republican and coal company candidate. Although Governor Shafroth didn't prove to be Colorado's greatest governor, he did live up to his advance billing in union circles. In March, 1909, when the master builders of Denver came to grips with the Denver Building Trades Council, partially tying up the building industry in the capital city, Governor Shafroth refused to interfere

[1] Conditions in the Coal Mines of Colorado, hearings before a sub-committee of the Committee of Mines and Mining, 1914, Part IX. P. 2811.

though repeatedly importuned to do so. That he would have a difficult decision to make in a coal dispute became apparent in January, 1910, when the United Mine Workers international convention voted to seek a wage increase of 12.5 per cent, a half holiday on Saturdays, and a bank-to-bank eight-hour day.

Many miners believed the convention had been overly zealous and that a conservative course, designed merely to obtain a renewal of the northern contract with a view to consolidating the union's position in the entire area, should have been adopted. Although there had been no hitches in the contract or disputes of consequence, the miners knew the northern operators had been subjected to pressure by their competitors in the south for treating with the union. Offers of price agreements, improved markets, and advantageous working agreements had been made to the 17 companies on condition they would pull away from the United Mine Workers. When the union's new demands were presented, it became apparent that the C. F. & I. and the Victor American had succeeded in their ardent wooing. The northern operators refused to consider either the demands or a renewal of the contract.[2] Lawson and Frank Smith, newly-elected president of District 15, met with them April 1, 1910, in the Denver offices of F. F. Struby, president of the Northern Coal & Coke Co.

"We have made a careful study of the earnings in the northern field and we feel our demand for an increase of 12.5 per cent is not unreasonable," Lawson told the operators. "Our study shows that the average earnings in this field have varied from $350 to $500 a year. I think you gentlemen will agree that a 12.5 per cent increase is extremely conservative."

The operators looked at each other. Amusement showed on the faces of several of the gentlemen. One or two, who had opposed the original contract most vigorously, appeared hor-

[2] Conditions in the Coal Mines of Colorado; hearings before a sub-committee of the Committee on Mines and Mining, U. S. House of Representatives, 1914, Part 1. P. 20.

ror-stricken. Like a well trained chorus, they shook their heads in the negative. Struby acted as the spokesman.

"No," he said. "We are willing to talk about better ventilation, pay days on the 10th and 25th of each month, and the sprinkling of walls and roof to keep down the dust."

"You know those are required by law and have been for years," Lawson said in a low voice. "On these three we are not asking you to do anything except obey the laws of this state. When you refuse to even consider the other points you are not bargaining in good faith."

The operators were firm. The union negotiators offered to compromise for a wage increase of 5.55 per cent for men who worked by the day and three cents for those who worked by the ton.

"We won't do it," Struby said. "Nothing is to be gained by further discussion."

When the conferences ended, 3,000 men were instructed to lay down their picks and walk out of the northern mines.

Coal company strategy in the 1910 strike developed within a few hours after the last man had left the mines. Application was made to the sheriffs of the northern coal counties for deputies, arrangements were made for importation of strike breakers, and the Baldwin-Felts Detective Agency, an organization with an ugly record in West Virginia, was engaged. In a public statement, the operators promised their mines would be reopened and that non-union workmen would be protected by private guards. They gave a full explanation of their reasons for refusing to bargain with the mine workers.

"The operators conceal the point raised by the miners that the constantly increasing costs of living necessities is a just and sufficient reason why the price of their labor should also be advanced," Lawson said in a public reply that was a bid for favorable public opinion. "The State Railroad Commission has just handed down a decision granting the coal operators of

Northern Colorado a reduction of 25 cents a ton on their rate
to Denver. The operators appear to be very sensitive when it
is suggested that the price of lignite coal will be, in the near
future, advanced 25 or 50 cents a ton. They evidently would
have the public believe there is no danger of the cost of coal
going up, but let us stop a minute and see why the cost was
reduced from $5 to its present rate. The coal operators in the
northern field had a falling out among themselves; the result
was a coal war, but the war ended and the white winged dove
of peace once more hovers over the coal operators' council
chambers."

Lawson's prediction that the price of coal would be advanced
was borne out a few days later when C. L. Baum, president
of the Consolidated Coal and Coke Co., announced the price
would jump from $4.50 a ton to $5 effective Sept. 1 because
"we cannot get proper aid from the sheriff of Boulder County."

"The consumer pays the cost of mining coal under existing
ing conditions," he explained. "If the people knew the conditions there would be no advance in price and there would be
no trouble."

The sheriff of Boulder County, MP Capp,[3] was an independent sort of fellow with a sharper political eye than most
of his brother officers. He had an innate honesty that appealed to his constituents and earned him the repeated support
of elements that had little in common. He incurred the enmity
of the coal operators at the outset of the strike by refusing
to deputize private guards for the mines. The story was told,
and not denied, that an agent of the operators offered Sheriff
Capp $1 for each man to whom he would issue a deputy
sheriff's commission, and a flat guarantee of $80,000 in cash.
A similar plan in Southern Colorado had made a county sheriff
wealthy during the 1903 strike.

When they failed to win over Sheriff Capp, the operators
sought to move deputies from neighboring counties into Boulder

---

[3] Sheriff Capp did not have a first name. He used the letters MP.

County. Sheriff Capp promptly ran them out and threatened to jail any others who trespassed in his jurisdiction. The miners, through Lawson, promised Sheriff Capp they would refrain from violence. The promise was given in good faith, but the arrival of strike breakers in the field made it difficult to keep. There was constant friction, and minor disturbances were the inevitable result.

The operators built stockades around their properties and housed their imported miners inside. Armed guards manned the gates and served as escorts for strike breakers who arrived from the East by every train. The guards lacked authority of deputy sheriffs, however, and could not act as freely as those maintained by the C. F. & I. and the Victor-American Fuel in the southern coal fields. To correct this situation, the Baldwin-Felts detectives launched a campaign designed to force Sheriff Capp to deputize them. Their strategy, based upon long experience in industrial conflicts, was to provoke the miners to violence. Lawson sensed the danger and attempted to meet it by calling the miners together and warning them of the futility of fighting with the Baldwin-Felts.

"When you slug a Baldwin-Felts the fellow has justification for his job," he said. "If they can get you into enough fights, the operators will ask for troops. They want nothing more than to have the state bear the expense of their guard system."

The first break came, however, in an unexpected manner. Barney Fowler, captain of the guards at the Standard Mine, assaulted a striker on the streets of Lafayette. John Cassady, the town marshal, sought to arrest Fowler. The guard resisted, and was shot and wounded in the ensuing struggle. Coal company officials immediately charged that the shooting was the first step in a program of lawlessness by the United Mine Workers of America.

Edwin V. Brake, state labor commissioner, asked the coal operators and union leaders to meet with him. Lawson immediately agreed, but the coal companies, in a letter signed by the Northern Coal & Coke Co., the National Fuel Co., the Parkdale Fuel Co., and the Evans Coal and Fuel Co. refused, saying: "Since our former employes on April 1 last terminated their relations with us and went on strike, we have employed other persons to take their places and, as stated, our relations at this time with our present employees are perfectly satisfactory to us and to them."

Brake then proposed an arbitration committee composed of one representative of the miners and one of the operators, the two to select a third member or, failing in that, the third to be selected by Governor Shafroth. The miners agreed and the operators refused.

"It can be seen that while the miners were at all times ready to submit the matters in dispute to a board of arbitration, the operators assume the attitude there is nothing to arbitrate," Brake said in his report to Governor Shafroth.[4]

Brake sent his deputy, Eli M. Gross, into the northern field to investigate charges that strike breakers were being held in the stockades against their will. The superintendent of the Superior Mine assured him the men could leave any time they wished.

"However, while wandering around the camp," Gross wrote to Brake, "I encountered a guard stationed under the tipple who, under a mistaken idea that I was a company official, admitted to me that his orders were to stop all of the men from leaving the camp wherever possible. He said he had had no trouble with the foreigners, for all he had to do was to order them back to camp, but that some of these Virginians and Kentuckians and Americans in general were so game that they could not be run back by a display of arms, and that he had no authority to shoot anyone for failure to go back, only to threaten. A number of workmen, upon learning that a state official was in camp, came to me and signified their desire to leave; all those who desired to leave I took out with me."

[4] Biennial Report of Colorado Bureau of Labor Statistics, 1909-1910.

Constant desertions from the stockades plus the efficient picketing system of the union kept the mines crippled, though some coal was produced. By late Fall, when the fields turned brown and chill winds swept down out of the north, the operators were desperately in need of coal. The miners, too, were in a serious plight as their funds were running low. Tempers became short on both sides. Baldwin-Felts detectives rode each day through Lafayette in their automobiles, rifles in hand. Union and non-union men were beaten in sudden forays.

Using the disturbances as an excuse, the coal companies went to Denver District Court with a petition for an injunction to restrain union men from interfering with the Northern Coal & Coke Co., its employes or agents, and from picketing, congregating or posting notices. Judge Greeley W. Whitford, a stalwart Republican, granted the petition and obligingly named the coal company's imported Baldwin-Felts detectives as officers of his court to enforce it. They did a thorough job. They arrested Marshal Cassady for contempt of court because he searched two detectives for concealed weapons. A few days later, the gunmen arrested 16 strike leaders, including Ed Doyle, on a charge of congregating on the streets of Lafayette, posting notices and flying banners in violation of the injunction. Judge Whitford conducted a two-day hearing in Denver and then sentenced each of the leaders to a year in jail. As he pronounced the sentences the afternoon of Dec. 23, 1910, the scales in the hand of a figure of justice atop the Denver County courthouse fell with a crash.

The sentences had an effect the coal operators had not anticipated. Union organizations in Denver and their sympathizers paraded the streets in protest and persons who had no connection with the dispute roundly denounced Judge Whitford. Governor Shafroth announced he was "convinced an injustice had been done these men." Demands were made on the Legislature for impeachment of Judge Whitford. Before the protests could materialize into more concrete action, Judge Whitford had the miners brought from jail. The only attorney present was James Blood, the author of the injunction and the chief counsel of the Northern Coal & Coke Co.

"There were many criticisms heaped upon the court for its action," Judge Whitford said sternly. "A demonstration took place in the street of five thousand men who marched by the courthouse and capitol. That was shameful and un-American and should never have been tolerated in this community. It was an attempt to intimidate the court by fear from doing what it thought was right and just in this case."

After calling them "anarchial" and "revolutionary" he released them with a warning. Fifteen minutes after the miners had left the courtroom, Ralph Talbot, Judge Whitford's attorney, appeared at the State Capitol and informed a legislative investigating committee of the action.

With the injunction still in force, the Baldwin-Felts detectives became the virtual rulers of the northern field. Minor clashes involving nothing more than a broken nose or split scalp became more frequent. The Denver Trades and Labor Assembly, a militant organization with an established background, called for a boycott against Denver business houses and firms in which coal operators held interests. The wives and mothers of strikers gathered daily in Lafayette and Louisville churches and schools to pray for peace. Each disturbance, however minor, brought from the coal operators charges that the incident was proof of lawlessness on the part of the strikers. Lawson and Doyle used the same incidents to prove that the operators were seeking to provoke riots and murder. Despite the frequent clashes, there was no bloodshed until April 15, 1911, when T. J. "Teddy" Wycherly, an official of the Lafayette local, was stabbed to death on a Lafayette street by four Mexican strike breakers from the Simpson Mine a few minutes after he had helped Ed Doyle pay out weekly benefits to hundreds of miners.

Doyle saved the Mexicans from an angry mob with pleas

that the coal operators would welcome a lynching. The mob screamed at him, taunted him with his jail term at Whitford's hands, and called him a traitor, but in the end he succeeded in staving them off until Sheriff Capp arrived and spirited the Mexicans out of town.

The Legislature took cognizance of the action in a resolution praising Doyle and Sheriff Capp for "restraining citizens, laboring under intense excitement and anger on account of the unprovoked crime, gathered to avenge the killing of a useful, worthy citizen. This House also congratulates the good people assembled under a strong impulse to do violence on the occasion, and that they yielded to the appeals and persuasion of Sheriff Capp and Edward Doyle and obeyed their better judgment and their law abiding instincts."

Judge Whitford's injunction was invoked a second time late in June after a group of Lafayette miners pummeled Albert Crabb, a strike breaker. Sheriff Capp arrested Doyle and 15 other leaders and took them to Denver. Judge Whitford refused their request for a jury trial under the civil code and proceeded with a hearing of his own. Attorney Blood quizzed the union men and forced them to admit they knew the import of the Whitford injunction. Witnesses were called by Blood to prove the injunction had been violated. The star witness for the Northern Coal Co. was Charles Sherratt, a former member of the Lafayette union local. He had helped to organize the local, but had left it because of rather pointed intimations that he was a spy for Northern Coal. He had gone to work immediately in the Simpson Mine.

He told Judge Whitford a story of villification and abuse, but admitted the miners had confined themselves to hard words and had not prevented him from working.

"I've been called a lot of names by these fellows," he testified. "On June 16 I met a lot of the women and Mrs. Newcomb drew some eggs from under her apron and threw them at me."

Judge Whitford frowned heavily and nodded to Sherratt to continue.

That same night, Sherratt said, he heard a noise and went to his front door. William Crawford, one of the arrested leaders, who lived directly across the street, was standing on his front porch yelling.

"What did he say?" asked Attorney Blood.

"He yelled 'scab' and 'baa-baa.' "

"Did he say anything else?"

"Yes sir, he did. He said, 'Go down to your bull pen and bring your thugs and body guards up here and I'll tell them what I think of them too.' "

Judge Whitford frowned again and stared at Crawford.

Another witness, Elmer Bush, a bookkeeper at the Simpson Mine, testified he heard Crawford's yelling. He went on to say he had discussed his testimony with Detective Felts, head of the Baldwin-Felts, and that he had written it down "so I wouldn't get rattled on the stand."

The miners refused to be sworn. Judge Whitford made them stand up and all be sworn at once. The first miner questioned, Antone Cochinas, contended he could not speak English. An interpreter was secured and while the examination was underway Mr. Cochinas became greatly excited and started talking English.

"Where did you first hear of the Whitford injunction?" Attorney Blood asked in an angry voice, waving the interpreter aside.

"Yes, yes, I know of some junctions," Cochinas replied, speaking very rapidly. "I come here by Grand Junction. I worked seven years at Louisville Junction. I know Utah Junction. Me, I never heard of Whitford Junction."

Judge Whitford, flushed with anger, hurried through the hearing and then pronounced sentence. He gave Doyle a jail term for referring to the court as "old injunction Whitford," and found Crawford guilty of contempt for indiscreetly remarking he would "see Whitford and his injunction in hell."

Robert McBernie, Guy Gordon, Martin Koenig, Grover Wiseman, John Bolton, John H. Newcomb, Walter Gaboury, Andrew Burt, Joseph Carr, Kay Gardjurgis, George Badonis, and Cochinas were each fined $500 and remanded to jail for failure to pay. Daniel Williams was fined $200 for encouraging lawlessness and Marshal Cassady drew a suspended fine of $250 for permitting violation of the injunction. Judge Whitford ordered that the miners were not to be released for any reason until authorization was received from him. Not even an executive order from the governor was to be recognized. Then he delivered a lecture:

"At the former citation for the violation of the injunction by members of the defendant union, the court imprisoned 16 men for one year or until the further order of the court. The court had repeatedly stated its warnings of the court's firm determination to see that its orders were obeyed. The court talked to the sheriff of that county and the court believed then and believes now that if he performed his full duty order could be restored in that community. Lives have been lost in that community since the former order of the court was issued, and would be lost unless order was restored. It is the court's firm determination to enforce the obedience of its orders. Idleness begets lawlessness. Here is organized refusal to work. Bitterness and animosity are in the breast of each against those who do work. This must be remembered as a general condition in the place when we examine the evidence and determine the truth or falsity of the charges. Declarations have been made by members of the union that they will yet win the strike despite Judge Whitford's orders. These declarations have come from those high in the councils of the union."

Having lectured to his evident satisfaction, Judge Whitford denied an application for a stay of execution pending an appeal, denied there was a right to appeal in a contempt case, and denied bond. The miners were marched off to the Denver County jail.

CHAPTER III

AN IMPIOUS JOAN OF ARC

Old Mother Jones, a veteran mine worker organizer, who had been sent to Colorado by the international board to assist John Lawson with the strike, had little patience with either the "damn fool lawyers" or their "sissified mumbo jumbo and pussyfooting." Mother Jones was a woman of direct action, and she decided it was up to her to get Doyle and his union friends out of the Denver jail.

An old hand at the strike business, Mother Jones had taken part in practically every major industrial war in the United States for more than 30 years. Viewed through the eyes of union men, she was a sort of impious Joan of Arc disguised as a kindly old Irish grandmother. If you looked at her through the eyes of employers, particularly those of coal operators, she was a contentious witch who deserved nothing more than some refined, country club version of the stake and a pile of faggots. The Colorado coal operators made a point of whispering that she was a worn out strumpet, and Polly Pry, a newspaper writer, amplified the whisper by broadcasting it in the lascivious columns of Frederick G. Bonfils' Denver Post. No doubt Mother Jones' only connection with the ladies of the night was to give comfort to those who had been kicked out of coal towns and camps when their days of usefulness had passed. Mother Jones had an intense dislike for women, but she could put up with them and even be civil to them if they had contributed in any way to the welfare or happiness of the grimy-faced sons of labor.

Mother Jones paid as little attention to the libels against her name as she did to the established rules of industrial warfare. No matter what was said about her, she went her way, a dynamic, go-to-hell type of fighter with a bagful of tricks, a vocabulary that caused many a mule skinner to hang his head in shame, and a voice that could out-shout a whole platform of bull-chested orators. A born actress, Mother Jones could, when the occasion demanded, take the part of a genteel lady and speak in a refined, semi-cultured manner.

In her years of marching up and down the land, Mother Jones had been known to reach into her old black purse many times to feed an enemy, be he scab or just plain ornery, but she had never been known to retreat. She had taken an active part in the 1903 strike in Colorado and had been twice deported from the state by Gov. James H. Peabody at the behest of harassed coal operators who found her stinging tongue more nerve-wracking than picket lines, closed mines and diminishing dividends. Strangely enough, she was ready now to do business with the other side. In company with several leaders of the Western Federation of Miners, a metal miners' organization, who feared the coal strike would imperil their own union, she worked out a scheme whereby the jailed miners would simply apologize to Judge Whitford and be released. The strike would be called off.

Mother Jones didn't bother to inform Colorado leaders of the United Mine Workers of her plan, but there is some evidence that one or two national leaders were a party to it in an effort to get rid of a costly struggle. John Lawson learned of the scheme from a union attorney who had been summarily discharged by Mother Jones. He found her at a union man's home in Denver, and she readily admitted the plan.

"Those poor boys," she said. "I have to get them out of that filthy jail."

"Mother, if those men stay in jail until they apologize they'll stay there until they rot," Lawson said angrily. "They haven't done anything wrong. If President White approves this idea I'll blast him from one end of this country to the other."

"Now, my boy, you wouldn't do that."

"That is just what I will do, Mother."

Lawson left her with that, and on his return to his home found a telegram summoning him to the UMWA offices in Indianapolis. He crumpled it, and threw it into a waste basket.

"I'm staying right here in Colorado," he told Mrs. Lawson. "Someone is trying to kill this strike off from the inside."

His decision proved a fortunate one for he learned the next day that President White was enroute to Colorado. Had Lawson answered the call to Indianapolis, they would have passed each other in Nebraska or Iowa. Mother Jones asked Lawson to go with her to meet White's train.

"Nothing doing," he replied. "Let White come and see me."

White's train was late, and before it arrived the Denver Times carried a story that he had arrived in the city and was taking steps to settle the coal strike. The story was furnished the paper by Orrin N. Hilton, a former Illinois judge, who was serving as chief counsel for the Western Federation of Miners. The story was discussed heatedly when President White found John Lawson in the lobby of the Markham Hotel and insisted that he join a conference in the offices of the Western Federation of Miners.

White was apologetic about the story, as was Judge Hilton when the conference opened.

"I'm sorry about the Times piece," Judge Hilton said. "It was premature in view of Mr. White's delay in getting here."

There were no interruptions while Judge Hilton explained the proposed settlement plan in detail. When he had finished, Mr. White turned a questioning eye to Lawson.

"Judge Hilton, do I understand you to say these miners are to apologize?" Lawson asked.

"Well, they won't have to do it themselves," Judge Hilton replied. "I'll do it for them, and the judge will release them immediately."

"I'll see them rot first," Lawson said savagely. "Decent men don't have to apologize in this country for something they didn't do."

Lawson explained his position fully to President White, giving the international executive a complete picture of conditions in the coal fields and of the need for complete organization.

"We have had many setbacks in this field," he said. "If we fall down this time we may as well get out of Colorado and stay out."

White turned to Hilton.

"This thing is off," he said. "I guess I didn't understand it fully. I'll talk to the coal operators as you planned, Judge, but the strike goes on. It didn't originate in my administration, but I will see it through if the miners want it."

President White met with the coal operators the next morning. They told him they would dismiss all charges against strikers in the northern field and have the jailed miners released if the men would go back to work. They refused to consider bargaining meetings with the United Mine Workers. President White finally ended the conference with the statement: "We cannot afford to go back to work for the consideration of releasing our men. The courts of Colorado will do that."

"So far as we are concerned there is no strike," Attorney James Blood replied for the operators. "We have refused to deal with the United Mine Workers as an organization and do yet."

"These operators of yours are tough babies," President White told Lawson that night. "I thought I had run across some bad ones in the East, but they are wishy-washy compared to the kind you breed around here."

"They're bad, Mr. White, but we can beat them if we can have a little money for more organization work," Lawson replied. "The south has to be organized completely before we can do anything worthwhile."

"I believe you. And we'll get it to you as fast as we can muster our strength for the effort. Colorado should be a good proving ground for the whole nation."

Before he left for Indianapolis with a chastened Mother Jones, White issued a public statement for the benefit of the coal operators.

"The United Mine Workers will ultimately succeed in organizing the entire state," it said. "When this is done, industrial peace will prevail. The public will be fairly treated and not compelled to pay exorbitant prices. I can cite the experiences of other states as proof of this. We'll continue to spend money in Colorado to support this strike and we may spend more for an even greater strike, because it is certain that recent moves of the operators will do nothing except bring further unrest upon the state."

President White had hardly settled himself comfortably in his Indianapolis offices before the Colorado Supreme Court, acting on an appeal from the Whitford sentences, released 13 of the jailed miners. Doyle and William Crawford were released a short time later. With the release of the miners and the complete failure of the settlement plan, the coal operators intensified their opposition to the strike. The Rocky Mountain Fuel Co. absorbed the Northern Coal and Coke Co. and a determined campaign was launched to import non-union miners from eastern states. Recruiting agents sent 8,000 men into the northern field in a few weeks. The union strengthened its picket lines at railroad stations and mine approaches. Hundreds were dissuaded from entering the mines, but the majority of the newcomers went to work under the protection of armed guards. Before many weeks had passed, the non-union workers began to desert and large numbers of mines were again severely crippled. The operators, in a last effort to end the strike, called on Governor Shafroth with a demand for troops. He refused.

The indignant operators then issued a bulletin, signed by the presidents of the 10 largest companies, for public consumption. Designated as a preamble and resolutions "adopted by the operators of the northern Colorado coal fields," it explained the demand on the governor and the operator complaints against picketing, adding:

"Resolved, That we, the operators of the Northern Colorado coal fields, have fought what we believe to be an unjust strike since March 31, 1910, and now wish again to assure our employes and their families, regardless of whether or not the municipal officers, the sheriff of Boulder County, or the governor of the State of Colorado fail, neglect, or refuse to protect you in the exercise of your rights to work where, when, and for whom you may desire, that we will provide you with adequate, full and complete protection, and be it further

"Resolved, That it is the unalterable purpose of the undersigned operators not to enter into a contract with the United Mine Workers of America, or any other union of coal miners; that all of the mines in the Northern Colorado fields will hereafter be operated exclusively on the 'open shop' policy, just as the mines are now being operated in the southern field; and be it further

"Resolved, That we, the operators of the Northern Colorado coal fields, desire to thank our present employes for their loyalty and full obeyance of the law as true American citizens, without which no just cause can succeed, and we wish again to assure you of our true and loyal protection."

Lawson replied in an open letter to the Colorado public, the men and women who had to do the worrying about empty coal bins and cold nights because of a dispute they did not fully understand. His letter read:

"Inasmuch as the operators of the Northern Colorado coal fields have flooded the public press with malicious falsehoods and misrepresentations as to the real conditions existing around the mines and have sought to inflame and prejudice the minds of the

people so as to create a sentiment which would tend to force
Governor Shafroth to send troops into the coal camps to aid the
mine owners, we believe that it is our duty to give the facts
which show that the latter, goaded to desperation by constant
defections from the ranks of the deluded and misinformed strike
breakers, have not only stooped to the basest falsehoods and
villification, but have openly encouraged lawlessness."

The letter accused the operators of injuring the "fair name of
Colorado," and of being frantic because of a stampede of strike
breakers from their camps. The letter also charged that the
operators had forced up the price of coal to build sentiment
against the union.

"Not only have these men attempted to bulldoze the governor
of the state, but we can prove that operators, at an early stage
in the prolonged struggle, tried to bribe certain officials and
offered them thousands of dollars to use the power and influence
of their offices against the miners," the letter said. "But to get
to the facts as to who are the lawbreakers, thugs and undesirable
citizens. We can furnish hundreds of instances and give days
and names and data sufficient to convince any fair-minded
citizen that it is the hired gunman of the detective agencies who
is responsible for nine-tenths of the assaults. He is brought to
Colorado because he is a trouble-maker. There are few places in
the country where the detective agencies are now needed for any
length of time. They have to start something to stay on the
corporation payrolls. The operators have always seemed blind to
this fact, or do not care."

A list of assaults and shootings followed and the letter wound
up with the statement:

"We can prove that one of the most prominent operators of
the northern field made the statement many months ago in the
presence of reliable witnesses that the 'operators would have no
trouble winning if we had a few killings.' Their fondest dreams
as to the killings have been realized, and in each case we can
prove that it was not the fault of our men. We have always

counselled moderation, sobriety, and strict adherence to law. We still continue to do so. Colorado is the only state in the union where there is a coal strike on, and we are backed by the entire membership of our order. We hope the public will withhold judgment and not be misled by such unmanly and un-American methods as the operators are now resorting to."

The verbal chest thumpings made little impression on the man in the street or his wife in the home as they had come to the conclusion that both coal operators and coal miners needed a little expert exorcising. Governor Shafroth was shrewd enough to sense this public reaction and order an investigation of both sides to the controversy. Secretary of State James B. Pearce, in his capacity as state labor commissioner ex-officio, went to the coal fields with two deputies and gathered enough data to fill out a hefty report. Although it is true his report served to endear himself and Governor Shafroth to voting unionists, his observations were nonetheless pertinent.

"Certain interests have for so many years been accustomed to break strikes with the militia that it is a difficult thing to break them of the habit," he wrote. "It is much the cheapest and speediest method for them, as the taxpayers of the state pay the bills. A striking illustration of this is given in the bond issue of over $950,000 issued to settle the Cripple Creek war debt."[1]

He found that the prospects of severe conflict in the northern field were lessening as "both sides seem to have exhausted themselves." It was true that the operators and the union had spent large sums, but there remained ample reserves on the one hand and a strong, dues paying membership scattered through the entire country on the other.

The union re-opened its Trinidad office and John Lawson and John McLennan, president of the State Federation of Labor, took up their headquarters in the southern field as the first step in a concerted drive to organize C. F. & I. and Victor-American miners. Lawson was convinced neither side could win in the

[1] Biennial Report of Colorado Bureau of Labor Statistics, 1911-1912. P. 139.

northern field and that the real war would have to be fought in
the south. His presence in the Trinidad area caused a number of
irregular strikes by miners who were eager for a show down with
their employers, but in each case Lawson forced the men to go
back to work.

"Get back to your mines," he told one group of belligerents
who called on the union for assistance. "Work your heads off
for the United Mine Workers. Organize your fellow workers
in every camp and be prepared for the day when we call you."

Detective Reno and his men watched every move and kept
C. F. & I. executives supplied with daily reports. When it became apparent the union movement was becoming potent in the
southern field, the company began a series of cautious adjust-
ments in an effort to forestall further organization and alleviate
unrest. The wages of 10,000 miners were suddenly boosted 10
per cent.[2] Individually, the men were due to receive an additional 15 to 25 cents per day. The Rocky Mountain Fuel Co.
and the Victor-American followed suit in their mines in Las
Animas, Huerfano and Fremont counties as did the Consolidated Coal & Coke in the northern field. The majority of those
who benefited from the pay increases gave credit to the United
Mine Workers, and the immediate result was a sharp rise in the
number of UMWA secret memberships.

Alarmed by the drive in the south and the failure to break
the northern strike, the coal operators held a meeting in Denver
to discuss their position. After some argument, it was agreed
the northern operators should again attack. They obtained a
dissolution of the ineffective Whitford injunction and went into
Federal District Court with a petition for an injunction against
the miners, contending that neither Governor Shafroth nor
other state or county authorities were willing or able to maintain
order in the strike-bound area.

Before Federal Judge Lewis heard the application, trouble
flared in Lafayette between union men and strike breakers em-

[2] Denver Express, April 5, 1912.

ployed by the Rocky Mountain Fuel Co. Each side claimed the other fired the first shot. In all, more than 400 rounds were exchanged before Sheriff Capp, with a force of deputies, arrived from Boulder and restored order. Only one combatant, George Michoff, a strike breaker at the Simpson mine, was injured. He had two minor flesh wounds in the leg.

The union and company versions of the disturbance were quite different. The union side was contained in a statement by Rev. John Calloway, a Baptist minister, who charged that non-union miners precipitated the shooting. J. V. Sickman of Louisville, attorney for the Rocky Mountain Fuel Co., said a "man on a bicycle" rode rapidly by a house occupied by Greek strike breakers and fired through the door. The official report, prepared by Secretary of State Pearce, gave the union men the best of it.

"Warrants were issued for 27 union miners charged with offenses connected with these disturbances and they, without a single exception, went into Boulder and surrendered themselves to the sheriff," the report said. "Tony Morello, the man who started the trouble, however, in spite of the fact that Mr. Slater, the man who was in charge of the Baldwin-Felts contingent of gunmen employed by the Rocky Mountain Fuel Co., gave Sheriff Capp an order stating that he should be surrendered, never gave himself up, but by some arrangement with the district attorney's office was allowed to remain at large. These occurrences, together with the fact that all the trouble happened just prior to the application of the Rocky Mountain Fuel Co. for a federal injunction, caused grave suspicion in the minds of union men; and the union officials openly express their belief that they were deliberately planned for the purpose of influencing the federal courts in the matter."

Judge Lewis listened patiently to arguments for an injunction when he held the hearing. Jesse G. Northcutt of Trinidad, representing the coal operators, spoke for an injunction, and Horace Hawkins, the union attorney, gave his objections. Without delay, Judge Lewis held that picketing was lawful. He denied the petition.

"The court is inclined to believe that the firing in the Simpson Mine brawl was precipitated from within the stockade," Judge Lewis said. "The federal authorities should be appealed to only as a last resort. The local authorities should be appealed to first; when they fail, the state authorities, and lastly the power of the nation. It appears that both the local and state authorities claim to have the situation in hand. Therefore, the peace officers must be given credit for the faithful discharge of their duties and under no circumstances, as an independent proposition, will this court take it upon itself to unarm citizens of that community."[3]

Judge Lewis' ruling was, of course, a major victory for the United Mine Workers. By eliminating an operator hope of a federal anti-picketing or strike injunction, it left the union free to picket the northern mines with all the strength it could muster, and experience had taught the union leadership that forceful picketing would eventually wear down or win over the most callous strike breaker. Lawson, Doyle, McLennan, and several other strike leaders believed the repeated failures of coal company strategy would force the operators to meet with them in the near future, but they under-estimated their opponents.

[3] Denver Express, Oct. 7, 1912.

CHAPTER IV
THE 1913 STRIKE CALL

Intense public interest in the 1912 political campaign shoved the northern coal strike into the background for a time as this was the first year that Colorado selected its United States senators by popular vote. Both the coal operators and the miners had important stakes in the national and state campaigns. Politics and industry were loving bedfellows in Colorado, and the group with the greatest number of stooges in public offices had the same strategic advantage as that enjoyed by the Confederate general who attributed his successes to reaching the field of battle first with the most men.

The operators, through long practice, were skilled in political arts. They were not particularly disturbed by the fact that their usual vehicle, the Republican Party, was hopelessly split by the progressive movement headed nationally by Theodore Roosevelt. They were willing to support a Democrat if he was amenable to their type of reasoning. On the other hand, John Lawson and his miners were naive on the subject of politics. They invariably regarded the Democratic Party as the champion of the downtrodden, a position that could not have been sustained had they had the experience to draw obvious conclusions from the party's record in the state.

The Democrats nominated and elected Governor Shafroth to the long term in the United States Senate and Charles S.

Thomas, a party veteran, to the short term. They also elected Fred Farrar, an attorney from an agricultural district, as attorney general, and Elias M. Ammons, a rancher and former Republican, as governor. Ammons defeated Clifford C. Parks, the Republican candidate, and Edward P. Costigan, the young union attorney, who sought the governorship under Roosevelt's Bull Moose banner. The miners concentrated their fire against Parks, but made the fatal mistake of splitting their vote between Ammons and Costigan. Lawson, as a member of the Democratic State Central Committee, and a number of his followers, supported Ammons, while the rest gave their support to Costigan. Ammons was a political unknown as far as Lawson was concerned. He supported a label and was chagrined at the close of the campaign to find evidence of coal company support for his candidate. He decided the operators had turned to Ammons on the theory that Parks was certain of defeat and Costigan was too dangerous to corporation control. This explanation was plausible as there was nothing in the Ammons background to attract the operators insofar as Lawson could learn. The new governor was a mild, sun-tanned man with pleasant manners that contrasted oddly with his love for profanity. Although he had little formal education, he had worked as a newspaper reporter until failing eyesight had forced him to turn to other fields, cattle and politics, some years before.

Before Governor Ammons took office, the United Mine Workers Executive Board met in Chicago. Lawson was summoned and asked for a detailed report on the northern strike and conditions in the southern field. It was the opportunity he had long wanted, and he made the most of it.

"Our last report shows we have spent $791,418.02 in the northern field," he told the board. "That may seem like a lot of money; but we've got to spend many times that sum in the southern field before we make Colorado a union state."

The board members, after a careful study of Lawson's report, ordered the organization campaign speeded regardless of cost.

It was agreed the rest of December would be spent on the necessary ground work and that the public drive would begin early in 1913.

"Financial assistance will be yours," President White told Lawson. "We are in shape now to take those Colorado operators into camp once and for all."

Lawson went back to Denver for a brief conference with United Mine Workers officials and leaders of the Colorado Federation of Labor. They received his news with enthusiasm and promised secrecy, a promise some were apparently not able to keep for when Lawson arrived in Trinidad to open a permanent headquarters, a reporter for the Chronicle-News, a daily newspaper owned by Judge Jesse Northcutt, counsel for the coal operators, caught him within an hour.

"We have advices out of Denver that a big strike is to be called in the southern field," the reporter said. "How about it?"

Lawson smiled. He knew someone had given the plans away unwittingly or the company spy system had purchased them from a weak and needy brother.

"There is no cause for alarm," Lawson replied ingenuously. "An industrial war is to be deplored at any time, and invariably innocent third parties suffer. The organization I represent is not contemplating a strike as conditions at this time do not call for action of that kind. We believe that a campaign of education will be advantageous to both miners and operators."

The reporter went away satisfied, unaware of the smirks of Lawson's aides in the new headquarters.

"What do you mean, John, when you say conditions in this field don't warrant a strike?" McLennan asked with a broad grin on his face.

"You know what I meant," Lawson said. "Our condition, of course."

He remained in Trinidad until February when he went north to Louisville for the annual convention of District 15. McLennan was re-elected president of the miners, Thomas Scott was named vice president, Ed Doyle was chosen as secretary-treasurer, and Lawson was re-elected to the international board. There was no discussion of the approaching organization campaign as the leaders knew company spies were present in the guise of delegates. When the convention ended, Lawson delayed his return to Trinidad to attend sessions of a legislative investigating committee on the northern strike.

The United Mine Workers appeared before the committee with a number of charges against the operators which were immediately denied by President Shumway of the Rocky Mountain Fuel Co.

"We have plenty of labor and have applications for work which we cannot care for," Shumway told the committee members. "It is untrue that we have imported undesirable citizens. We have imported no miners. Those who have come from the outside did so without our connivance or knowledge."

Asked if his company received a rake-off from beer sold in the camps and if beer was at the root of disturbances, Shumway laughingly replied: "Without beer it would be as impossible to operate a coal camp as it would be to operate a mine without men. Some of these foreign miners find their only recreation in song and beer, but there have been no disturbances because they are allowed to drink it. They get so much pleasure out of it that I don't think it would be fair for the company to taboo it."[1]

The legislative investigation had not been sought by the coal companies and it was met by them in a manner entirely unexpected by Lawson and his aides. The C. F. & I. suddenly announced it had abolished the lucrative scrip system, and that the eight-hour day would go into effect in all southern mines March 1. Both the Denver Post and the Rocky Mountain News, Colorado's largest newspapers, overlooked the fact that the eight-hour day had long been required by law. They stressed the statement that "the change from the existing system is,

[1] Denver Republican, Feb. 26, 1913.

according to officers of the company, purely voluntary and not influenced in any way by the activities of union organizers." It was explained in the newspapers that the scrip system of the Colorado Supply Co., subsidiary of the C. F. & I. Co., was being replaced by a credit system "whereby debits for purchases will be allowed with the overplus of the wage check paid in cash."

The improvements, the public was informed, were the work of Jesse F. Welborn, president of the C. F. & I. Co. Mr. Welborn was the executive head of John D. Rockefeller's extensive enterprises in Colorado. He had started with the C. F. & I. Co. as a humble bookkeeper of humble farm origin. His rise in the business world, once he had become general sales agent of the company, had been rapid. Welborn was impetuous for an executive. He made his decisions quickly and established his own justification for them later regardless of the evidence. He understood the social amenities of life as represented by the exclusive Denver Club and the Denver Country Club, but he had no understanding of his coal miners as human beings. Those who had occasion to contact Welborn in the social or business worlds found him friendly and likeable, while the workers in his mines thought of him as a harsh, stuffed-shirt executive who cared nothing for their broken heads and empty bellies, a man who applied the jungle rule of tooth and claw to industry.

Welborn dominated his brother coal operators and the politicians by force of personality and his commanding position as Rockefeller's Colorado manager. Opinions on matters of business and business policy originated with Welborn or his superiors in the Rockefeller offices at No. 26 Broadway in New York City. It was up to him to produce the dividends demanded by C. F. & I. directors and stockholders, and he went about the task in a relentless manner. As the leading operator of the state, Welborn couldn't afford to show any signs of softness for it was up to him at all times to set the pace for the other coal companies. The United Mine Workers were mere obstacles as far as Welborn was concerned. He looked upon the organization as an unholy aggregation of anarchists who were, or ought to be, outside the law. His action in abolishing the scrip system was a strategic move against the UMWA, and was not motivated by any belief that the system was undesirable as it had justified itself many times in his eyes through handsome returns to the Colorado Supply Co. and indirectly to the C. F. & I.

The Welborn strategy had the desired effect and the legislative investigators hastily ended their work with the obvious conclusion that "little good could come of an investigation unless it should furnish an opportunity to bring together the operators and the striking miners."

Before the legislative fiasco was forgotten, the UMWA international board formally voted the promised funds for Colorado and sent its international vice president, Frank J. Hayes, west to take charge of the final drive for organization in the southern field. A big, red-haired young fellow with a persuasive tongue and a rapidly growing fondness for the cup that both cheers and befuddles, Hayes was an experienced administrator who could plot a rough-and-tumble battle or write a better than average poem with equal ease. He was well-read and intelligent, and the miners of the nation looked to him as their future leader, an anticipation that was not realized in later years when he was superseded by John L. Lewis.

Any lack of staying power in Hayes was compensated by Lawson and Doyle. At their first meeting in District 15 headquarters in the German-American Trust Building in Denver, they formed a policy committee. This committee, under the terms of a resolution adopted by the international board in Indianapolis, was vested with dictatorial powers. It could organize, bargain and call strikes. It could call out all of the miners in Colorado or any part of them as it saw fit. Hayes was elected chairman and Doyle was named secretary-treasurer. The committee's first act was a written appeal to the coal miners of District 15. The letter, which was correctly interpreted by the coal operators as a declaration of war, read:

"Greeting:

"This is the day of your emancipation. This is the day when liberty and progress come to abide in your midst.

"We call upon you this day to enroll as a member of the greatest and most powerful labor organization in the world, the United Mine Workers of America."

The background and purposes of the union were set forth in detail along with Colorado laws that prohibited corporations from interfering with or coercing employes.

"We feel sure we have your support," the appeal said. "We know that for years you have appealed to us for help. Now we are answering with all the power and wealth of our great union. We ask you to join or help organize a local at once, if none exists in your locality. We ask you to help lay the foundation of the splendid movement we are building in this field. Do not delay a moment, but make haste to join your fellows and help win the victory. If you are discharged for exercising your legal rights, we will begin court proceedings against the offending company and will pay you strike benefits from the moment you quit work."

The letters swamped post offices in every mining town, and they were followed by organizers who opened branch offices in Aguilar, Walsenburg and Florence to supplement the Trinidad headquarters. The strike in the northern field was almost forgotten. Predictions of a bigger and more important strike were on every tongue. None of the miners believed the operators would meet with Hayes and Lawson.

The operators held a secret meeting in Denver at which they raised a defense fund and ordered their mines put in readiness for battle, if need be. Guards were doubled at the properties in the southern field, and barbed wire was strung around the closed camps. Additional gates were placed across public roads to control travel, and huge quantities of arms and ammunition were purchased. Large sums of money were used to employ spies who were sent to join the union, and other sums went to bribe weaklings in the swelling union ranks. With ample funds of its own, the union in turn paid coal company men for desired if not always authentic information.

Once the drive was launched, the policy committee sent a letter to the newspapers attacking the coal corporations and informing the public that the union was determined "to exhaust all honorable means in an endeavor to bring about a settlement before a strike order is issued. We are for Colorado; we are for good citizenship; we are for enforcement of the law; we stand for justice. We hope the situation may be cleared up without a strike and that the disgraceful scenes of years gone by that have placed a blot upon the fair name of Colorado will never be enacted in this state again."

The letter was mostly front, as the union leaders had no intention of meeting with the operators until such time as a vast majority of the miners were enrolled in and supporting the United Mine Workers of America. Twenty-one pairs of organizers were put through a special course in the Denver office and then sent into the southern field. Their operation was simple, but effective. One member of each team was known as the active organizer; the other was the passive organizer. The so-called active organizer moved in the open and was known to everyone, including Major Reno and Sheriff Farr, as an organizer. His passive team mate posed as a miner looking for work. He cussed the unions and their leadership, and obtained a job in the heavily guarded mines. He made friends with officers of the company and, where possible, hired out as a coal company spotter. Miners who served as spotters were paid from $10 to $30 extra each month by the coal company to report fellow workers who were either union members or disposed to join the union.

Once the passive organizer was installed in the mine, his active team mate sought new members in that mine. If a miner joined, the active organizer kept the man's membership secret and sent his card directly to the Denver office. Despite the public plea for organization of locals, there was no need for them nor would they have been desirable. There were too many spies about. If a working miner refused to join, his name was sent to the passive organizer who immediately reported to the company that John Cotino had joined the union. The result was always the same. The company sent John Cotino packing down the canon, with or without the preliminary of a kangaroo. In this manner a constant stream of anti-union and non-union men, the confirmed strike breakers and scabs, were kept streaming down the canons. The companies unwittingly sent the faithful out, while the active organizer sent carefully coached men of union affiliation to apply for the jobs that had to be filled.

The active and passive organizers were paid $1 a day and expenses while they were on someone else's payroll, and $3 a day and expenses when they were forced to rely solely on their union pay. In one month, the active-passive system caused the operators to send more than 3,000 non-union men down the canon. Their places were taken by 3,000 union men.

When complete organization of the mines appeared a certainty, Hayes and Lawson called on the new governor with a request that he use the influence of his office to arrange a conference between coal operators and union leaders. Governor Ammons was much disturbed by the recurring rumors of industrial warfare, and he had little idea of what he ought to do, if anything. He did, however, consent to talk with the operators. Welborn, J. C. Osgood, head of the Victor-American, and A. D. W. Brown, president of the Rocky Mountain Fuel Co., were summoned to the executive offices in the State Capitol. They met with the governor in a back room while Hayes and Lawson sat in an ante room. When Governor Ammons had finished with the operators, he called Hayes and Lawson.

"It didn't do any good," he said. "They won't meet with you men at all. They claim a meeting would be the same thing as recognition of the union. I'll keep working on the proposition, though, and I'll send Brake to Southern Colorado to make an investigation."

Deputy Labor Commissioner Brake left the next day at 12:15 p. m. and arrived in Trinidad at 7:45 p. m. He obtained a cab at the station and went directly to the Toltec Hotel on Commercial Street. Trinidad was three times as large as Walsenburg and was a much older town. It had been settled originally by cattlemen and still had more diversified interests than the Huerfano County town though coal was the dominant factor in the life of Trinidad. The citizens of the town did not have much use for the rest of Colorado and proudly referred to Las Animas County as the kingdom of King Coal. The county sported a special seal which contained a crown for the mythical king, a piece of coal, a pick, a shovel, and the wording: "The Kingdom of Las Animas." The citizens also took a certain pride in the fact that Trinidad had been under martial law oftener than any other city in the United States. Brake found the crooked streets packed with the usual Saturday night crowd, but the picturesque community seemed calm and peaceful.

"This looks like a pretty quiet place to me after what I've heard about it around Denver lately," he told the hotel clerk as he signed the register. Brake glanced up just in time to catch a fleeting look of fear on the clerk's face.

"What's the matter, son?"

"Nothing, sir, nothing. We just hope it will stay quiet."

Just outside the hotel, two Baldwin-Felts gunmen, George Belcher and Walter Belk, sauntered along Commercial Street. They walked with an arrogant air. Their chests were puffed out and their right hands swung loosely. In their manner was the warning, "Just let some damned miner start something with us."

Belk was known as "Big Hearted" to his friends. The union men of Trinidad knew him only as "that damned gunman from West Virginia." Both he and Belcher were feared. As they swaggered along, a third figure came limping down the street. Gerald Lippiatt was a striking miner from the northern field. He was serving as an organizer out of the Denver office. As he came up with and started to pass the two gunmen, they butted him with their elbows and cursed him. Other gunmen appeared in the vicinity. They leaned against nearby buildings and puffed at their cigarettes. Lippiatt took in the situation at a glance. A John Lawson would have gone on and awaited an opportunity to meet these gunmen under more favorable circumstances, but a burning hatred welled up in Lippiatt. He cursed back, and then turned and crossed the street. He went to the Packer block on the opposite side of the street and secured his gun. Then he came back. Belcher and Belk were waiting hopefully. These two men understood guns and killings. They were professionals and knew their business thoroughly. Several organizers ran out of the union office in the Packer block and called to Lippiatt. He shook his head angrily and walked straight up to Belk.

"All right, you rat, let's have it out," Lippiatt cried shrilly.

Belk slapped the organizer with his left hand as his right slid under his coat. Lippiatt drew his gun and fired, but he was too slow. Belk's heavy revolver roared and Lippiatt fell back, a shudder running through his frail body. His own shot struck Belk in the soft part of the leg about six inches above the knee, but the gunman remained cool and deliberate. He fired again and again, taking careful aim as Lippiatt, his face a chalky white, backed away. In the center of the street, he crumpled and pitched forward with six slugs in his body.

Commissioner Brake reached the sidewalk as Lippiatt fell. The Saturday night crowd stampeded toward the shelter of doorways. A woman screamed. Brake pushed his way down the sidewalk past Belk who was limping toward the hotel with Belcher and two gunmen supporting him.

"He's dead," a bystander told Brake as he reached Lippiatt's side. The labor commissioner stared at the figure in the street and listened to the crowd mutter "murder" and "the dirty sons-of-bitches."

The killing threw the coal miners of Las Animas and Huerfano counties into a frenzy. Hotheads demanded that the gunmen be wiped out. McLennan and a half dozen organizers worked frantically to quiet the enraged men who gathered in the Trinidad headquarters.

"There must be no trouble," McLennan pleaded. The State Federation of Labor was scheduled to open its annual convention in Trinidad Monday morning, and an outbreak on the part of the miners would react against them in the federation and with the public. When the crowd had finally quieted down, McLennan called Lawson at his home in Denver to inform him of the shooting. The news left Lawson sick at heart. Three days before Lippiatt had called him on the telephone.

"I am leaving for Trinidad tonight, John, and I want to tell you goodbye," Lippiatt had said. "I think I am going to be killed."

"Killed? What do you mean?"

"The gunmen have been pressing me pretty hard down there, John, but I am going back. I've got a hunch they are going to get me this time."

"Then you mustn't go," Lawson had told him. "Stay here and we'll send someone else down; someone who isn't so well known to them."

"No, John, I'm going back. It is my job, and I want to go. But this is my last trip. Goodbye."

Brake met with the Chamber of Commerce early Sunday morning. The businessmen were alarmed. They admitted they were not satisfied with industrial conditions in the area, but insisted that, while they didn't blame the miners, a strike must be avoided. Brake agreed to use his influence with the federation in an effort to avoid any drastic action.

When the labor convention was called to order the next morning the meeting hall was filled with angry delegates. The Lippiatt killing had excited the men of labor as nothing had in many months. They saw in it a new reign of terror. Lippiatt was to have been a delegate to the convention. His chair was draped in black. Every delegate was mindful of it during the convention, but the speeches were far less belligerent than might have been expected. There was a certain grimness about the way the delegates went about their work once the first anger had passed. They indorsed the United Mine Workers and pledged assistance of labor throughout the state to any action the miners might see fit to take.

The bullet-riddled body of Lippiatt accompanied the Northern Colorado delegates when they left Trinidad. At Colorado Springs, where Lippiatt was to be buried, the delegates left their coaches and stood with bared heads while the flag-draped coffin was removed from the baggage car to a waiting hearse. Ten days after the killing, the policy committee wrote a letter[2] to each operator in the southern field:

"Dear Sir:

"For many years the coal miners of Colorado have been desirous of working under union conditions, and as you no doubt know, have made this desire known on innumerable occasions, a large number of them being discharged because of their wishes in this respect.

"While we know your past policy has been one of keen opposition to our union, we are hopeful at this time that you will look at this matter in a different way, and will meet with us in joint conference for the purpose of amicably adjusting all points of issue in the present controversy. We are no more desirous of a strike than you are, and it seems to us that we owe it to our respective interests, as well as the general public, to make every

---

[2] Conditions in the Coal Mines of Colorado; Hearings Before a Subcommittee of the Committee on Mines and Mining, U. S. House of Representatives, Government Printing Office, 1914, Part IX, P. 2539.

honest endeavor to adjust our differences in an enlightened manner.

"It ought to be evident to yourself and your associates that Colorado cannot stand alone in opposition to our movement. The operators of Wyoming, Montana, Washington, Oklahoma, Kansas, Arkansas, Missouri, Texas and Iowa, embracing all the important coal producing states west of the Mississippi River, have been working under contracts with our union for years, and it goes without saying that the operators in the above mentioned states, who once held the same opinion concerning our union that you now seem to hold, are at this time well satisfied with our union, and are much pleased over the security and stability given to the industry through the medium of the trade agreement.

"Why oppose us here, spending millions of dollars in an industrial conflict for no good purpose? Why is it not possible and practical for you to do in this state what the operators in all the neighboring states have already done?

"We feel sure that you will appreciate the gravity of this situation, and will do your part to meet it at this time, when no sting will be left behind, which is always the result of a strike settlement.

"Let us meet now as friends and proceed to settle this entire controversy with honor to ourselves, with credit to our people, and with faith in each other.

"Hoping you will favor us with a prompt reply, we beg to remain,

"Sincerely yours,
"POLICY COMMITTEE."

The committee hoped the letter would force the operators out into the open. It was anxious to avoid a strike, but determined that Colorado should not remain a monument to the open shop in an organized West. The committee members stayed close to their Denver office, watching each incoming mail for a reply, but only two small operators deigned to answer.

Meanwhile, the U. S. Department of Labor, through Secretary of Labor William B. Wilson, sent Ethelbert Stewart to the offices of John D. Rockefeller in New York in the hope of enlisting the capitalist's aid in averting a strike. Stewart did not get to Rockefeller, but a member of his legal staff, Starr J. Murphy, informed Stewart that the "matter was being handled" by the executive officers of the C. F. & I. in Colorado. At almost the same hour, Brake called at Governor Ammons' office in Denver to make a report.

"What did you find?" the governor asked without ceremony.

"Plenty," Brake replied. "The feeling is most intense in Trinidad, and the town is filled with armed men, guards and detectives. This Lippiatt killing has created bad feeling among the miners and it is my firm belief that if something is not done quickly there will be a disastrous outbreak down there."

"What do you recommend?"

"I'd ask the sheriffs of Las Animas and Huerfano counties to come up here and then I'd demand that they disarm every man in the two counties, guard or miner. If they wouldn't agree, and frankly Governor I don't think they would, I'd put the two counties under martial law immediately."

Governor Ammons dismissed the commissioner with a wave of his hand and, in due time, Brake wrote ruefully:

"The governor did not accept any of my suggestions; in fact did nothing to allay the trouble. Other advisers were stronger evidently with him than myself."[3]

On September 8, when it was apparent the major operators did not intend to reply to the August 26 letter of the policy committee, a second letter was sent, notifying them that the miners would meet in convention in Trinidad September 15 and inviting them to attend. The committee stated that the letter was its final effort and expressed belief that if the operators

[3] Biennial Report of Colorado Bureau of Labor Statistics, 1913-1914, P. 166.

would meet with the miners in joint convention all differences could be adjusted. Not a single operator replied to the letter. The only effect was an increase in the number of guards at the various camps. Spies, camp marshals, and gunmen swarmed through the company towns and into Trinidad. Miners knew they would be discharged if they left camp to attend the Trinidad convention. Beatings and blacklistings would follow. Sheriff Jefferson Farr, flanked by 326 deputies, many of whom were imported from other states, swore that not a miner from his district would get to the convention. His deputies, employed, armed and paid by the Colorado Fuel & Iron Co., were scattered about Walsenburg and along the roads to watch for delegates.

Before the convention met, Doyle, as agent for the policy committee, perfected plans for a strike. Through a dummy real estate office in Denver, he handled all business with the organizers and paid them with checks which were apparently for real estate transactions. Acting on Lawson's theory that the miners would be ejected from the various camps the minute a strike was called, Doyle leased land near the mouths of the mine canons and bought up tents which were stored in Pueblo pending the day of eviction. Inasmuch as it was impossible to communicate freely with miners inside the camps, newspaper reporters were induced, for a consideration which amounted to $75 a month in several instances, to work union messages into their stories. Some of the more enthusiastic writers gave extra service in the form of jabbing the operators in tender spots.

"That is all right, boys," Doyle told them. "If the operators really show their hand and shoot off their mouths enough, we'll take every man out when we call the strike."

Doyle worked out a thousand little details. He had to be prepared to cash benefits, and to provide shelter, clothing, doctors, nurses, and hospital care. The union had $1,000,000 on hand and a promise from the national organization of an additional $250,000 per month if needed.

Despite the vigilance of armed guards, more than 300 miners made their way into Trinidad from the various mining camps for the convention. Not a single operator appeared. Hayes sat on the platform for two days, neither urging the miners to strike nor counselling them to remain at work. This was a popular convention and it was up to the miners to decide. The machinery was in readiness if they wanted to test their strength against the coal barons.

With another international officer it was different. Mother Jones, scenting a fight, had returned to Colorado. Her part in the attempt to call off the northern strike was both forgiven and forgotten, but the aged organizer seemed to feel she must rise to new heights to prove her unionism.

"Rise up and strike!" she screamed from the platform. "If you are too cowardly to fight for your rights there are enough women in this country to come in and beat hell out of you. If it is slavery or strike, I say strike until the last one of you drop into your graves. Strike and stay with it as we did in West Virginia. We are going to stay here in Southern Colorado until the banner of industrial freedom floats over every coal mine. We are going to stand together and never surrender."

She paced up and down the speaker's platform, and waved her arms dramatically.

"When I get Alabama and Colorado organized I will ask God to take me to my rest," she cried. "But first I am going to force the operators to concede that human life is to be regarded above property."

She scored the private detectives and guards, and told the cheering miners that any man who would not defend his home and fireside from thugs had no right to live on the free soil of America.

Lawson sat on the platform and listened to the fiery old woman work the miners into a pitch of frenzy. She was good, he had to admit, but strikes were won by headwork, not oratory. Let her talk, though. She was a good show and the headwork had been done. Everything was ready for the strike.

The scale and policy committee, composed of Chairman Lawson, Pete Miller, Thomas Dennison, John Sidle, John Burke, George Collier, Charles W. Gould, and James Noon, Jr., sat for two days listening to the grievances of miners. They complained they were robbed of from 400 to 800 pounds of coal on each ton they dug; that they were paid in company scrip which was worth only 90 cents on the dollar and expendable only in a company store or saloon; that they were charged from 25 to 40 per cent more for goods than they could be purchased for in the open market; that they were forced to vote according to the wishes of the company superintendent regardless of their own political beliefs; that they were kangarooed and discharged if they joined a union, and that they were sent down the canon if they asked for a checkweighman of their own to protect them from short weights or sought other relief from camp conditions.

When the committee had heard all who wished to be heard, Lawson read its report to the convention.

"In view of the failure of our efforts to secure a peaceful solution of our differences, and in view of the fact that the operators have even refused to answer any of our invitations for a joint meeting, we hereby instruct that a strike call be issued by the District Policy Committee to all the mine workers in Colorado to take effect Tuesday, September 23, 1913.

"We further recommend that any member who is discharged because of affiliation with our movement shall be promptly supported by the organization.

"In conformity with the policy of the organization, which has worked so successfully in other districts, we recommend that we sign with all companies that agree to our demands, provided, however, that they agree not to furnish coal to fill contracts of companies on strike, and that companies that sign up must do so for all the mines they operate."

The demands were seven in number. The first called for recognition of the union and the second set up a scale of wages for mine workers in the various classifications: $3.45 a day for miners; $4 for shot firers; $1.60 for trappers (boys); $3.30 for pumpmen, and so on. The remaining demands were as follows:

"Third: We demand an eight-hour work day for all classes of labor in or around the coal mines and at the coke ovens.

"Fourth: We demand pay for all narrow work and dead work, which includes brushing, timbering, removing falls, handling impurities, etc.

"Fifth: We demand a checkweighman at all mines to be elected by the miners, without any interference by company officials in said election.

"Sixth: We demand the right to trade in any store we please, and the right to choose our own boarding places and our own doctor.

"Seventh: We demand the enforcement of the Colorado Mining Laws and the abolition of the notorious and criminal guard system which has prevailed in the mining camps of Colorado for many years."

A cheer broke from the delegates; then another. There was no doubt of the vote and a few minutes later the convention cast a unanimous ballot for strike. Once the vote and call were on the records, Vice President Hayes told the delegates that most of the demands were nothing more than demands for compliance by the coal operators with statutes which had been on the books for many years.

"I was never more hopeful for success than I am in this strike," he said. "I do not think it will last long. The operators cannot fight an organization of 450,000 men for long. I think we shall realize in Colorado the greatest victory in the history of our organization. I know we cannot lose because our demands are just, and, having made every honorable effort to adjust the differences, the responsibility rests not on us, but on the operators. I hope that when next Tuesday comes every miner will lay down his tools and never take them up again until they take them up as United Mine Workers, recognized by the operators."

While the delegates dispersed to their homes to work the few days remaining, the operators met in Colorado Springs. They decided to stand together and resist the UMWA demands to the last. The die was cast.

CHAPTER V
EXODUS AND THE DEATH SPECIAL

The miners of Southern Colorado, 12,232 in number, began a mass exodus from the narrow, twisting canons September 23, 1913. With them went their women and children. Rain and snow, driven by a biting wind from the north, made progress slow. The long lines of wagons and push carts, hub deep in the soft mud, moved at a snail's pace toward the plains below, bound for the tent cities at Ludlow, Suffield, Sopris, Starkville, Walsenburg, Rugby, Monson, Aguilar, Forbes, El More, Pictou, Cokedale, Oak Creek, and other strategic points at the mouths of the canons. Drenched and shivering, the evicted miners and their families were filled with gloom and fear now that the strike had actually started. Snatches of forced song came from many of the wagons as work-worn women strove to encourage their men and keep their tiny ones from crying.

Lawson, dressed in rough clothes and high-topped boots, moved swiftly from one tent colony to another. There had been a hitch somewhere along the line and 1,000 tents, enroute from West Virginia, had been lost or delayed in transit. Not all of the families could be cared for immediately. As he sped from colony to colony, Lawson met company officials along the roads.

"A good day for a strike," one superintendent called tauntingly.

"Any strike-day would look good to the people from your mines," Lawson shouted back and went on about his business.

In the camps, armed guards trudged from house to house. Wherever they found a striker who had not obtained a conveyance, they threw striker, family and household possessions into the mud-filled street. Mothers, with nursing babies at their breasts, sat on mattresses and furnishings in the freezing rain, awaiting some means of transportation. The camp streets were piled high with tables, chairs and brass bedsteads. Treasured family Bibles, brought from the old country, clothing, pictures, dolls, and other possessions of the strikers and their families were tossed into the rain and mud.

As the families reached the tent colonies they were cared for as rapidly as possible. Each tent had been floored and walled, and arrangements had been made for water and fuel. In the center of each colony was a large tent designed to serve as a school for the children during the day and as a recreation and meeting hall at night. Due to the loss of the thousand tents, many families were housed in the central tents the first night. But there were not sufficient accommodations for all. Hundreds of Greeks, men without families, camped out in the storm. Still others were housed temporarily in union halls and the homes of sympathizers in nearby towns. Those without shelter or fires were fed from special kitchen tents.

Don MacGregor, staff reporter for the Denver Express, a pro-union daily newspaper, was the only newspaperman who even attempted a detailed account of that first day. He wrote:

"No one who did not see that exodus can imagine its pathos. The exodus from Egypt was a triumph, the going forth of a people set free. The exodus of the Boers from Cape Colony was the trek of a united people seeking freedom.

"But this yesterday, that wound its bowed, weary way between the coal hills on the one side and the far-stretching prairie on the other, through the rain and the mud, was an exodus of woe, of a people leaving known fears for new terrors, a hopeless people seeking new hope, a people born to suffering going forth to new suffering.

"And they struggled along the roads interminably. In an hour's drive between Trinidad and Ludlow, 57 wagons were passed, and others seemed to be streaming down to the main road from every by-path.

"Every wagon was the same, with its high piled furniture, and its bewildered woebegone family perched atop. And the furniture! What a mockery to the state's boasted riches. Little piles of rickety chairs. Little piles of miserable looking straw bedding. Little piles of kitchen utensils. And all so worn and badly used they would have been the scorn of any second-hand dealer on Larimer Street."[1]

Fifty additional gunmen were employed for the C. F. & I. Co. by Detective Reno at an office opened for the purpose in the Dover Hotel, 1744 Glenarm Place, in Denver.

"We'll hire 200 more at least to supplement the men we have," Reno announced. At the same time he ordered construction of an armored automobile in the company's steel plant in Pueblo. The Denver Express said most of the newly enlisted guards were scarred veterans of industrial wars in Chicago, Kansas City and St. Louis plus "barrel house bums" from Denver's own saloon and red light district.

Ethelbert Stewart, Secretary of Labor Wilson's mediator, arrived in Trinidad the day the strike began. A heavily-built man of commanding appearance, Stewart was known as an intelligent, conscientious worker, but there was little he could do in Southern Colorado as the time for soft words had passed. He joined with two agitated state officials, Secretary of State Pearce and Labor Commissioner Brake, in a tour of the coal camps. They found the public road into Primero closed and company guards, rifles in hand, barring the way. After a heated argument, they succeeded in getting into the camp with a surly captain of guards as an escort. Before they left, the would-be peace makers discovered that strikers who wanted to leave were

[1] Larimer Street is a run-down thoroughfare in the older part of the Denver business district.

being detained by force.[2] Brake finally obtained an order from the Las Animas County sheriff and succeeded in getting several families past the guards and out of the camp. Stewart talked about conferences, but to no avail. The miners were willing, but the coal operators refused even to listen to his suggestions.

Mother Jones ignored the mediators, the union leaders and the operators. She sensed this was the big show for her, and she put on her best act. On the desolate plains east of Walsenburg, she shook her bony hand at 3,000 upturned faces and challenged them to fight.

"You men, you great, strong men have been enslaved for years," she cried. "You have allowed a few men to boss you, to starve you, to abuse your women and children, to deny you education, to make peons of you, lower and less free than the Negroes were before the Civil War. What is the matter with you? Are you afraid? Do you fear your pitiful little bosses? Are you great, strong men, with so much latent power in you, afraid of your masters or the Baldwin-Felts thugs hired by your masters? I can't believe it. I can't believe you are so cowardly, and I tell you this, if you are, you are not fit to have women live with you."

Dispatches from the coal fields brought forth hysterical editorials in the newspapers. The Rocky Mountain News evasively called for protection of the public's rights. The Express championed the strikers. Governor Ammons, as jittery as the News' editors, warned that violence would be met with immediate action. And violence came quickly. The day after the strike began, Bob Lee, camp marshal at Segundo, was shot and killed as he attempted to herd four strikers with his horse. The companies charged the killing was the beginning of anarchy. Governor Ammons decided Lee died as a result of a deliberate plot, and issued a manifesto warning that any more lawlessness would be met by prompt punishment "no matter by whom committed."

[2] Biennial Report of the Colorado Bureau of Labor Statistics, 1913-1914, P. 166.

Paralysis crept over the state. Non-union miners in the northern field, who had worked through the long strike in that section, laid down their picks. One hundred and twenty-five strike breakers marched out of the Simpson and Standard mines near Lafayette and registered with the union for strike benefits. Throughout the northern field, mines which had been operated by non-union labor were crippled by the sudden swing toward the UMWA.

Judge Northcutt circulated a petition among Trinidad businessmen, asking for troops. Lawson immediately protested, and Edward Keating, congressman from the southern district, called Governor Ammons from Pueblo to ask that the petition be denied.

"We are opposed to sending troops down here," Keating told the governor. "We believe the local authorities are able to cope with the situation."

The Northcutt petition was unsuccessful. The businessmen of Trinidad didn't want the militia. J. J. Abercrombie, an independent mine operator, said he hadn't even bothered to find out if the miners had walked out of his mine, but that if they had it was all right with him.

"As for the shooting of Lee, it seems to me that Bob Lee died from natural causes," he said wryly.

Mayor Dunlavy of Trinidad characterized the proposed request for troops as ridiculous.

"The only serious thing has been the shooting of Lee," Mayor Dunlavy said. "The people here understand that well enough even if those in authority in Denver do not. So far as I can make out, and from everything I've heard, the companies have done more that might make trouble than the miners have up to date."

Lawson deprecated the violence in a public statement which was printed in the Denver newspapers.

"We desire law and order above all things," he said. "We shall try to conduct this strike in a manner that will command public respect. We depend for success on the justness of our cause. We request the operators to warn their imported gunmen to respect the law and to cease their intimidation of union miners. We have cautioned our people in this respect and we expect the operators to do likewise. Our responsibility in this regard is the same and we ought to meet it like men. There is no occasion for the employment of 500 gunmen for the alleged purpose of protecting property."

The operators pooh-pahed public fears that the gunmen would cause trouble and insisted the guards were necessary to protect the mines and camps. They further insisted, in a statement issued by their attorney, Frank Gove, that less than 30 per cent of their miners had walked out.

"For obvious reasons the operators are unwilling to give the strikers and agitators the figures for individual mines," Gove said. "Many willing men were kept from returning to work by means of threatening letters received by them from strikers."

The company contention that the miners wanted to work, but were prevented by small radical groups was repeated in a letter[3] sent to John D. Rockefeller by L. M. Bowers, a C. F. & I. official, six days after the strike began.

"It is safe to say that out of an estimate of 8,000 men who are out, 7,000 of them have quit from fear of the blackhand and similar organizations, who, through letters or face to face, threaten to kill the men, do violence to their wives and daughters, and practice all the hellish villainy that these creatures possess," Mr. Bowers wrote his chief. "One of our marshals, who was one of the best men in our employ, was deliberately shot by Greeks when he undertook to stop them from tearing down a bridge. A bus, carrying a few men, was held up by twenty-five or more strikers and the occupants ordered to leave camp. . . . Old Mother Jones has been on the ground for two weeks. . . . "

[3] The letter was later printed in the report of a congressional investigating committee.

The men ordered to leave were three Negro strike breakers brought into the state from Texas. They were ordered off the bus, fed in the union camp at Ludlow, and sent home—at union expense.

A federal grand jury, sitting in Pueblo, began an investigation of the strike and of conditions in the coal fields at the request of the operators.

The next serious trouble came October 7, 1913, when several Ludlow strikers walked up the canon to Hastings, intent on getting their mail from the United States post office. Guards refused them admittance to the camp. The miners argued for several minutes and then, seeing they could not enter, turned and started back down the winding road. A guard laughed and fired two shots over their heads. A few minutes later, B. S. Larson, chief clerk of the C. F. & I., accompanied by Belk and Belcher, drove close to the Ludlow colony and fired more than a dozen shots into the tents.[4] Furious, shouting men poured out of the colony and made for the automobile. Here and there was a gun, but most of the men carried sticks or stones. They rushed toward the company men who sped off. The appearance of the miners was a signal, however, for a volley which crashed from a hill near Hastings and from a stone house near the mouth of Hastings canon where a force of guards was stationed. Miners secured guns from secret hiding places and the firing became general. The women and children rushed from the colony and crowded close against a fence on the Hastings side of the tents. Although they stood on the plain, fully exposed to the fire, they seemed to have no fear. They cheered when they saw a mounted guard go down. Every shot from the miners that seemed to take effect brought another cheer from the women and children.

John Lawson, panicky at the thought that women and children might be killed, ran along the fence, forcing them back to the colony.

[4] Conditions in the Coal Mines of Colorado, Hearings Before a Subcommittee of the Committee on Mines and Mining, U. S. House of Representatives, 1914, Vol. 1, P. 37.

"Get back to the tents," he shouted. "Get back, every one of you."

Gradually the women and children drifted back, singing the union songs as they went. Before the furious onslaught of the crazed miners, the guards retreated to the hills. The miners straggled back into camp, swearing vengeance against the guards. Their leaders promptly talked them out of it.

A few shots were fired at the camp the next morning from a passing Denver & Rio Grande Western railroad train, a mile east. Again the men ran out with their rifles and started toward the distant right-of-way. John Lawson stopped them.

"Are you fellows crazy?" he cried. "While you fellows run down there a mile or so the Hastings guards will come down and take the tent colony."

The strikers saw the logic of that and returned to the colony with muttered threats.

Early the next morning, a shot was fired from Hastings Hill at a number of miners who were playing baseball at the edge of the colony. The bullet kicked up dirt in the middle of the diamond. Once more the miners roared with anger and ran for their weapons. In the ensuing fight, the guards were driven back into the hills. Mack Powell, a former union miner who was working as a cowboy on a nearby ranch, was killed as he sat on his horse watching the battle.[5]

The coal companies again demanded state troops. They accused the strikers of carrying on a merciless war against them. The claim was made despite the fact that company guards had to travel some distance from company property to come to grips with the colonists.

Two days after the disturbance, Bowers, who had left his home in Binghampton, N. Y., to establish headquarters in Denver, again wrote to Rockefeller.

"It is now proven beyond any sort of question that Win-

[5] Witnesses later told a congressional committee they heard the guards brag they had killed a miner during the battle.

chester rifles in large numbers and revolvers with large quantities of ammunition are being supplied to the sluggers whom these men have brought in from other states together with the blood-thirsty Greeks who have just returned from the Turkish wars," Mr. Bowers said in his letter. "We also find that Ethelbert Stewart, representing Commissioner of Labor Wilson, has been for years connected with labor unions. . . .

"When this government places in the cabinet men like Commissioner of Labor Wilson, who was for many years secretary of the United Mine Workers of America, which has been one of the unions that permitted more disorder and bloodshed than any class of labor organization in this country, we are not skating upon thin ice, but we are on top of a volcano.

"When such men as these together with the cheap professors and still cheaper writers in muckraking magazines, supplemented by a lot of milk-and-water preachers with little or no religion and still less common sense, are permitted to assault the business men who have built up the great industries and have done more to make this country what it is than all other agencies combined, it is time that vigorous measures are taken to put a stop to these vicious teachings which are being sown broadcast throughout the country.

"I know of no journal or magazine published in this country today that is doing the good work that is being done in Leslie's Weekly and I know of no better expenditure for the common good and for the safety of this country that you could direct than to make it possible for the publisher to distribute a million copies a week of this magazine.

"I am personally doing all I can, when attending directors' meetings of the several companies I am in and whenever I meet business men, to call attention to Leslie's Weekly."[6]

While Mr. Bowers happily planned to right conditions in Colorado with a flood of Brahminish magazines, Lawson sought

[6] Report on the Colorado Strike, United States Commission on Industrial Relations, 1915, P. 146.

ways and means of protecting the tent colonies. Breastworks were thrown up around the Ludlow colony and pits were dug under most of the tents to provide shelter for women and children in case of attack. While the precautionary steps were being taken, Lawson learned the coal operators had purchased four machine guns and shipped them into Colorado. They had been sent to the southern field.

"This puts a more serious aspect on these attacks," he said soberly in a council with McLennan and Hayes. "We've got to protect the women and children at all costs."

"But they can't conduct a war against us with machine guns," Hayes protested. "They wouldn't turn guns like those on defenseless people."

"I am afraid they would," Lawson replied. "They'd apparently do anything if they thought they could get away with it."

They sent a letter to the operators protesting against the killing of Mack Powell and against the purchase of machine guns. A second letter was sent to Governor Ammons informing him of the presence of machine guns in Southern Colorado. No replies were received. Eight days later the C. F. & I. Company's armored automobile, The Death Special, equipped with a machine gun, appeared on a road near the Forbes tent colony. The colony had been fired upon several times by snipers and the strikers, fearful of a more serious attack, had built a separate colony for the women and children, 300 yards distant. There were 25 men in the colony. They had seven rifles and shotguns, six revolvers, all of different makes, and very little ammunition. The men were sitting around a blanket in the colony street, playing cards, when the armored car approached. At the same moment a dozen horsemen galloped over a slight elevation just north of the tents and headed for the card players. The strikers jumped to their feet and picked up their guns.

The horsemen stopped a few yards away and one of their number, Charles W. Kennedy, dismounted and approached the miners on foot. He carried a white handkerchief as a sign of peace. Kennedy walked confidently. This was old stuff to him. He was a man of experience. Although listed on official records as a resident of Prowers County and a deputy sheriff of Las Animas County, Kennedy was far from being a green, country peace officer. He had served three years in the 19th Infantry, Philippine Islands; three years in the Second Infantry, Philippine Islands, and several months with a British regiment, the Dublin Light Infantry, on the Pabenegmay River in Upper Burma. Alarm was written on the faces of the strikers as he stepped up to them. They could see his white flag plainly enough, but they could also see the carbines of the horsemen and the black snout of a machine gun protruding from the armored car, some 150 yards away.

"It's all right, boys, we're union men," Kennedy called out loudly. The miners lowered their guns and clustered around him as he drew a union card from his pocket.

"I want to tell you something," Kennedy said. "What I want to say is that we're going to teach you damned red-necks a lesson."

He tossed the handkerchief aside, dropped to the ground, and rolled.[7] As he did so, the horsemen fired a volley into the astonished strikers. Luke Verhornik pitched forward on his face, a bullet through his brain. The strikers turned and ran toward a small gulley. The machine gun chattered at their backs. A little boy, who had been visiting his father, ran toward the women's colony. The machine gun swung in his direction and he crumpled midway between the two colonies. He attempted to drag himself away, but lay quiet when the rapid fire gun turned back to him. John Ure, an aged striker, who had been unable to run with his companions, huddled under a cot in his tent while bullets ripped the canvas into shreds. A small girl, the daughter of a neighboring farmer, who was on her way home from school, was shot in the face. The firing kept up intermittently from 2 p. m. until nightfall when the

[7] Kennedy later testified before an investigating committee that the strikers threatened to kill him.

attackers withdrew. The strikers crept stealthily out of the protecting gulley and made their way to the moaning boy. He had
nine bullet holes in his legs.[8] They carried him to the women's
camp and then returned to their gulley where they kept guard
the rest of the night.

A message was sent to Ludlow to John Lawson and when he
arrived at the Forbes colony early the next morning he saw
Felts, Belcher, Judge Northcutt, the C. F. & I. attorney, and
three guards, all heavily armed, hiding in a railroad cut 200
yards from the tents.

The Ure tent was found to have more than 85 holes in it.
It was taken down and sent north to union headquarters in
Denver from where it was shipped East to exhibit to miners
and unionists in other organizations—a ragged sample of a
ragged warfare. None of the attackers had received so much
as a scratch.

Fearful that a similar attack would be made on the large
Ludlow colony, Lawson left Trinidad and took active charge.
He felt he should keep in close personal touch with the colony
and secondly he had Governor Ammons' expressed wish that
he be in charge. Lawson's first task was to organize the colony
on military lines. Guards were posted on the outskirts, day and
night. The tents were in a strategic position at the crossing of
two roads leading to Berwind and Tabasco on the one hand
and Hastings and Delagua on the other. Strike breakers could
not very well reach the company camps without passing near
the colony. The chief weakness lay in the complete exposure to
attack. Lawson called the men together in the big tent.

"From now on we have to protect this colony every minute
of the day and night," he said. "Every man will have a part.
Some of you will guard the tents and some of you will be
assigned to patrols outside. We have 1,200 people here and we
have to have both order and protection."

He appointed a leader for each of the 21 racial groups and

[8] Report on the Colorado Strike, United States Commission on Industrial
Relations, 1914, P. 104.

gave instructions that each leader was to be obeyed in everything by the people of his nationality. The leaders, in turn,
were to be responsible to him.

"Let every miner wear his red bandanna around his neck,"
Lawson said. "It is our uniform." He had already set an example by knotting his own bandanna around his neck. A .45
caliber revolver was strapped to his waist.

Despite the constant fear of attack, the people of Ludlow
seemed happier than they had in the coal camps. Racial an-
tagonisms began to disappear in the close intimacy of the
colony and in the need for united action. Men and women of
different nationalities began to learn each other's languages. A
pidgin tongue was developed. The melting pot was finally at
work.

"You know," a little Welsh woman told Lawson, "I never
had much use for these foreigners, but I am beginning to like
them now. They're just like us only they can't talk our
language."

"That's right, mother," Lawson replied. "They're human
beings and loveable, too."

Lawson arranged for regular dances in the big tent. The
Italians supplied the music. It was a wedding of the races.
Over-worked, beaten men and women, who had never had time
to get acquainted in the dreary camps, had time to know one
another and to appreciate each other's qualities.

There were a few guns in the colony, rifles, shotguns, and
revolvers, but not more than 30 or 40. The union had purchased some rifles and ammunition, but the supplies had been
distributed over a wide area. Large purchases had not yet been
made as the coal companies had cleaned out the stores of the
state to equip their private armies.

The colonists' guns were used by the Ludlow men who stood
guard during the long freezing nights while coal company
searchlights, mounted on nearby elevations, played over the
roads and tents. One particular light at Hastings was a source

of constant irritation as the operator would often keep it on the Ludlow tents throughout the night. Women and children could not sleep. Nerves were shattered. The problem was finally solved by an enterprising striker who borrowed a high-powered rifle from a Trinidad dentist and carefully shot out the Hastings light as well as several others in the vicinity. They were replaced, but the guards used them with more discretion.

The clashes between strikers and guards became more frequent with the appointment of a new commander of company guards who was more brutal and bloodthirsty than any of his predecessors. He was K. E. Linderfelt, a lieutenant in the Colorado National Guard, a soldier of fortune, and a veteran of the Philippine campaign and the Mexican revolution. A swaggering, blustering man, Linderfelt was a rare combination of bully and bulldog. Cruel and mean, he was a braggart, but he could back his boastfulness with courageous fighting. Under his leadership, the guards went to new lengths to intimidate and harass the strikers.

Three guards in a company automobile raced by the Sopris tent colony, emptying their automatic pistols at the camp as they sped along the highway. A searchlight was mounted on the hills above the town of Segundo. When a guard, who had insulted a Segundo woman, was beaten, a machine gun opened on the town and sprayed bullets along the streets and over the houses for ten minutes. The next morning, 48 strikers, who were peacefully picketing the Starkville mine, a property owned by James McLaughlin, brother-in-law of Governor Ammons, were arrested and marched on foot between double rows of armed guards into Trinidad, three miles distant, where they were jailed. In Walsenburg, a band of six thugs, led by Lou Miller, went up and down the streets, assaulting strikers and union sympathizers.

CHAPTER VI

CALL OUT THE MILITIA!

The brutal assaults brought vigorous protests from labor organizations throughout the state. The Pueblo Trades and Labor Assembly called for a federal investigation and intervention. The assembly's announcement was sufficient to send Cass Herrington, political manager of the C. F. & I. Co., a Father Malone, and Caldwell Yeaman, a corporation attorney, to Washington to forestall any such move. The Denver Trades and Labor Assembly, the Typographical Union and a dozen other labor organizations protested to Governor Ammons. The bewildered executive summoned Ed Doyle to his office for a conference on conditions in Las Animas and Huerfano counties.[1]

"You'll have to do something about these shootings," the governor said.

"Are you going to hold us responsible for individual cases and for cases provoked by the guards?" Doyle asked in surprise. Governor Ammons toyed with a letter opener nervously.

"Well, you'll have to control your men. That is all there is to it."

Doyle explained, or rather attempted to explain, the union's position, but Governor Ammons would not listen.

"Sheriff Farr and Sheriff Grisham telephoned me that they

[1] Conditions in the Mines of Colorado, Hearings before a Subcommittee on Mines and Mining, U. S. House of Representatives, 1914, Part VII, P. 2215.

are afraid to make arrests," Governor Ammons said. "I've told them I will give them any aid they need. There seems to be nothing left to do but send troops down there."

"You had better be cautious, governor. If you shoot half the miners and deport the other half we'll have the same thing over in ten years."

"Well, we've got to do something, Doyle."

"May I make a suggestion, governor? Why don't you throw Welborn, Osgood, Brown, McLennan, Lawson and myself in jail and keep us there until we can agree to come out and sit down in a conference like gentlemen?"

The governor was startled. He peered sharply at the young Irishman to see if he were joking. Doyle was serious.

"If you've offered these two sheriffs assistance," Doyle went on, "would you offer John Lawson assistance if he appealed for aid?"

"I should say not," Governor Ammons replied shortly. "I would not give him assistance while he had armed murderers shooting at innocent people on the roads."

"Why, governor, you have offered to give assistance to the Baldwin-Felts detectives—to the deputies—knowing as you do that you have no control over them, yet you refuse a citizen of the state, Mr. Lawson, assistance."

The governor's face flushed with anger. Argument was not a strong point with him. He sought refuge in high indignation.

"You fellows can't tell me what to do," he shouted.

"No, governor," Doyle said smoothly. He tried to hide a smile. This man was as transparent as glass. Doyle could see right through him. "If you send troops into the southern field what will be your attitude?"

"I want peace; the armed guards will be taken away and those people will be disarmed. We must have peace."

"Fine, governor, fine. That is what we want. I presume there will be no objection to two men meeting on the street and talking if one has a union card in his pocket and the other hasn't?"

"There will be no picketing," the governor replied. "There will be no picketing. That is positive—that is where the trouble will start."

"If there is no picketing, strike breakers have a free road," Doyle replied. "If you want to avoid trouble, why don't you strike at the seat of the trouble? Why don't you stop the cause of the trouble and shut down the mines?"

"No, they have a right to operate those mines."

"Then you are going to recognize the rights of the operators to operate those mines, but you are not going to recognize the right of the citizen to talk, one man to another?"

Governor Ammons arose in a sign of dismissal.

"We cannot have picketing," he said. "We cannot have any picketing; that is all there is about it."

Doyle went back to his office and telephoned Lawson.

"This fellow Ammons never knows what to do or when to do it," he said sadly.

"I've noticed that," Lawson replied, "and I am afraid he will get worse as time goes by."

The next day, Governor Ammons, in company with several state officials, went to Southern Colorado to make a personal investigation. At one company gate he was refused permission to pass along a public highway leading into the C. F. & I. Company's Ravenwood Mine. An Oklahoma gunman, who stopped the party, told the chief executive:

"You may be the governor and again maybe you ain't. I dunno. But you ain't got no pass to get in here and you ain't going in, see?"

Governor Ammons saw, and turned around and went back.

While the governor was riding back to Trinidad, Denver bankers announced that they were willing to give the state financial assistance to put the militia in the field. At almost the same hour, Congressman Keating introduced a resolution in the House asking Congress to make an inquiry in the strike district.

Mother Jones decided a demonstration was in order. She called the women and children in from the colonies for a parade in Trinidad. The aged organizer tried to charter cars on the Colorado & Southern railroad to carry the Ludlow contingent into Trinidad, but the railroad refused cars. She finally got her forces assembled in Trinidad, however, and started her parade with a brass band out front. Governor Ammons was at the Cardenas Hotel. On the pretext that the paraders should have a word from the state's chief executive, Mother Jones marched her women and children to the hotel. They couldn't get the governor to come out so they filed into the hotel and through the hallways to his room, packing every corridor. Governor Ammons refused to see them.

"Unlock that door and come out here," Mother Jones yelled, beating on the door. "These women ain't going to bite you."

Her remarks made a hit with the crowd, as she intended, but Governor Ammons cannily stayed in his room.

A series of dynamitings at Sopris, up the river from Trinidad, brought renewed demands from the operators for troops. Lawson made a speedy investigation and found that Antone Langowski, secretary of the Sopris union local, who was receiving $3 a week in strike benefits, was responsible for the disorders. The operators were right; it was a union man and a striker who must bear the blame for the explosions on company property. Lawson was nonplussed. In most everything the strikers followed him faithfully. He had specifically asked them to refrain from violence. On further investigation, he found an answer. Mr. Langowski was receiving $3 per day from the operators to start trouble and throw discredit on the United Mine Workers.[2]

[2] Conditions in the Coal Mines of Colorado, Hearings Before a Subcommittee of the Committee on Mines and Mining, 1914. Part VIII, Pages 2305 to 2346.

A new high in terrorism was reached in Walsenburg October 24, 1913, when thirty heavily armed guards rode into town from the Walsen Mine. They trotted their horses down Seventh Street to a group of houses where strike breakers were preparing to move their furniture to the C. F. & I. stockade. A crowd of strikers and their women and children stood on the sidewalk and in the street jeering.

"Scabs! Scabs!"

As the guards rode up, cursing and threatening, the unarmed strikers and their families started a new chant:

"Scab herders! Scab herders!"

Without the slightest warning, the guards opened fire. The crowd scattered. Women, with children in their arms, ran screaming toward the shelter of nearby buildings. The guards fired several rounds and then rode away, toward the mine and its stockade. When the miners crept back into the street, they found three of their number—Kris Kokich, Andy Auvinen and Cisto Croci—riddled with bullets. The strike breakers had fled.

Frenzied strikers and union sympathizers armed themselves and marched through the Walsenburg business section calling for vengeance. Guards stood in a line across the gateway of the Walsen Mine property at the head of Seventh Street. Sheriff Farr, with 50 deputies, barricaded the court house. Men were posted at every window; a machine gun covered the main approach to the gray stone building. Four hundred citizens milled in the street outside, calling on the sheriff and his deputies to come out and fight. Sheriff Farr telephoned Trinidad for help. Judge Northcutt and A. C. Felts, with ten armed guards, climbed on a northbound pullman that night. The brakeman objected.

"Gentlemen, you can't bring guns into this car."

Judge Northcutt signaled to Felts and then politely held the door open while the detective kicked the railroader off the train.

On their arrival in Walsenburg, Judge Northcutt and Felts were unable to get near the court house, and Sheriff Farr was forced to remain in his fortress until the mob wearied of the siege and drifted away.

In Denver, coal company press agents glibly explained away the Seventh Street killings. They sent out stories to the effect that the 30 mounted guards were sent to Walsenburg to rescue the wife of a strike breaker, and that the miners had attacked the armed men. Regret was expressed at the three deaths, but the stories explained they were necessary to preserve law and order.

The men of Ludlow and other colonies demanded arms from their leaders and when they didn't get them went to Trinidad to beg from door to door for anything that would shoot. Billy Diamond, the union official charged with handling the Trinidad office, ordered 300 rifles from the East, but someone tipped off the coal companies and the shipment was seized as it entered Colorado. A number of strikers intimated Diamond might have had something to do with the tip-off. They finally received a shipment of arms, however, through Charles Snyder, an organizer, who brought 71 rifles, all of .30-.30 caliber, and 5,000 rounds of ammunition from Denver. These guns, together with the personal arms of the miners, raised the number of weapons in the Ludlow colony to approximately 200. Lawson brought three rifles and a small amount of ammunition into the colony for the office tent. Of the arms on hand, approximately 60 rifles were carried regularly by Lawson's colony police.

Each pay day approximately $2,000 was distributed to the Ludlow men. The money was sent out from Denver by Ed Doyle and paid out from the office tent. The same practice was followed in each tent colony. On the afternoon of October 25, Lawson sat in the Ludlow office with the paymaster and Louis Tikas, leader of the Greeks. A table blocked the doorway of the tent and served as a counter for payments. Outside the tent, more than 500 men were strung out in a long line waiting for their benefits. It was cold and blustery and the men were anxious to be gone. As each man stepped up for his benefits, he handed his card to Tikas who read it aloud while the pay-master checked his lists. Then the money was paid. Lawson sat a little to the side. If there was a dispute over the amount, Lawson had the man step aside and wait until the rest were paid.

The men were paid as rapidly as possible, but it was slow work.

Shortly after two o'clock, Lawson heard several shots.

"Did you hear them?" he asked Tikas.

"Sure, I heard them," Tikas replied. "It is probably some of the guards up the canon wasting company bullets on tin cans."

Lawson motioned for the paymaster to go on with his work. Minutes later more shots were heard. The men in the long line became fidgety and restless. Lawson rose from his chair and went around the table. He saw a miner running along the line.

"The colony is being attacked," the miner cried. "The colony is being attacked."

The line broke and the miners ran in every direction. Leaders of the police squads called to their men to assemble. There were cries and orders in a dozen tongues. Lawson's first thought was of the women and children. He saw several miners, rifles in hand leave the camp and head for a deep cut a short distance away. The women and children were milling around in the colony streets.

"Be quiet," Lawson called, moving among the women. "There isn't anything unusual taking place. Return to your tents. There isn't any danger."

He knew the guards rode to meet the Colorado & Southern train at this hour. They had probably fired the shots and gone on their way. He heard the whistle of the locomotive, and the firing seemed to die away. He went to the office tent and called Trinidad to inform the headquarters office of the shooting. As he replaced the receiver, Frederick Huppert, telegraph operator at Ludlow station, came to the door of the tent.

"Mr. Lawson, there is a young woman up here near the railroad tracks," Huppert said. "Her name is Anna Cameron. She is the daughter of the superintendent at Hastings."

"Yes?" Lawson replied.

"She just came in on the train and there wasn't anyone to meet her. She wants to get home."

"We'll take her to her friends," Lawson said. ` He snatched up his gun belt from the cot, buckled it around his waist, and went with Huppert to the tracks. Miss Cameron was near tears.

"I telephoned for a rig," she said, "but no one has come. I would like to get up to Hastings."

"You come with me," Lawson said. He picked up her suitcase and took her arm. They walked up the road toward Hastings.

"Don't be alarmed," Lawson said gently. "I haven't found out what the shots are about, but I don't think there is any danger."

"You are very kind," Miss Cameron replied.

Several hundred yards from the Ludlow station they met Carl Bayes, driver of the regular hack, who had been sent down the canon for Miss Cameron. Lawson helped her into the hack, tipped his hat politely and bade her goodbye. By the time he returned to the colony the firing in the distance had increased in volume. He immediately called several of the men together.

"This is beginning to look serious," he said. "Get several tents and we'll move as many of the women and children as possible to that arroyo just north."

The men fell to willingly. Tents, stoves, coal and food were placed on a big wagon. There were no horses available so the men picked up the tongue and pulled the cumbersome vehicle to the sheltered arroyo. The women and children would be out of range, and could be more easily guarded in this protected spot. The tents were pitched and the little camp made ready for the night shortly before dark. A detail of miners brought a number of women and children to the new camp.

On his return to the colony, Lawson found dozens of strikers, rifles in hand, straggling in from the prairie. A light snow was falling and visibility had been reduced to a few yards.

"The guards have give up," an Italian told him. "There was a big bunch and they had what you call reinforcements. The clerks came down from Berwind after the shooting start. I guess they go back now."

"How did it start?"

"The gunmen shoot when they go to the train."

"Anybody injured?"

"Naw, nobody she got a scratch."

It was not until the next morning that Lawson learned that a guard named John Nimmo had been killed.

The miners were infuriated by the afternoon-long exchange of shots. Despite pleas from Lawson that all they could hope to do against the guards was defend their tent homes from attack, most of the men took food and slipped away into the hills during the night.

Lieutenant Linderfelt, in command of a detachment of guards at Ludlow section house during the impromptu battle, had several scouts out on the prairie watching the colony and maintaining contact with other detachments. When they informed him that the rest of the guards had withdrawn up the canon and that large numbers of strikers were leaving the colony Linderfelt knew the miners had played into the company's hands at last. He telephoned Trinidad for aid, pleading a desperate situation, and wired Adjutant General John Chase of the Colorado National Guard in Denver, telling him that a virtual rebellion existed.

At 2 a. m., with strikers slowly closing in around the section house, Linderfelt abandoned it and marched up the canon. As he entered the canon, the section house went up in flames. He took his men to Berwind, obtained provisions from the company store, and moved on to the pump house which could be easily defended if the hoped for attack took place. Linderfelt kept urgent telegrams going into Trinidad and Denver.

Late in the morning, the strikers attacked the Tabasco mine. Entrenched on hillsides above the mine, they sent a steady rain of bullets down on the property. The guards barricaded themselves in the mine buildings and returned the fire.

"Sheriff Grisham phoned 8:30 this morning a sufficient force of deputies to relieve you about to leave Trinidad," General Chase telegraphed Linderfelt. "They should be in contact with strikers by 10 a. m."

Thirty-six coal company guards had been rushed from Walsenburg to Trinidad and deputized by Sheriff Grisham as Las Animas County deputy sheriffs, but train crews refused to take them back to Ludlow. When he was informed the guards couldn't get a train, Lieutenant Linderfelt played his trump card. He wired General Chase: "The only solution to this is troops and at once. No help can be expected but from troops."

Meanwhile, the miners tired of the battle. They had no organization and no leadership, and they began to wander back toward the Ludlow colony, singing and laughing at the discomfiture of the guards. They had driven the thugs into their holes. There was much loud bragging. A grand banquet was arranged. The warriors told great stories of their prowess. Lawson sat glumly apart. He was angry at them for their disobedience and he feared they had given the coal company a strong case for militia.

Early the next morning, while the strikers were sleeping off the effects of their celebration, union headquarters in Trinidad telephoned that a locomotive, drawing three steel coal cars and a box car and caboose, mounted with machine guns, was enroute from the county seat town to attack the colony.

"They can't do that," Lawson yelled. "We'll stop them before they ever get here." He called his various captains together and told them to rout out their men. Within a half hour, five hundred men, with red bandannas around their necks and carbines in their hands, streamed out over the plains to meet the train. Guards in the hills to the west opened a steady fire on them, but the miners ignored it. They had to stop that train.

The miners moved in a semblance of order. Louie Tikas commanded the Greeks, many of whom had seen military service in their own country and knew the meaning of discipline. Still others among the various racial groups were veterans of European or Balkan wars and were now under the direct command of young men who had been trained to direct troops. The miners were ready when the steel train arrived. A Baldwin-Felts detective was at the throttle of the locomotive and another Baldwin-Felts was the fireman. A third, Felts himself, was the conductor. Two machine guns were mounted in the steel coal cars which were filled with riflemen.

The Ludlow men, hidden along the sides of Water Tank Hill and on the Green ranch, sighted the train as it drew near. Just as it rounded a curve and the cars were broadside to the miners they fired a heavy volley. The guards ducked down, but the cars had been built to carry coal, not to stop bullets. The train coughed to a stop. Then it started to back away. While the miners cheered triumphantly, the train backed to Forbes Junction where the guards, five of whom had been wounded, detrained and made their way on foot over the hills to join Linderfelt's men. The lieutenant, who had witnessed the rout of the train from the hills, hurried back to his position where he received reports from his scouts and then hastily wired General Chase in Denver:

"Large body of men leaving Aguilar to reinforce. Rebels at Ludlow make statements they are going to clean up Berwind and Hastings. Situation looks hopeless. No hope can be expected only from troops, as there is nothing left to hope for."

The miners were more jubilant than ever when they marched back to the Ludlow colony from the steel train victory. Again they feasted and danced, but the celebration came to an end at an early hour when a blizzard screamed out of the northeast and blotted out Southern Colorado. In the midst of the storm, 300 strikers slipped out of the tent colony and turned toward the hills, determined to prevent the guards from making another sortie out of the canons. Before dawn of October 28, 1913, they attacked Berwind and Hastings. All the pent-up hatred of weeks was concentrated on these two mining camps. The shooting of the miners was accurate and vicious. Ten mine guards and deputies fell before noon. Telephone and telegraph wires were cut. A special detail blew up the railroad tracks. Another detachment attacked Tabasco, driving the guards and their families into the mine. While the battle was at its height, couriers came running from Ludlow with messages from John Lawson.

"Stop your fighting and return to your tents quickly," the messages said.

"But why for we do this?" a huge Slav asked. "We come to feex these guards and we stay now and feexum good."

"Lawson says to come back and you'd better do it," a breathless messenger said. "The governor has called out the militia."

The miners put their rifles away and slowly moved back to Ludlow. They walked in little groups, talking excitedly. What did this mean? Would the soldiers be neutral? Would they take the rifles of the miners? Would they disarm the company guards? What protection would the miners have from the imported gunmen? Those who had been in other strikes were sick with fear. They dreaded "the melish" above all things.

When they reached the camp, an angry Lawson addressed them.

"You've got to stop this fighting, boys," he said. "You have a perfect right to fight in defense of your families and your homes, but you have no right to attack. You are just playing the company's game when you do."

The men moved restlessly. They trusted Lawson, but they hated and feared the gunmen.

"What about the soldiers?" a man called.

"They'll be here soon," Lawson replied. "I've talked to Doyle and there is no doubt they have been called out by the governor."

Doyle had telephoned the colony a few minutes after Governor Ammons had issued an executive order to General Chase. The general, a physician who specialized in eye, ear, nose and throat ailments in Denver, was a sanctimonious man of past middle age and a militarist of the old school. He had first earned a reputation with the notorious Adjutant General Sherman Bell in the Cripple Creek strike of 1903. When General Chase wasn't busy practicing his profession or playing the organ in the York Street Presbyterian Church in Denver, he was in uniform.

Governor Ammons' order had been brief. It read:

"It having been made to appear to me by the peace officers of the counties of Las Animas and Huerfano and other counties of the State of Colorado, by numerous civil officers and other good and reputable citizens of said counties, that there is a tumult threatened, and that there are bodies of men, acting together by force and violence to break and resist the laws of this state, and that a number of persons are in possession of deadly weapons and are in open and active opposition to the execution of the laws of this state in said districts, and that the civil authorities are wholly unable to cope with the situation in the preservation and maintenance of order, and the laws of the State of Colorado,

"I, therefore, direct you, in pursuance of the authority and power vested in me as governor by the constitution and laws of the State of Colorado to forthwith order out and assume command of such troops of the National Guard of Colorado as in your judgment may be necessary to maintain peace and order in said districts, and that you use such means as you may deem right and proper, acting in conjunction with or independently of the civil authorities of said districts, as in your judgment and discretion are demanded, to restore peace and good order in

the communities affected and to enforce obedience to the constitution and laws of this state.

"Given under my hand and the executive seal this twenty-
eighth day of October, A. D. 1913." [3]

The governor's intention to call out the militia was known
to the labor leaders several days in advance, but they made no
objection. They knew troops would be advantageous to the
coal companies in that it would enable them to hand much of
the cost of their guard systems over to the state, but they felt
the rights of the miners would be protected by a state statute
which forbade the importation of strike breakers into the state.

General Chase was dressed in his best uniform and ready to
take to the field by the time the executive order was signed.
He went to Governor Ammons' office with a group of National
Guard officers for a conference. It was agreed that the militia
would be strictly neutral, and that company guards and gunmen would not be enlisted under any consideration.

"I think that is very important," Capt. W. C. Danks, an
attorney, told the conference. "These company gunmen and
guards are pretty much riff-raff, and I don't think we should
allow any of them to be in uniform."

Governor Ammons agreed. When the officers left, everyone
understood that corporation gunmen would not be allowed to
become part of the military organization. The agreement was
based upon strikes of an earlier day when corporations shifted
gunmen from their own payroll to that of the state.

At Ludlow, and in the other colonies nestled along the Southern Colorado foothills, the union leaders assured their people
that the militia would not injure them or their cause. The assurances quieted the strikers for a few hours, but when the troops
failed to arrive promptly, the miners became restive again. Wild

[3] Conditions in the Coal Mines of Colorado, Hearings Before a Subcommittee of the Committee on Mines and Mining, U. S. House of Representatives,
1914. Part IX, P. 2528. Governor Ammons was entirely justified in calling out
the militia. It was only after the militiamen got out of hand that criticism, some
of it proper and some not, was heaped on his head.

rumors spread from tent to tent and from colony to colony. One report said armed men, traveling in seven automobiles, were enroute from Trinidad to the Ludlow colony to attack. The miners and their families milled in the streets of the colony, cursing the guards and the coal companies and demanding revenge on the guards before the troops arrived. Lawson was anxious to get away to Denver for a conference with President White, who had arrived from Indianapolis to receive progress reports, but first he had to quiet the men. He called the leaders of the colony police together and ordered them to keep the miners in the colony.

"You tell every man, in his own tongue so there will be no misunderstandings, that he cannot leave this colony," Lawson said. "Not a man must go outside of the boundaries. If the guards attack, the men will be turned loose to defend themselves."

When Lawson reached Denver, the policy committee met immediately with President White. Their first accomplishment was the launching of an advertising campaign to offset a similar program sponsored by the operators. For several days, Denver newspapers had carried advertisements designed to make the public believe coal miners earned from $4 to $5 per day. The policy committee ran a series of its own in the Denver dailies. The first advertisement contained a reproduction of time slips which showed the miners had not averaged more than $1.60 per day. The public was asked to decide if the miners would spend a winter in tents to secure the demanded wage of $3.45 per day if they could make $4 and $5 as the operators contended.

"If these operators are paying $4 and $5 a day why do they persist in refusing to pay $3.45 a day?" the advertisement asked.

Lawson was forced to leave the policy committee before its conferences were ended because of a new outbreak in the southern field. Guards at Aguilar, a few miles north of Ludlow, fired on strikers who retaliated with a heavy volley. In the ensuing battle, the guards were driven back into the mine buildings. Before the fight ended, several buildings and the post office were smouldering ruins. The Denver newspapers played up the battle in sensational headlines. The UMWA immediately arranged a mass meeting in the Denver municipal auditorium, and 10,000 persons crowded into the building to hear President White and Vice President Hayes discuss the strike.

"The miners of this state have not fired a single shot except in self defense," White told the throng. "That is our policy and will continue to be our policy."

Lawson was speeding back to Ludlow.

CHAPTER VII

GUNMAN IN ARMOR

A long troop train, carrying General Chase and the state militia slowly came to a stop on a siding three miles north of Ludlow October 31, 1913. General Chase occupied one car with his officers—Major Pat Hamrock, a Denver saloon keeper; Major Edward J. Boughton, tall, slim and immaculate, an attorney for the mine owners' association in Cripple Creek, who would act as judge advocate of the miltia; Captains Danks and Van Cise, and others. Lieutenant Linderfelt was waiting with two automobiles and a handful of company guards. After a hurried conference with Linderfelt, General Chase, flanked by several officers, left the train and went by automobile to Ludlow. The machine bore a flag of truce. Lawson and McLennan, along with Hayes, who had arrived a few minutes earlier, and the leaders of the various nationalities, met the military commander at the edge of the colony and conducted him with proper ceremony to the headquarters tent.

"I suppose you have seen a copy of Governor Ammons' order?" General Chase asked.

"Yes, we are familiar with it," Lawson replied.

"Very well," the general said. "I will disarm both sides to this controversy as soon as possible. Order will be maintained at all times. The military will not be used to aid either side."

The leaders communicated the promise to the men in a dozen tongues and a cheer went up.

"Will the troops camp near here?" Lawson asked as the cheering died away.

"Yes, the camp will be established in the immediate vicinity."

"Then we would like to greet them formally when they come in," Lawson said.

Before General Chase left the colony, it was agreed that the troops would march into the area in full dress and that the strikers would meet them along the road.

When the general and his officers had gone, Lawson gave hurried orders and telephoned Trinidad headquarters.

"Notify the other colonies to have as many people here as possible tomorrow," he said. "We want to give the militia a proper welcome."

The next morning, as the troops tramped toward Ludlow, miners and their wives, led by a brass band, marched across the sun-lit plain to welcome them. Eighteen hundred men and women carried American flags. Ahead of them danced a thousand children dressed in white and singing Vice President Hayes' composition to the tune of The Battle Cry of Freedom:

> "We will win the fight today, boys,
> We'll win the fight today,
> Shouting the battle cry of union;
> We will rally from the coal mines
> We'll battle to the end,
> Shouting the battle cry of union.
> The union forever, hurrah! boys, hurrah!
> Down with the Baldwins, up with the law;
> For we're coming, Colorado, we're coming all the way,
> Shouting the battle cry of union."

The militia moved in a steady stream along the rutty road. The marching men showed their appreciation of the hearty welcome. There were broad grins on the faces of the officers and the men in the ranks. These miners didn't look like blood-thirsty devils who would cut a man's throat without the slight-est compunction. They looked to many of the militiamen like poor, uneducated foreigners who had had few opportunities to improve their lot. The heavily-equipped soldiers marched smartly by the gaily decorated colony. They crossed the Colo-rado & Southern railroad tracks and turned south a short dis-tance to a quarter section that had been selected as the site of the military camp. Wagons bearing tents and other camp equipment lined the road behind the troops.

As soon as the military camp began to take shape, General Chase went to Trinidad to open headquarters and supervise the location of other companies of militia. He opened offices in the Columbian Hotel, and immediately issued two orders. The first called for the closing of all saloons in proximity to tent colonies, and the second provided for disarmament of strikers, mine guards and detectives.

Coal company guards assembled at the Coronado Hotel in Trinidad by the dozens to turn in their guns. A large crowd of strikers and sympathizers gathered outside of the hotel to watch the proceedings. The guards were to be given safe con-duct out of the state, according to the military authorities. As the crowd in the street grew in size, General Chase became nervous. He ordered cavalry out and had the street cleared.

"It was apparent this crowd intended to massacre the guards," General Chase announced. "Notwithstanding assurances of Mr. Lawson and other union leaders that there would be no trouble, it was apparent there would be. Several leaders rather gleefully informed me they could not control their men where the guards were concerned." [1]

The first strikers to be disarmed were those in the Sopris and Segundo colonies, up the river from Trinidad. A few hours later a disquieting rumor reached the Ludlow colony. Strikers

[1] Report of the Commanding General to the Governor for Use of the Con-gressional Committee, 1913-1914.

who had given up their arms sent word that the weapons had been given to mine guards.

"We must know about this," Louis Tikas told Lawson. "The Greeks will not turn over their guns if this is true. We would be at the mercy of the gunmen."

"Let's see what we can find out before we decide anything," Lawson said thoughtfully. "If the guards are really being disarmed then every gun in the possession of our men must go to the militia."

Lawson made a careful examination of all reports and sent trusted men to make an investigation in the various colonies and camps where the militia were receiving weapons. As a result of his inquiry, when a detachment of militia arrived at Ludlow and demanded the miners' arms, it met with cool indifference. There was no refusal, however, as weapons were brought from the tents and placed in a pile. The lieutenant in charge of the detail asked for more. He was told there were no others in the camp; that he could look around and ascertain that fact for himself. He nodded and counted the weapons—thirty-seven in all. The discouraged officer carted them off to Trinidad.

"There are more guns than this in that colony," General Chase bellowed when he saw the small pile of miserable weapons. "I want every gun they have there."

The union leaders met General Chase's subsequent demands with shrugs. There were no more guns available. Would the general care to make a search? The strikers had decided to be cautious. They would wait, and keep an eye on the pompous adjutant general. They felt they had been justified when they learned the few serviceable guns among the thirty-seven given up at Ludlow were turned over to coal company guards at Berwind, Tabasco, Hastings and Delagua. The guards, who had supposedly been disarmed for transportation out of the state, appeared at company gates with rifles in their hands and revolvers buckled to their waists. Not a single guard had been sent out of the district. The miners remained silent, however, at Lawson's direction. He insisted they conduct themselves with the utmost propriety. They were not to badger the militiamen or furnish any pretext whatsoever for misunderstandings.

Lawson's instructions were followed and resulted in the best of relationships between the militiamen and the strikers. The soldiers camped near Ludlow came to dances in the big tent, and ate dinner with the miners and their families. Teams from the two tent cities cleared snow off the baseball field and played several games. They went hunting together and mingled freely in the two camps.

Within a few days, a number of professional and salaried men, who had looked upon the expedition as an outing, realized the troops were apt to remain in the field for many weeks or perhaps months. They became restive and asked to be relieved. Their requests were granted in almost every instance and new faces appeared in the ranks. Genuine alarm spread through the tent colonies when the strikers recognized a number of the new men as mine guards. Charles W. Kennedy, who had carried the white flag when the Forbes colony was attacked by the armored car and horsemen, appeared at Segundo in a national guard uniform. Enlistment of mine guards was sanctioned by General Chase despite the agreement made in Governor Ammons' office when the troops were first ordered to Southern Colorado. The coal operators were gleeful. It was much cheaper for the state to pay their men than for them to have to do it themselves.

Few guards were enlisted in Company K at Ludlow and the strikers remained on good terms with the men of this outfit which was commanded by Captain Philip Van Cise, a Denver attorney. Although details from K searched the colony for guns at regular intervals, there was no difficulty as both Captain Van Cise and his soldiers treated the miners and their families well. With Company B it was a different story. This company, led by Lieutenant Linderfelt, who bore the nickname Monte, was soon composed mostly of mine guards. Linderfelt, unlike most of the militia officers, had a blind hatred for "red-necks and Wops" as he called the strikers. Within a few days after the military occupation, Linderfelt and his men had to ride in parties, armed to the teeth, for protection while members of K Company continued to fraternize freely with the miners.

Violence broke out anew November 8 in a manner unfortunate for the union when a strike breaker at La Veta had trouble with pickets and called for company guards. Three guards, driven by a chauffeur, hurried to the man's aid. On the return trip to the mine, a force of strikers ambushed the car. The driver and two guards were instantly killed while the third was fatally wounded. On the same day, to make matters worse, a non-union miner was shot to death on the streets of Aguilar by a striker. Despite these indefensible incidents and repeated blasts from the coal operators, who renewed their cry of rebellion, the field remained comparatively quiet as Governor Ammons' order prohibiting the use of state troops to escort strike breakers remained in effect. However, the operators were engaged in a vigorous campaign to coerce the governor into withdrawing it and the killings gave added weight to their arguments. They contended if troops could be used to escort strike breakers to the mines the strike would be speedily broken and peace would return to Colorado.

The first indication that the campaign was gaining ground came when the attitude of the militia suddenly changed. General Chase ordered his men to stay away from the colonies and the miners. The general began to appear on the roads in an automobile owned by the Colorado Fuel & Iron Co. On November 12, militiamen and mine guards worked together in a sudden search for arms in what was called the old town of Segundo, as distinguished from a newer section. Windows were smashed, and money and jewelry were stolen. In other towns, strikers were ordered to stay away from railroad depots. Still another order forbade them to congregate on public highways. The orders were obviously designed to enable strike breakers to travel to the mines without having to run picket lines.

In Denver, Governor Ammons fumed and fretted in his office. There was no appropriation to pay the expenses of the militia. The coal operators offered to finance the state military department, but Governor Ammons properly refused. He did consent, though, to allow the Denver Clearing House, through its president, John C. Mitchell, to advance $250,000 to maintain the troops in the field. This was an indirect way of permitting the operators to do the financing, the union leaders felt, as the clearing house head was the same Mitchell who, as president of the Denver National Bank, had threatened to call the loans of the Juniper Coal Company when that firm indicated it would sign with the United Mine Workers. The governor's acceptance of the financing plan was more than pleasing to the coal operators. They felt it was a matter of time until they could get the order against importation of strike breakers from other states rescinded.

Mr. Bowers jubilantly wrote to Rockefeller:

"You will be interested to know that we have been able to secure the cooperation of all the bankers of the city, who have had three or four interviews with our little cowboy governor, agreeing to back the state and lend it all the funds necessary to maintain the militia and afford ample protection so that our miners could return to work, or give protection to men who are anxious to come up here from Texas, New Mexico and Kansas together with some from states farther east. Besides the bankers, the Chamber of Commerce, the Real Estate Exchange, together with a great many of the best business men, have been urging the governor to take steps to drive these vicious agitators out of the state. Another mighty power has been rounded up in behalf of the operators by the gathering together of fourteen of the editors of the most important newspapers in Denver, Pueblo, Trinidad, Walsenburg, Colorado Springs, and other of the larger places of the state. They passed resolutions demanding that the governor bring this strike to an end, as they found, upon most careful examination, that the real issue was the demand for recognition of the union, which they told the governor would never be conceded by the operators as 90 per cent of the miners themselves were non-union men, and therefore that issue should be dropped." [2]

Mr. Bowers complained of enormous losses, but found hope in the attitude of the state's newspapers and business men generally. He wound up his letter with the statement:

"Personally my hope is to be blessed with enough mental and physical strength to be able to stand four-square until we win a righteous victory."

Lawson did not let the meeting of the editors pass without a reply. He charged that only 14 of the 439 members of the state editorial association were present at the meeting and that 11 of the 14 were either subsidized or bulldozed by the coal operators. He singled out John C. Shaffer, editor of The Rocky Mountain News; Frank S. Hoag, Pueblo Star; L. C. Paddock, Boulder Camera; Fred Marvin, Pueblo Chieftain, and H. E. Bowden, Trinidad Advertiser, as anti-union editors who had framed the meeting in the Brown Palace Hotel in Denver to aid the coal operators for business or other reasons.

"I have reason to believe that Mr. Shaffer has been subjected to intimidation himself," Lawson said. "At the beginning of this strike the News was friendly to the workingman; then it changed suddenly. It is my understanding that John D. Rockefeller got to Mr. Shaffer through the Armours."

He praised George Hosmer, editor of the Morgan County Herald, and the editors of the Colorado Springs Gazette and Denver Express for refusing to concur in the editors' resolution. The attack on the editors was only an aside for the busy union leader as conditions were rapidly becoming more acute in the southern field. A reign of terrorism was being undertaken by

[2] Report on the Colorado Strike, United States Commission on Industrial Relations, 1915, P. 111.

the militia. Hundreds of persons were arrested. The public highways were no longer open to either strikers or other citizens without consent of the military. In most instances the arrests were mere intimidation. The civil authorities were pushed aside and men were thrown into jail for no reason other than that they were strikers or strike sympathizers. They were held in jail in Trinidad for days at a time without a charge being placed against them. The right of habeas corpus was ignored. General Chase set up a Military District of Colorado with himself in command and announced that military prisoners would be disposed of by men of his choice. Although martial law had not been declared and the civil courts were sitting in Las Animas County, General Chase ignored the local authorities completely. The first trouble came when militiamen arrested four strikers on warrants sworn out in the district attorney's office. In the regular manner, the men were taken before a justice of the peace and released on bond.

General Chase called District Attorney John J. Hendricks on the telephone.

"What the hell do you mean, turning our prisoners loose?" General Chase demanded.

"We haven't turned them loose," Hendricks protested. "They've merely been released on bond in the usual manner."

"How do you dare do such a thing?" General Chase stormed. "In the future you leave our prisoners strictly alone unless you want me to send a squad over to take care of you and the justice of the peace."

Hendricks immediately wired Governor Ammons, asking if martial law had been declared in Las Animas County.

"General Chase was directed to adopt all legal methods necessary to restore order and maintain law," Governor Ammons wired back. "Please consult him."

Hendricks replied that "Your telegram fails to give desired information. Have you as governor proclaimed martial law in Las Animas and Huerfano counties?"

Governor Ammons passed the buck again. He telegraphed:
"Referring to your telegram of yesterday, consult General
Chase concerning military status of Las Animas County."

The district attorney was furious at Governor Ammons' refusal to answer direct questions. Inquiries to General Chase
were insolently met. Finally General Chase put the district
attorney straight. He wrote:

"You are hereby notified that all persons arrested, incarcer-
ated, and held as military prisoners in the counties of Las
Animas and Huerfano, State of Colorado, are to be held subject
to the order of the commanding general, Military District of
Colorado, in regard to their confinement, trial, and final disposition of their cases, which notice you are respectfully requested to observe until further notice from the commanding
general, Military District of Colorado."

To all intents and purposes, the notice prohibited the district
attorney from handling the public business of the district or
from prosecuting cases in the courts as he had no means of
knowing who were military prisoners and who were not, nor
was he given the courtesy of a notification when arrests were
made. General Chase's action in hamstringing the civil authorities made the gunmen and guards more lawless then ever. They
got drunk, insulted women on the street, held up travelers on
the roads, and even threatened to shoot children. When citizens
complained against the militiamen or the gunmen, General
Chase promptly exonerated them. One mine guard, who had
foully abused a Mrs. Rampone, was arrested by the civil authorities. He was immediately declared a "military prisoner" by
General Chase and two days later was walking the streets of
Trinidad in a militia uniform.

Strikers and their wives were barred from the U. S. post
offices in the various coal camps. As many as a hundred men
and women were arrested at one time and held as military
prisoners without charges. Union men caught talking to strikers were clubbed over the head and hauled off to jail. At Gen-

eral Chase's headquarters in the Columbian Hotel, prisoners filed in and out day and night between militiamen carrying rifles with fixed bayonets. Adolph Germer, an organizer for the United Mine Workers, and his wife, were arrested as they stepped off a train in Walsenburg. He was taken to jail and Mrs. Germer was held in a hotel room. She charged she was insulted by drunken militia officers who tried to convince her that her husband was having an affair with another woman. A Mrs. Augusta Radlich was stopped by a militiaman when she tried to go to the Ludlow post office for her mail. When she protested, he cursed her and threatened to knock her to the ground with the butt of his rifle.[3]

Residents of Las Animas County were terror stricken. There seemed to be no limit to the depravity and cruelty of their oppressors. One of the most obnoxious of the gunmen was George Belcher, the Baldwin-Felts detective who figured in the killing of Lippiatt before the strike was called. He slugged strikers on the streets, took potshots at inoffensive citizens, and swaggered around Trinidad boasting of what he was going to do to the "damned red necks."

Belcher's name was on the tip of every tongue. Men looked over their shoulders before they discussed him, and then they cursed and spat on the ground when they mentioned his name. Now and then a hothead would brag of what he would do to Belcher when an opportunity presented itself, but such braggarts were shunned. Finally a little group of strikers met secretly to discuss Mr. Belcher and his future. They talked at length, but paid most heed to a Greek who had known Belcher in other days.

"You cannot even shoot thees Belcher," the Greek said when he made his contribution to the discussion. "Two men try in West Virginia. He is come walking up the railroad track. Two men hide behind the bush. When he comes close, they jump up

[3] Conditions in the Mines of Colorado, Hearings Before a Subcommittee of the Committee on Mines and Mining, 1914. Part II, P. 742.

with thirty-thirty guns and shoot him in the chest. He turn flip-flop like this."

The Greek demonstrated with his arms and hands, and then went on:

"He come up with gun in each hand. He kill both miners."

The conspirators shook their heads in wonder and shivered appreciatively. Truly this Belcher was a bad man. They debated how he could survive such an attack, and finally decided he wore armor.

Scores of miners gathered on Commercial and Main streets in Trinidad the night of November 20, 1913. They had their wives and children with them and they sauntered aimlessly up and down the streets, peering in shop windows and greeting each other in the manner of good neighbors. At the intersection of the two streets, Belcher stood on the high curb, as was his custom each evening. He rocked back and forth on his heels, sneering at the strikers as they passed by him. If one of them made a gesture, he'd give them the same thing his pal Belk had given Lippiatt. Now and then Belcher directed slurring remarks at some passing miner or sympathizer. Finally, tiring of the sport, he started to cross the street just as the big clock on the bank chimed the hour. The crowd seemed to thicken for a moment. The gunman disappeared from view in the mass of humanity that crowded into the street with him. Then a shot rang out. The crowd scattered. Belcher lay in the street in a pool of blood. Bits of brains protruded through an ugly hole in his head. Someone had placed a heavy caliber gun to the back of his head and pulled the trigger. General Chase and Major Boughton, who were standing in front of the Columbian Hotel a few yards down Commercial street, heard the sharp report and came running. They reached the gunman just as he died.[4]

---

[4] Belcher wore heavy steel plates over his chest and back.

Soldiers rushed to the intersection, guns drawn. Within five minutes, Louis Zancanelli, a miner, was taken into custody and hustled off to the Columbian Hotel headquarters.

"You did this outrageous thing," General Chase thundered.

"I don't know anything," Zancanelli replied, over and over.

Five days later, General Chase announced Zancanelli had confessed he was hired to kill Belcher and Walter Belk by two United Mine Worker organizers. Orders had been issued for the arrests of the two men, but they were not to be found.

"These two organizers first offered the job to Zancanelli," General Chase announced. "He declined so they offered it to his tent-mate in the Ludlow colony, Mario Zeni. This man accepted and came to Trinidad to do the job. He did not find the right opportunity, however, and the organizers went back to Zancanelli. They told him Zeni was no good, but that he, Zancanelli, could do the job if he would. They told him also that, if he succeeded, the union would take care of him the rest of his life, so that he would not have to work. They promised him $1,000; that is to say, $500 for each murder."

Zeni was also jailed. For five days and five nights a militiaman, with fixed bayonet, sat outside Zeni's cell and kept him awake. Every time the striker fell asleep, the guard jabbed him with the bayonet and threw cold water into the bare cell. The guard was changed every few hours. Each morning a militia officer called at the jail and asked Zeni if he wanted to make a confession.

"I know nothing to say," the Austrian replied each time. "What do you want me to say?"

He was told he had better confess an organizer offered him $1,000 to kill Belcher and Belk.

"No, no," the Austrian protested.

"I will call the organizer in here," the officer said the fourth morning. "He will tell that he offered you $1,000. What are you going to say then?"

"I say then he is God damned liar," Zeni replied hotly. "Organizer never give me any thousand dollars; never give me twenty-five dollars; he never give me a damn cent."

Zeni stayed in jail 45 days. Zancanelli remained in another cell, charged with murder. Dozens of miners were jailed as suspects in the killing and held for investigation for varying lengths of time.

The day after the Belcher killing, General Chase created a military commission of seven officers to hear and consider cases brought before it. Officers assigned to the new body were Cols. C. B. Carlile, Edward Verdeckberg, George F. Lingenfelter, Majors A. H. Williams and Boughton, Capt. A. D. Marshall, and Lieut. W. A. Spangler.

Mother Jones, protesting at the top of her voice, was deported with the admonition to stay out of Colorado, particularly Southern Colorado; still other leaders were seized by the militia and put out of the state.

Andrew Colnar, a Croatian miner, who was living in the tent colony at Pryor, wrote a letter late in November to a relative, Paul Antovitch, the fire boss at the Pryor Mine, inviting him to quit work and join the colony.

"If you want to come down, nobody is bother you," Colnar wrote. "You be just the same as anybody else. Besides that I guarantee you from trouble."

The letter fell into the hands of the militia. Colnar was arrested and taken to the national guard quarters in Lester where he was handcuffed to a bed over night. The next morning he was interviewed by Capt. Allison C. Drake who demanded that Colnar recompose the letter.

"I no remember it," the striker protested.

"Then sit here until you do," Captain Drake replied. He left the miner in the assembly room with a piece of paper and a pencil throughout the day. That night, Colnar was placed in the Lester jail. Next morning he was put to work digging a new latrine for the troops. The militiamen decided to have a little fun with the Croatian. The latrine was to be six feet long, two and a half feet wide, and eight feet deep.

"We'll give this red neck son-of-a-bitch the scare of his life," one of the sentries told his mates. They agreed. Colnar was first asked his religion. He told them he was a Roman Catholic.

"All right, we'll get you a priest tonight," they said. "You are to be shot at sunrise."

Colnar began to sweat profusely.

"By gosh, I ain't going to dig this hole for my own," the striker said in his broken English. "Let somebody else digging it."

"Hurry up," the guards said menacingly. "This has to be done soon."

During inspection later in the morning, Colnar was ordered out of the hole and made to stand in the center of the detachment. He was certain he was to be executed at once, but as soon as the inspection was completed he was ordered to resume his digging.

A short time later a soldier stepped up and said in Polish.

"How are you, friend?"

Colnar understood the tongue.

"Not much good," he replied. "I am afraid I am digging my own grave."

"Yes," the soldier said. "I am sorry to tell you that I am sent here to tell you the truth; you are digging your own grave. You are to be shot tomorrow morning."

Hearing the words in a language he understood better than English was too much for Colnar. He fell fainting in the hole. When he recovered, he asked his grave-faced tormenter:

"What have you heard about it? What am I going to be killed for?"

"I don't know. You must have done something pretty bad."

By the time the miner was finished with the latrine, he was sick with fear. He was led back to the jail, and a short time later was released by Captain Drake with a warning not to

write any more letters to working miners. Colnar fell on his
knees and thanked God for his deliverance.[5]

When he arrived at the union office in Walsenburg and told
his story, the union leaders recognized it for what it was—
a cruel hoax on a simple man. The story was given to the
press along with a condemnation of the militia for terrorism.
General Chase refused to take action against the troopers responsible, and within a few days the militia had a new and
entertaining pastime. Miner after miner was compelled to dig
a hole "For your own grave, you good for nothing red neck."
Tom Ivanitch, a Pole, was pulled off a train at Ludlow station
and told he must dig his own grave. The militia later said it
was all in fun. They allowed Ivanitch to write a last letter to
his wife before they turned him loose. The letter, which they
forced him to write in English, read:

"Dear Wife:

"Best regards from your husband to you and my son and
my sister Mary and little Kate and my brother Joe. I am under
arrest and not guilty and I am digging my own grave today.
This will be my last letter, dear wife. Look after my children
you and my brother Joe. There won't be anything more of me
unless God helps me. With this world that men have to go
innocent and lie in the ground and God bless the ground where
I lie. We are digging the grave between the tents and the
street. Dear wife and brother Joe, I am telling you to look
after my children. Best regards to you and the children and
brother Joe and mother in law and sister in law Mary Smiljimie
and all that's living. If I don't go tonight go to Trinidad and
seen the head man and see if something can be done for us. I
don't know what to write anymore to say goodbye forever.
I see now that I will have to go in the grave. God do justice.
I got $5 to put in the letter if somebody don't steal it. I got
$23.50 from Domenic Smircich. That there is written in a

[5] Conditions in the Coal Mines of Colorado, Hearings Before a Subcommittee of the Committee on Mines and Mining, 1914, P. 2052.

book. Let Joe get that. Best regards to all I know if they are living. Your husband.

"I am sorrow and broken-hearted waiting for the last minute. When you get the money from the society for the children divide it equally."

An Italian striker, who was the victim of similar terrorism, wrote to his wife:

"Dear Louisa:

"Best regards from your broken hearted Carlo. This is the last letter I am writing. That's all I have to say. Sorrow. Goodbye. Goodbye."

While the militia intimidated miners and terrified military prisoners with ghastly pranks, Governor Ammons made a new effort to bring peace to the coal fields. He asked the policy committee to submit a proposition for settlement of the strike. The committee informed the governor that it could not deviate from the instructions of the Trinidad convention, but proposed that the operators meet with a special committee of five union men—John Lawson, McLennan and three striking miners. Any proposed settlement would be submitted to a specially called convention of miners. The operators refused to consider this proposal.

Governor Ammons then asked Secretary of Labor Wilson to come to Colorado and lend a hand. When the federal official arrived, he was subjected to attack by the operators who contended he was biased against them because of a past connection with the United Mine Workers. Finally, Welborn, Osgood and Brown agreed to meet with three striking miners. The conferences were held in Governor Ammons' offices with the operators insisting that the question of union recognition not be raised. Secretary Wilson sat in on the meeting. After each controversial point was thoroughly discussed, Governor Ammons called for a vote of the operators and the miners. All proposals were tentatively agreed to except those relating to wages and adjustment of future disputes. It was finally decided that Governor Ammons should write a letter proposing a settlement along the lines discussed at the meeting, leaving the two unsettled issues to be discussed at a later date.

When the letter was given out, it developed, much to the surprise of the miners, that it was substantially the same proposition as the one offered by the operators before the strike. There were no provisions for wage increases, contracts or machinery for settlement of future disputes. Secretary Wilson wrote a letter condemning the proposal and urging that specific plans be made to settle future labor troubles. This suggestion was rejected by the operators. They announced they were willing to accept the Ammons plan.

Mass meetings of strikers were called throughout the troubled areas. The governor's proposal was read in English, Spanish, Italian, Slavic and Greek. The miners voted to a man to reject it. The operators immediately charged that the United Mine Workers leadership had railroaded the rejection, and that the miners would have accepted the plan if they had been let alone by "the outside agitators." The spirit in which the operators entered the conference was shown, however, by a report sent by Welborn to New York after the conference ended. It read:

"At the urgent request of the governor and under some newspaper pressure, we met three of our striking miners in conference with the governor, November 26th. There has never been any substantial objection to meeting our own employes for the purpose of discussing proper matters, yet we have felt that such a meeting might be construed as an indirect recognition of the officers of the union.

"We succeeded, however, in yielding to the requested meeting in such a manner as to have the selection of the men, nominally at least, in the hands of the governor, who acted as chairman. The miners, in answer to questions, stated that they represented only themselves directly and would be obliged to take back to the miners for their approval or disapproval whatever understandings, if any, might be reached. We reached no direct understanding; in fact we wanted none, as we were almost sure that had an understanding between the miners and ourselves been reached it would have received the stamp of approval of the officers of the organization and in that way been twisted into an agreement between us and the organization." [6]

Governor Ammons' troubles were not limited to double dealing in conferences with the operators. He had increased difficulty paying his militia. State Auditor Roady Kenehan, a big, dark-haired man of powerful physique, didn't like Governor Ammons or the militia. He scanned every militia bill minutely and repeatedly charged that bills for horses, mules and feed were being padded.

"Some of these horses and mules have been purchased as many as three times," Kenehan announced indignantly. "I am going down south and look at them. They must be wonderful animals."

A native of Queens County, Ireland, Kenehan was a fighting man himself. He disliked management and this dislike and his antipathy for the militia had their roots in his own adherence to a union. A blacksmith by trade, he was something of a power in the strong International Brotherhood of Blacksmiths, Drop Forgers, and Helpers, and in the Denver Trades and Labor Assembly. It was said of him that he didn't leave his bellows until 30 minutes before he was sworn in as state auditor, and that he "took his hammer and anvil to the Statehouse."

He held up all militia vouchers until he had made a tour of Southern Colorado and forced sullen militiamen to point out brands and other identifying marks on their livestock while he watched with a practiced and experienced eye. Before he arrived in Trinidad, the militiamen angrily hanged him in effigy and then buried the effigy some distance from their camp. Roady

[6] Report on the Colorado Strike, United States Commission on Industrial Relations, 1915, P. 91.

demanded to be taken to the grave. With a group of militiamen as his audience, he stood on top of the grave, hands in pants
pockets, and bellowed: "Sure and I am the only man in this
world who ever stood on his own grave."

He turned to the soldiers and grinned at them.

"You boys have had a lot of fun," he said with a great laugh.
"But remember, you can only buy your horses once if you don't
want me to burn your backsides for you."

By December 1, however, Kenehan had to approve issuance
of scrip to pay the soldiers. The bankers had agreed to accept
it, and Kenehan could hold out no longer. When a messenger
went to his office in the Capitol for the paper, Roady pounded
his desk with his huge fist and roared:

"The laws of this state say the governor has to come for this
stuff, and by golly he'll have to do it in person as long as Roady
Kenehan is auditor."

Trembling with anger, Governor Ammons went for the
scrip.

CHAPTER VIII

A POMPOUS GENERAL

The federal grand jury, which had launched an investigation of the strike at the request of the C. F. & I. Co. shortly after the miners had laid down their tools, completed its work in Pueblo, December 2, 1913, with a report that made excellent reading in the newspapers for both sides to the industrial controversy. It indicted 25 officers and members of the United Mine Workers for violations of the Sherman anti-trust law and at the same time accused the coal barons of violating state laws, controlling elections and debauching their employes.

Those indicted were John P. White, president of the United Mine Workers; William Green, the secretary-treasurer; John Lawson, Adolph Germer, Robert Uhlich, James Morgan, A. B. McGary, Charles Batley, Edgar Wallace, Sam Carter, Zancanelli, Zeni, Charles Richard, Edward Richards, Sam Dejon, Daniel Richards, Frank Krupa, Teter Rich, Charles Shepherd, Marcus Marculich, John Flockhart, Daniel Martinez, D. A. Durand, and Peter Gonzales.

U. S. Attorney General McReynolds had instructed U. S. District Attorney Harry E. Kelly not to go into the strike matter when the demand was first made by the operators for an investigation. Kelly had then refused the offer of the operators to assist in the investigation whereupon Judge Northcutt, representing the coal operators, had appeared before the grand jury with a direct demand.

As soon as the indictments were announced, U. S. Attorney Kelly stated that the "government did not summon the witnesses, and the government did not instigate or take part in presenting the evidence upon which the indictments were based."

The union leaders branded the indictments as a publicity play on the part of the operators. The Denver Express carried a banner line to the effect that "Grand Jury Indicts 25 Union Miners at Command of Coal Barons Who Were Branded as Violators of State Laws in the Past."

"This marks the first attempt of capital to destroy all organized labor by means of the anti-trust law," The Express declared. "The indictments charge the miners with violating a federal law by doing something the Colorado law recognizes as legal."

That part of the jury report dealing with the operators must have surprised Judge Northcutt as it found state laws had not been observed; that the coal companies nominated, elected and controlled county officers; that camp marshals, whose appointments were controlled and whose salaries were paid by the companies, had "exercised a system of espionage and had resorted to arbitrary powers of police control, acting as judge and jury and passing sentence" and that camp marshals had brutally assaulted miners. It was also found that the scrip system was still in effect, that miners were obliged to trade at company stores, and that check weighmen had been denied. The report said in part:

"Saloons in the mining camps produce a deplorable situation among the miners, habituating them to the improper use of strong drink and thereby impairing their efficiency by lessening the production and increasing the hazard in operating the mine."

Vice President Hayes issued a statement to the effect that the indictments were no surprise.

"They may indict us, but they cannot indict the principles for which we stand," he said. "They will prevail until human slavery ceases to exist. We are accused of organizing a conspiracy in restraint of trade. If they mean by the term 'restraint of trade' that we have restrained John D. Rockefeller and a few other eastern millionaires from plundering the miners of Colorado, then we plead guilty to the indictment and we are proud of the achievement. It is rather strange that no grand jury has ever indicted any company officials in this state although it is an established fact that they have violated the laws for many years."

The justice department stepped in and quashed the indictments before warrants could be issued. The union men never were served.

Lawson paid little attention to the Pueblo grand jury or the statements and counter-statements as he had a serious situation to face in the southern field. Between December 1 and 6, Colorado experienced its greatest snowfall. The flakes buried the entire state under a heavy blanket that varied from four to six feet deep. At the tent colonies, men worked in relays to keep the streets open as high winds whipped the snow into drifts that attained heights of twelve to fifteen feet. The great storm brought new trials and tribulations to the colonists. With the suffering, however, came a measure of peace for the movements of the militia, the guards and the gunmen were also impeded. Despite the severity of the blizzard, not a person deserted the colonies. The strikers and their wives accepted the storm as part of the burden they had to bear in their war against the coal companies.

When the roads opened, Lawson went to work on a new problem. He knew strike-breakers were coming into the field despite the prohibiting state law and he knew, too, that troops were aiding and escorting them. Each day the militia were lining up more and more with the coal barons. They were worse than the gunmen in that they wore uniforms and were cloaked

with the authority of the state. Lawson talked the matter over
with Hayes, and Hayes, in turn, laid it before the State Federation of Labor. The federation moved swiftly. A call was
issued by President McLennan and Secretary W. T. Hickey for
a special convention in Denver. The call said in part:

"The strike of the miners has grown to a real war in which
every craft and department of organized labor is threatened
with annihilation unless they take a positive and decided stand
for their rights. The uniform of the state is being disgraced and
turned into an emblem of anarchy as it was in the days of
Peabody.[1] In the southern fields, military courts, illegal and
tyrannical, are being held for the purpose of tyrannizing the
workers. Leaders of labor are being seized and arrested and
held without bail. The homes of union miners have been broken
into by members of the National Guard and property stolen. In
order that members of organized labor in every part of the
state, whether affiliated or not, may become familiar with conditions in this struggle, a convention is hereby called to meet
in Denver, Tuesday, December 16, 1913, at 10 o'clock. The
purpose of the convention is the protection of the rights of
every worker in this state and the protection of the public from
the unbridled greed and outrages of the coal operators."

More than 500 delegates assembled at the appointed time, including a number of United Mine Worker officers such as President White, Secretary Green, Lawson, Hayes, Doyle, and
Mother Jones who had slipped back into the state in violation
of a militia order. The National Guard was assailed for persecution and brutality. Mother Jones outdid herself with a speech
in which she urged that Governor Ammons be hanged forthwith. The delegates demanded that a march be made on the
State Capitol to learn the future policy of the state from Ammons' own lips.

Late the second day, the demand for a march became irresistible and 2,000 persons, with Mother Jones and Louis Tikas,

[1] James H. Peabody (R), governor of Colorado during the 1903 coal strike.

carrying a Ludlow banner in the lead, marched on the State-house. Governor Ammons agreed to meet the convention delegates in the chamber of the State House of Representatives. The huge room would not accommodate more than 500 persons, so it was agreed that only the delegates would attend. A crowd estimated at 4,500 persons waited in the corridors and the snow-banked driveway outside.

Eli M. Gross, vice president of the state labor federation and a factory inspector for the state commissioner of labor, presided. Governor Ammons was understandably ill at ease. He knew these men well. Many of them had indorsed and supported his candidacy. He knew something, too, of the bitterness they now held against his administration. He whispered to Gross.

"Governor Ammons will answer any questions," Gross told the assemblage. "I will rule that the questions must be written."

Dozens of pencils appeared. The governor answered question after question, slowly and hesitantly. Outside the big building, Lieutenant Governor Stephen R. Fitzgarrald and Attorney General Farrar addressed the demonstrators briefly.

Lawson, Hayes, and the other leaders of the miners did not take an active part in the meeting in the House of Representatives chamber. They stood in the back of the great, high-ceilinged room on the theory it was best for the federation and the governor to deal directly.

As from afar, Lawson heard the governor's voice:

"I do not believe many of the charges that have been made against the National Guard, but I would be glad to have a committee of the federation investigate and submit any proof."

Then Lawson heard Gross thank the governor and adjourn the meeting. The demonstrators marched back to their meeting hall.

The last day of the convention saw the adoption of a lengthy resolution which again outlined abuses, condemned the operators vigorously, and called for the removal of General Chase and Judge Advocate Boughton who were characterized as petty tyrants "who have been mere tools and lickspittles for the mine owners."

After outlining grievances against the operators and the military, the resolution said:

"This convention declares now and gives fair warning, in the name of millions of American workingmen, that these things will no longer be tolerated. No surer or more certain course can be followed if it is desired to turn workingmen into anarchists. We call upon the great body of Americans not to drive workingmen into the ranks of the anarchists. The law was not made simply for the rich. There is not a man who will read this declaration but knows that if Osgood, Brown and Rockefeller, who are fighting the strikers with a malignity hitherto unknown in American history, were arrested, they would not be held incommunicado or denied counsel. Can any fair-minded man blame us for bitterness when the laborer is thus, by the officers of the law, denied the rights granted to the rich? We have no quarrel with the rich man, and we seek to prejudice no one against him. We do, however, demand for the laborer every privilege before the law which the rich man has. We frankly avow intention to get these rights for laboring men. We intend to get them lawfully if we can. Again we say, if this be treason, let the coal operators make the most of it."

The resolution called for the release of all military prisoners, the removal of Chase, Boughton, Major Charles E. Townsend, and Captain Householder. Governor Ammons was given five days to carry out the intent of the resolution or face a recall petition. At the same time, the federation's executive board was given authority to call a statewide strike of workingmen at any time it saw fit.

While the convention was completing its work, General Chase revealed he had obtained oral permission from Governor Ammons to permit the importation of strike breakers. A train, loaded with out-of-state workingmen, arrived in Trinidad the same day under military escort. Employment agencies of the coal companies were busy gathering more unorganized workmen in the eastern states, and in Kansas, Oklahoma and Texas.

Before he left Denver for Southern Colorado, Lawson hurled a last threat at Governor Ammons and the militia for good measure.

"The convention was undoubtedly the greatest in the history of the Colorado labor movement," he said. "It conclusively demonstrated several things. First, that organized labor is going to demand that the liberties of the people be protected. They are not willing to permit any military despot to arrogate to himself privileges that have been denied the czar of Russia. They are going to stand first, last and always for trial by jury. They will not permit Major Boughton, General Chase, the governor or anyone else to abrogate this right. It might be well to call the attention of the Democratic Party and the state administration to the fact that the appointment of such tyrants as General Chase and Sherman Bell during the Peabody regime brought a great political revolution and changed the entire aspect of state politics. And it would be well for the present administration to remember that it was the united forces of labor that brought about this revolution. If the present administration insists on serving the corporations instead of the people, the labor forces will bring about another change."

Governor Ammons paid no attention to the threats incorporated in the convention resolution nor to any of the demands. At the end of the five day period of grace, the executive board of the federation met to consider recall of the governor. The plan was dropped when it was found that the cost of circulating petitions would be approximately $8,000.

"It is an uncertain proposition and that large a sum can be better used for the strikers and their families," Hickey said. The other members of the board agreed. They still had a trump card, however. They named an investigating committee to accept Governor Ammons' challenge for a federation probe of the militia. Lawson, Gross, Frank Miner, James Kirwan, and

Prof. James H. Brewster of the University of Colorado School of Law were named to the committee. Once empowered, the committee asked Governor Ammons for a letter of authority to be shown to the military command in Southern Colorado. Governor Ammons wrote:

"You will please give this committee every assistance within your power to the end that they may secure what information they desire. Please have them furnished with any information you may have or direct that any one who has information shall give it to them. I will appreciate it if you could, if they so desire, send some one with them wherever they want to go."

The letter was directed to General Chase.

With Lawson serving as chairman, the committee began its work in Trinidad, December 23, the day after Governor Ammons penned his letter. The members of the committee were union men with the exception of Professor Brewster. A high-strung, articulate man, who nourished anti-union sentiments, Professor Brewster had taught conveyancing at the University of Michigan in Ann Arbor for many years before tuberculosis forced him to move to Colorado in search of health. He was liberal in his political views, but his opinion of the United Mine Workers was scarcely higher than that entertained by officials of the C. F. & I. Co.

An attempt was made at the outset of the investigation to interview General Chase, but inquiries at militia headquarters met with a cool reception. General Chase could not see the committee that day. Perhaps he could see them the next day.

"We may as well start," Lawson said. "We can call as many witnesses as possible today and then we'll try and see the general tomorrow. He can't ignore the governor's letter very long."

The first witness called was Mrs. Maggie Dominske of Ludlow. She told of being with a group of women who were stopped by militiamen when they attempted to go to the Ludlow post office.

"What did they say to you?" Lawson asked.

"They put up their guns and said, 'God damn you, don't you go another step. If you do, we'll shoot you. We're getting tired of these sons-of-bitches coming up here and we're going to put a stop to it.' "

"Was this on the public highway?" Professor Brewster asked.

"Yes, it was."

Mrs. Dominske and the other indignant women who were in the party testified at length.[2] Professor Brewster was angry when they had finished. He rubbed his hands together. He turned to Lawson eagerly.

"I am surprised," he said. "Surprised. I wouldn't have believed it if I had not heard it straight from these women. It is plain they are telling the truth."

Lawson smiled grimly. Only a start had been made. Professor Brewster would get many surprises before the inquiry was ended. A shorthand reporter was keeping a complete record of the proceedings.

The second day the committee went to General Chase's headquarters in the Columbian Hotel again. He received them coldly.

"Sit down, gentlemen," he said in a tone that indicated he would rather they wouldn't.

"I suppose you have a copy of Governor Ammons' letter?" Lawson asked.

"Yes, I have it." General Chase was abrupt.

"As you know, General, there have been many complaints against the conduct of members of the National Guard," Lawson continued. "We want to go into everything thoroughly, and we would like to talk to any of your men who are involved in these complaints."

General Chase reared back in his chair. He glanced toward the window where Major Boughton stood looking down into the street. Then he answered:

[2] A complete transcript of the hearings was later made available as a public document.

"I know very well what you men want to do down here.
I may as well tell you right now that you are not going to talk
to any of my men. You'll get everything directly through me."

"But, General, we need first hand information for our report
to Governor Ammons," Lawson protested. "Surely you can see
there would be matters on which you would not have reports."

General Chase glared at the big labor leader.

"I said you'll get any National Guard information directly
from me."

"What about the governor's letter?" Lawson asked. "It is
rather plain."

"I said you'll get your information from me. A state of war
exists here. My soldiers, in line of duty and honor, stand ready
to bear criticism without a murmur."

Lawson tried once more.

"We would like to talk to the guardsmen involved in the
Colnar case and . . . "

General Chase cut him short with an airy wave of his hand.

"Colnar was digging a privy vault. That is all there is to it,
and I consider the entire matter disposed of."

"We are not so obtuse as to suppose Colnar was really digging
his own grave," Lawson said. "But it is evident Colnar thought
he was. That is what is important and the reason we want to
talk to the men involved."

Chase turned from Lawson and shook his fist in Professor
Brewster's face.

"And you are a college professor," he snorted. "I am
ashamed of you. Running around with a lot of damned red
necks. You ought to know better. I don't see how you ever
got on the University faculty. It is a disgrace to our university
to have a man on such a committee as this."

Professor Brewster flushed. He reached across the desk and
wagged his finger under the mighty general's nose.

"You can't talk to me that way, sir!" he roared.

General Chase arose.

"Anyway, you will not be allowed to talk to the men. If you want anything, you may come here. Good day."

The committee filed out. Professor Brewster was too enraged to speak. Lawson, Gross and the others were amused. They knew the general of old.

In the days immediately following, the committee went by automobile to the various colonies. More than 160 persons, of whom approximately one-third were not connected with the strike in any way, were interviewed. The trips to the colonies were difficult as high snow drifts still covered many of the highways. It was biting cold and Professor Brewster had a severe cough. Several times Lawson suggested that he remain in his steam-heated hotel room, but Brewster refused.

Witnesses told the committee brutal, sordid stories. Young girls testified they had been grabbed by militiamen and abused; ranchers and home owners told of being held up and robbed in their own houses; much of the testimony was of such nature that women were barred while it was being given.[3] The Rev. James McDonald, Methodist minister at Aguilar, told the committeemen he had seen drunken militiamen on the streets of Aguilar in broad daylight with lewd women hanging on to them and that these same drunks, while their women laughed and screamed, pushed citizens off the sidewalks with bayoneted rifles.

"It was a shame and a disgrace," the Reverend Mr. McDonald said. "One drunken militiaman was going up and down the streets with his sleeves rolled up and hustling every citizen that he came to into the street. It was right after pay day and I was given to understand that these soldiers brought the lewd women from the railroad point at Lynn."

Bernard Stromberg, an inoffensive Trinidad merchant, testified he was arrested in the doorway of his clothing store while he stood on his own property, watching Chase's cavalrymen

---

[3] Specific instances of robbery and other criminal acts were contained in the committee's report to the governor.

herd men, women and children along the sidewalks on a busy
Saturday night. He said he was held two hours.[4]

While the committee was meeting in another part of the
district December 29, General Chase sent a detachment from
the Ludlow camp to the Ludlow colony and forcibly vaccin-
ated the colonists on the ground an epidemic was threatened.
Louis Tikas and James Fyler, who were in charge of the colony
in Lawson's absence, denied there was illness in the camp, but
were forced to allow the soldiers to carry out the vaccination
order. The Ludlow district was thrown into a furor the next
night when a cavalryman's horse stumbled and fell over a piece
of barbed wire near the colony. The trooper was bruised and
shaken. His companions took him to the Ludlow depot and
telephoned Hastings. Approximately 30 persons were in the
depot at the time. Among those waiting for the train were a
number of women and children who were not connected with
the Ludlow colony or the strike in any way. Tikas was also in
the station, waiting for the train.

A few minutes after the telephone call, Lieutenant Monte
Linderfelt stalked into the station with a detail. He talked to
the injured man a moment or two, and then seized a 15-year-
old boy who was staring round-eyed at the soldiers. Linderfelt
accused the boy of stretching wire across the highway, and,
when the youth denied it, hit him over the head with his gun.
Tossing his victim aside, Linderfelt strode up to Tikas. In the
presence of a dozen women, who were sitting nearby, the lieutenant shouted:

"There you are, you round-faced son-of-a-bitch. You're responsible for that wire."

Louie Tikas didn't answer. Linderfelt turned to one of his
men and asked him if he had a pair of wire cutters. The trooper
nodded.

[4] Conditions in the Coal Mines of Colorado, Subcommittee of the Committee
on Mines and Mining, U. S. House of Representatives, 1914. Part II, P. 724.

"You Tollerburg fellows beat it over to the colony and cut every God damned wire around the place," Linderfelt yelled. "The first man that interferes with you—shoot his head off."

He turned back to Louie Tikas and struck him in the face with his fist, screaming at the top of his voice:

"I am Jesus Christ, and my men on horses are Jesus Christs, and we must be obeyed."

Tikas made no effort to resist. He saw death in the faces of the militiamen who crowded around as Linderfelt, the vilest profanity spilling from his lips, beat him with heavy fists. The lieutenant finally tired, and ordered his men to take the bloody Tikas to the military camp. That done, Linderfelt stared for a moment or two at the people in the station and then stalked out into the night.[5]

A few minutes later, a striker killed a companion in the Ludlow colony during an argument over a crap game. There were angry words, the flash of a knife, and a dead man on the floor of the tent. It had nothing to do with the strike, but the militia trained guns on the tents and surrounded the colony with cavalry. Details of guardsmen turned the 275 tents and their interiors into jumbled messes, obtaining about 50 guns.

Informed of the assaults, the killing and the search, the committee went to Ludlow the next morning. While witnesses were being rounded up, Gross walked up the Colorado & Southern railroad tracks several hundred yards to take a look at a militia machine gun. No one bothered him. There were 10 guardsmen sitting around the gun. While he took in the scene, he heard voices and turned to see Lieutenant Linderfelt and a young boy standing a few feet away. A soldier was with them.

"This fellow wants to go up to the store," the soldier was saying. "I stopped him and he wanted to make some complaint."

"Go ahead, make it," Linderfelt said.

[5] Labor investigating committee report to Governor Ammons.

"Well," the boy began, "I was down here by the pump and I started up to the store with my lady—the lady with me—and they stopped me and I asked him how long they were going to hold us because I had business at the store, and he said, 'None of your God damned business.' Then I told this sentry he ought not to use that kind of language. I didn't like it. It made me sore—a lady with me and he talking like that, and we had some words and he brought me up here."

"You got business at the store?"

"Yes."

Linderfelt's face twisted into an ugly snarl.

"I am going to tell you fellows something," he said in a loud voice. "You are too God damned chesty, that's what's the matter with you. I am Jesus Christ down in this country, and all these fellows in uniform are Jesus Christs too. If this fellow had done the right thing he would have roughed you up with the butt of his gun. Now turn around and get the hell back down the track where you came from."

Gross walked back to the place where the committee was assembling and made out an affidavit. The boy and his woman companion were found and affidavits secured from them.[6]

After they had completed taking evidence from a score of witnesses who were in the railroad station when Linderfelt made the two assaults, the committee members rode back to Trinidad and wired Governor Ammons:

"We did not expect to report to you until we had completed the taking of testimony at all camps, but in our judgment the following serious matter should be reported to you at once: Lieut. K. E. Linderfelt, of the cavalry stationed at Berwind, last night at Ludlow brutally assaulted an inoffensive boy in the public railroad station, using the vilest language at the same time. He also assaulted and tried to provoke to violence Louie Tikas, head man of the Ludlow strikers' colony, and arrested him unjustifiably. Today, in the presence of one of our

[6] Labor investigating committee report to Governor Ammons.

number, he grossly abused a young man in no way connected with the strike, also making threats against the strikers in the foulest language. He rages violently upon little or no provocation, and is wholly an unfit man to bear arms and command men as he has no control over himself. We have reason to believe that it is his deliberate purpose to provoke the strikers to bloodshed. In the interest of peace and justice, we ask immediate action in his case."

The only result of the telegram was the release of Tikas from custody.

The committee's investigation had shown that Linderfelt had ordered fences around the colony cut so that his cavalrymen could cut across the fields, and that the injured man's horse had stepped on a loose piece of wire with one hoof and then caught the other in the wire, throwing itself to the ground.

"They cut the wire themselves and were too lazy to gather it up," Lawson said. "They were responsible for the fall."

The committee also reported to Governor Ammons that the militiamen sent by Linderfelt to cut and clean up wire around the colony after the horse incident had stuffed rusty barbed wire down the colony's well—the only place where the inhabitants of the Ludlow colony could obtain drinking water.

CHAPTER IX
"RIDE DOWN THE WOMEN"

While the committee pursued its investigation, train loads of strike breakers moved into the coal fields under military escorts. The corporations opened an office in Joplin, Missouri, and attracted hundreds of working men by offering fertile land at ridiculously low prices. No deposit was asked for the land. All the purchaser had to do was to go to Colorado, transportation furnished, and receive steady employment. Each man could pay for 20 acres of excellent land out of his earnings at so much per month. Applicants were not told they would have to work in strike-bound coal mines. Militiamen met the immigrants at the Colorado-Kansas line and stood guard over them until they were safely delivered to the closed camps. From the camps there was little chance of escape. Those who tried to leave were told they owed the company money for their transportation to Colorado, and that they would have to work it out. Guards, armed with rifles and clubs, made certain that none left. Despite the importations, the C. F. & I Co. admitted it could not produce enough coal even to supply the State Penitentiary and suggested that convict labor be used to provide the state government with needed fuel. Governor Ammons approved the plan, and Warden John J. Tynan took over the Number Five mine at Brookside in Fremont County, not far from the penitentiary.

Eight miners imported from Mexico escaped from the Primero mine near Trinidad and made their way to union headquarters. They said they had been promised $6 a day and did not learn that the wages were actually $1.50 a day until after they had been transported to Colorado from Mexico and put to work in the mine.

"We were held for 20 days," the spokesman for the Mexicans said. "We did not get away until the guards got their pay and got drunk. Then we slip away."

Meanwhile, Mother Jones, encouraged by the failure of the state authorities to remove her from Denver, announced she was returning to the southern fields.

"She will be jailed immediately if she comes to Trinidad," General Chase told newspapermen. "I am not going to give her a chance to make any more speeches here. She is dangerous because she inflames the minds of the strikers."

Mother Jones put her hands on her hips and made a statement of her own for the newspaper boys.

"Tell General Chase that Mother Jones is going to Trinidad in a day or two and that he'd better play his strongest cards—the militia's guns—against her," she said defiantly. "He had better go back to his mother and get a nursing bottle. He'll be better off there than making war on an 82-year-old woman in a state where women vote."

True to her word, Mother Jones went to Trinidad. General Chase arrested her and ordered her sent out of the coal fields. Lawson and the investigating committee saw her, Jan. 4, 1914, in Walsenburg as she passed through on a Denver-bound train under military escort.

A large number of union men, carrying an American flag, marched to the depot and stood under her car window during the train's brief stop. They sang lustily:

> "The union forever, hurrah! boys, hurrah!
> Down with the militia, up with the law;
> For we're coming Colorado, we're coming all the way,
> Shouting the battle cry of union."

Mother Jones nodded and smiled and tapped on the car window with her fingers to show her appreciation.

The investigating committee wired the state's two senators and four congressmen:

"As a committee appointed at the suggestion of the Governor of Colorado by the State Federation of Labor to investigate charges made against the militia in the coal strike district, we have learned of gross violations by them of constitutional rights. We shall report soon to the governor, but meanwhile we earnestly urge that every effort be made to secure a full congressional investigation, not only of the real causes of the strike in Colorado, but also of the conduct of the state militia in violating federal constitutional rights under General Chase's orders. Deportations are threatened. Mother Jones, a woman 82 years of age, on arriving in Trinidad was deported by the next train under escort of the militia. We ask you whether the equal protection of the laws is to be longer denied to citizens and others without investigation and action by congress?"

The telegram was signed by John R. Lawson, Frank Miner, James Brewster, James Kirwan, and Eli M. Gross.

Congressman Keating wired that he wanted a copy of the committee's report as soon as it was completed, and that he believed he could secure a federal investigation as soon as the Congress reconvened.

Back in Denver, under orders to leave the state, Mother Jones decided to return to Trinidad. She stayed several days with friends and then prepared for the trip in defiance of the orders of Governor Ammons and the military. The canny old organizer found that detectives had been stationed in Denver's Union Station to make certain she didn't take a train south again. By a circuitous route, she made her way into the railroad yards and had a friendly porter make up a berth for her. Once in bed, she called the porter again.

"Just tell the conductor that Mother Jones wants to get off this train in the morning on the outskirts of Trinidad."

"I sho' will, Motthah Jones."

Early the next morning, the Colorado & Southern train came to an unscheduled stop just outside Trinidad and an aged woman stepped off and started walking briskly down the cinder covered right-of-way. At the station in Trinidad, militia watched every passenger alight. When the train had gone, they went back to the Columbian Hotel to report that dangerous old Mother Jones was not among the arrivals. Mother Jones spent three hours in a hotel across the street from militia headquarters before the military learned of her presence.

"Impossible," General Chase shouted. He reached for a telephone and called Governor Ammons.

"Impossible," the governor said. "We had the depot and every hotel watched."

"She's here just the same," General Chase said crossly. "I am going to arrest her."

"Deport her," the governor replied. "Get rid of that woman."

A few minutes later a squad stood in front of Mother Jones' door. She was pleased, for her effectiveness was only increased by arrests and persecution. General Chase had heard of her readiness to go to jail and had another plan in mind. He first offered to send her out of Trinidad again.

"Nothing doing, General," she said. "I am free, white and a bit over 21. This is a free country and I've got a right to go where I damned please."

General Chase ordered her taken to Mt. San Rafael hospital, an institution on the eastern outskirt of Trinidad conducted by the Sisters of Charity of Cincinnati. She was placed in a room and two guards were assigned to keep watch over her.

"Lads, the great Standard Oil is certainly afraid of an old woman," Mother Jones cackled with evident satisfaction.

She was refused permission to see a union attorney and her mail was returned to the sender, opened or destroyed.[1]

[1] Conditions in the Coal Mines of Colorado, Hearings of the Subcommittee on Mines and Mining, 1914. Part IX, P. 2538.

"I am not making war on women," Governor Ammons announced, "but since Mother Jones is not a resident of the county
she insists on going to, she has no business there."

Horace Hawkins, the UMWA attorney, filed a petition for a
writ of habeas corpus with Las Animas County District Court.
Judge McHendrie, an associate of Judge Northcutt, the operators' attorney, refused to grant it. Hawkins made preparations
to carry the appeal to the Supreme Court.

Meanwhile, the investigating committee completed its report
and submitted it to Governor Ammons along with a complete
transcript of testimony taken in the various colonies and towns
in the mining district. It recommended the resignation of
General Chase, the discharge of all mine guards and detectives
serving in the militia, enforcement of the law prohibiting the
importation of strike breakers, and abolition of the practice of
allowing militia companies to elect their own officers.

The strongly worded report was lost in the howl of protest
over Mother Jones' incarceration. Nine hundred Fremont
County coal miners informed Governor Ammons that if he
refused to liberate her they would march to Las Animas County
and do the job themselves. A hundred women invaded the Columbian Hotel, brushed guards aside, and surrounded General
Chase, demanding her release. Although Lawson and other
union chieftains ducked when asked to confirm the story, union
press agents sent out a report that General Chase's husky son,
an officer of the militia, called to his father over the heads of the
irate women:

"Daddy, shall I blow the horn?"

On Jan. 23, the women of Las Animas County organized a
demonstration and parade in behalf of Mother Jones. Parade
permission was obtained from General Chase after great difficulty. The long line of shabbily-dressed women and children
moved across the Picketwire River bridge and up to Trinidad's
Commercial Street. They marched by the Columbian Hotel.
No militia were in sight. The traffic policeman on the corner of

Main and Commercial streets put his club behind his back and stepped aside as the parade reached the intersection and turned east on Main Street toward the hospital.

> "The union forever, hurrah! boys, hurrah!
> Down with the militia, up with the law;
> For we're coming Colorado, we're coming all the way,
> Shouting the battle cry of union."

The women sang with good will and the children did their part in high, shrill voices. Dozens of paraders carried banners, "God Bless Mother Jones" and "We're For Mother Jones."

Three blocks east on Main Street, opposite the post office, a line of cavalry was drawn across the street. General Chase, mounted on a fine-looking cavalry horse, sat in front of his men, facing the oncoming parade. The cavalrymen had their sabers out of their scabbards. A block behind them infantry filled the street. The line of women and children wavered for a moment. Then it moved again, straight toward the menacing troops.

"Don't advance another step," General Chase boomed. "You must turn back."

Again the line wavered and again it advanced.

> "The union forever, hurrah! boys, hurrah!"

Spectators, who had followed the parade, began to crowd forward for a better view. General Chase couldn't seem to decide what to do next. He spurred his horse forward to meet the women and then suddenly wheeled and rode back toward his men.

Sarah Slator, a 16-year-old school girl, who was watching with open mouth, caught his eye.

"Get back there!" General Chase roared. The horse brushed against her. The girl was completely flustered and stood frozen in her tracks.

"I said get back there," Chase yelled again and kicked at her. His foot caught her in the breast.[2]

[2] Conditions in the Coal Mines of Colorado, Hearings of the Subcommittee of the Committee on Mines and Mining, 1914. Part III, P. 987.

The head of the parade reached the cavalrymen. Part of the women were making their way between the mounted troopers. Several women gave a triumphant yell. An officer rode up to Chase, but before he could speak the general's horse became frightened and backed into a parked buggy.

General Chase fell off.

The women screamed with laughter.

Red-faced and angry, General Chase climbed stiffly to his feet and yelled at his men:

"Ride down the women."

Spurs sank home and the cavalry mounts plunged forward with snorts. Sabers flashed in the bright sunlight. Laughter turned to screams of terror. The women began to run back. Mrs. Maggie Hammons was slashed across the forehead with a saber; Mrs. George Gibson's ear was almost severed from her head. Mrs. Thomas Braley threw up her hands in front of her face and they were gashed by a sword.

A cavalryman leaned from his horse and struck Mrs. James Lanigan with the flat of his saber, knocking her to the ground. Another soldier leaned from his saddle and smashed 10-year-old Robert Arguello in the face with his fist. Pandemonium resulted. The paraders beat a disorderly retreat. Mrs. R. Verna, who had been marching in the van of the parade with an American flag, was pursued by a cavalryman who tore the flag from her grasp and knocked her down with his horse.

General Chase, mounted again, was yelling like a mad man. A thousand women and children scurried for safety.

Little Sarah Slator sought refuge on the elevated porch of a printing establishment with several other women and children.

"Get that bunch off there," an officer called. Sarah jumped down and a cavalryman swung at her with his saber. She stepped behind a telephone pole. The gleaming metal bit into the wood. Sarah laughed.

"Break your old sword, I don't care."

Then she ran back up Main Street. In front of the Zimmer-

man Book Store, several blocks up the street, she saw four
militiamen dragging two women along the sidewalk.

"Shame on you," she cried. "How many does it take to arrest
a man?"

Five militiamen stepped up behind her and she spun around.
One of them grinned and brought the butt of his rifle down on
her right foot.

"Now get along the street," he snarled.

She started to limp away, but Sarah Slator was a girl of
spirit. She saw a young woman with a three-year-old child at
her side.

"Hurry up," a soldier was yelling at the woman. "Hurry up.
Move along."

"I can't carry him," the mother protested. "He is too heavy
and he can't walk very fast."

"You'll get this bayonet if you don't hurry."

"You wouldn't dare," the mother cried.

"Oh, you think I am afraid?" the soldier growled.

Sarah Slator got herself in trouble again.

"I don't think you are afraid," she sang out. "You're so low
you could do anything."

Sarah went to jail along with six other women. Cavalry
patrols sent out to scour the streets arrested 12 men later in the
afternoon. The riot aroused the state as nothing had before.

"Great Czar Fell!" the Denver Express said in a double banner, "And in Fury Told Troops to Trample Women."

"A craven general tumbled from his nag in a street of Trinidad Thursday," the lead story read, "like humpty-dumpty from
the wall. In fifteen minutes there was turmoil, soldiers with
swords were striking at fleeing women and children; all in the
name of the sovereign state of Colorado.

"For General Chase, having lost his poise on his horse, also lost
his temper and cried, 'Ride down the women.'

"Then there was bloodshed.

"The French Revolution, its history written upon crimson

pages, carries no more cowardly episode than the attack of the gutter gamin soldiery on a crowd of unarmed and unprotected women."

Mother Jones stayed in the hospital under the vigilant eyes of her burly guards.

Congressman Keating was sorely troubled. He knew that something had to be done to restrain the Rockefellers, billionaire monarchs of American finance and industry. Although a freshman in Congress, he went directly to President Wilson and laid the problem before the executive. Congressman Keating was frightened when he was ushered into Woodrow Wilson's presence. He told his story though, swiftly and concisely. The President's secretary, Joe Tumulty, came in when the allotted time was up and glared at the Colorado representative. President Wilson smiled and waved Tumulty away. When Keating had finished, President Wilson spoke, with just a suggestion of doubt in his voice.

"But what do you think I can do?" he asked. "After all, this is a state matter and I am president of the United States."

"It won't be a state matter very long, Mr. President," Congressman Keating replied earnestly. "I have seen two of these strikes. They were not pink tea affairs. This will probably be worse than either of the others."

President Wilson repeated: "But what can I do?"

Congressman Keating had a plan.

"Call John D. Rockefeller to the White House," he suggested. "Urge him to meet the authorized spokesman of his employes."

It was a spectacular scheme. Congressman Keating, a former city editor of The Rocky Mountain News in Denver, was newspaperman enough to see the headlines in every paper in the country: "Rockefeller Called to the White House; Urged to Meet With Coal Miners in Colorado."

Even John D. Rockefeller couldn't resist that, Congressman

Keating believed. President Wilson hesitated. He was not a publicity hound. Perhaps he could see the newspaper headlines too, but if so, they didn't appeal to him.

"I can't do that," he said finally. "But I will help you. I will write to Mr. Rockefeller and ask him to do what you have suggested."

Congressman Keating was disappointed when he left the White House though he realized he had made some progress. His plan hadn't been accepted, but at least Wilson had agreed to enter the battle. Rockefeller fell back on statements of those who were in charge of his Colorado properties. The old, time-worn alibis were rehearsed—the men didn't want a union, agitators were responsible for the trouble, the strike would just collapse in a few weeks.

After an exchange of letters with Rockefeller, President Wilson summoned Keating to the White House. "We're not getting anywhere, Mr. Keating," he said. "There is only one possibility left, a congressional investigation."

Congressman Keating had anticipated that. He had introduced a resolution calling for an investigation. He had a copy in his pocket and showed it to the President.

"That is the idea," President Wilson said.

"Mr. President," Keating replied, "I have canvassed the members of the House. I think we have enough votes to pass this resolution, but it is tied up in the Rules Committee. That committee will not permit us to have a vote unless you use your influence with the Democratic members."

President Wilson agreed to do so. As Congressman Keating was leaving, the President pressed his hand and whispered, "Damn those coal operators."

The representative from Colorado was shocked. He didn't imagine that a man who had been president of Princeton could be induced to use profanity.

President Wilson redeemed his word. He sent for the Democratic members of the Rules Committee and urged them to

make a favorable report upon the resolution. They turned him
down. They had to make a choice between the President of the
United States, the leader of their party, and the mighty John
D. Rockefeller, and they sided with Rockefeller. But Congressman Keating was a resourceful man. He had a hunch and played
it hard. He decided to call a caucus of the Democratic members
of the House for the purpose of considering the resolution and
instructing the Rules Committee to make a favorable report
on it.

Nothing like this had ever been done before. Keating was
afraid to mention his idea to President Wilson for fear he might
veto it. For the same reason, Keating concealed it from Speaker
Champ Clark and the Democratic floor leader, Underwood of
Alabama. He called in a few members, who were then as obscure as himself, and prepared a petition for a caucus. They
then slipped around among their friends to get the requisite
number of signatures. It didn't take long, and the moment the
names were secured, Keating filed the document with the clerk
of the House. It created a sensation. Members of the Rules
Committee were indignant, but the caucus had to be called. The
opposition was nervous, and finally decided to advise its friends
to stay away, hoping to deprive Keating of a quorum. This
strategy failed, and the caucus was held in the House chamber
with 170 Democrats present.

Members of the Rules Committee appeared and said in substance:

"The Rules Committee was created to hold up undesirable
legislation. On many occasions we have acted as goats for the
leaders of this House. We have been criticised, but we have not
complained. Now we have voted not to report a resolution to
investigate the Colorado coal strike, and this young gentleman
from Colorado is asking you to over-rule us. If you do, some of
us feel that our self-respect demands that we resign from the
committee."

Prominent conservative Democrats followed, urging that

members of the caucus "stop, look, and listen" before they offered such an affront to the most powerful committee in the House. Keating felt his courage ooze, but he did not falter. A colleague, the elderly Graham, who represented Lincoln's old district in Illinois, came to Keating's assistance as did "Davy" Lewis of Maryland, chairman of the House Committee on Labor. Lewis closed the debate in a stirring appeal in which he described his own life in a coal mine from the day he entered the underground at the age of nine. There were moist eyes in the chamber when he had finished.

Keating won overwhelmingly and immediately dispatched a telegram to Trinidad. He did not know that the message would avert a great tragedy in the Southern Colorado city. The coal miners, angered by the Main Street riot, had decided to wipe out the militia and the private guards. Fierce-eyed Greeks, led by Louie Tikas, crept through the pinon trees on the hills above the militia camp near Trinidad. Plans had been carefully laid. At dawn, the miners would close in on the militia from all sides and annihilate them with one mighty blow. Other groups of miners—the Segundo, the Tercio, and the Sopris men—had filtered into Trinidad under cover of darkness and unobtrusively manned the roofs of business buildings. General Chase's headquarters was covered by a hundred picked sharpshooters. Not a man could live in the streets when the attack opened. Mop up detachments of 25 to 30 men hid in buildings of mine sympathizers, waiting for the dawn to sally forth.

The Keating telegram reached Trinidad about the same moment that a miner informed John Lawson of the contemplated attack. He raced to find Tikas. When he finally located him, the Greek leader was armed and equipped for the field with a gunny sack containing food and ammunition slung across his shoulders. Tikas did not deny the attack was planned and about to be executed.

"Call the men off," Lawson ordered. "Send them home."

"But, John . . ." Louie began. Then he looked into Lawson's face and saw something he had never seen before.

"All right, John," he said meekly. "I send word. I call the men back."

The miners were still drifting in from their positions in the hills the next day when the House formally authorized its Committee on Mines and Mining to investigate conditions in Las Animas, Huerfano, Fremont, Grand, Routt, Boulder and Weld counties in Colorado, and a bitter strike then in progress in the copper producing counties of Michigan. Members of the House committee, who would conduct the inquiries, were Reps. Martin D. Foster of Illinois, a physician; James F. Byrnes of South Carolina, John M. Evans of Montana, Richard W. Austin of Tennessee, and Howard Sutherland of West Virginia. The committee was granted full powers to subpena witnesses and documents, and to engage any clerical assistance it deemed necessary.

Lawson cheered the approaching investigation, while the Colorado operators remained silent.

"I am certain the congressional committee will find, just as our federation committee did, that every charge that has been made against the operators and militia can be sustained," Lawson announced. "We have great hopes for the committee."

General Chase announced the same day that "someone unknown to us" had thrown a bomb into the military camp at Walsenburg. The bomb, it developed, did not explode, but "if it had it would have killed a great portion of the soldiers about the headquarters of the camp," General Chase's announcement to the press said.

"Fake," Lawson replied. "They are doing everything they can to prejudice the public against the union by every conceivable type of malicious trickery." Fortunately, General Chase never learned of the narrowly-averted attack on his troops.

Mine worker attorneys filed new petitions in Las Animas County District Court for writs of habeas corpus for military prisoners. General Chase and Judge Advocate Boughton successfully resisted them.

"I'll hold these prisoners as long as I like," General Chase announced.

"The question of the guilt or innocence of these men is of no importance," Major Boughton explained. "It was deemed necessary for purposes best known to General Chase to lock them up and they will remain locked up until General Chase orders them released."

Alarmed by the approaching federal investigation, several of the large operators began to get rid of their strike breakers. One hundred men were shipped out of the Sunnyside and Gresham mines January 31. Other mines sent strike breakers out of the district in small parties under the protection of armed escorts.

Twelve hundred men and women paraded the streets of Trinidad February 1. They sang their union songs and marched up and down in front of the Columbian Hotel without interference. General Chase had heard enough of the Main Street riot and kept his troops in their camp. Although paraders were not bothered, General Chase continued his policy of wholesale arrests of strikers and organizers. James T. Davis, Aguilar marshal, and Albert J. McGuire, secretary of the Aguilar union local, were arrested and hustled off to jail for no apparent reason. William Diamond, in charge of the union headquarters in Trinidad, was held in jail for three days without a charge being made against him. Frank Miner, who had served as a member of the federation's investigating committee, was jailed when the militia intercepted him as he was enroute to the Starkville and Morley tent colonies with food, clothing and shoes for the colonists. P. Tomca, a striker at Starkville, was dragged out of his house and carted off to jail because he refused militiamen permission to open a package of meat while they were making a search of his home. His three motherless children were found near death from freezing the next morning when neighbors entered the house.

Lawson held his own men in line with the result that most of the arrests were illegal. There was not so much as a pretext for military action in most instances. He made a final plea to the men through their leaders whom he called together Feb. 6, 1914.

"The congressional committee arrives in Denver tomorrow and I have to go up there," Lawson told them. "During my absence I want you to keep every striker walking the chalk line. Don't let the men do anything that could be twisted by the militia or the coal operators."

They promised that the strictest order would be enforced.

Early the next day, Chairman Foster of the congressional committee met in the Brown Palace Hotel in Denver with Frank Gove, attorney and publicity man for the operators.

"We'll meet with the representatives of the operators and the union immediately," Doctor Foster said.

"My clients won't meet with the union leaders," Gove replied.

"I think they will this time."

"If you get them together in one room, Doctor, you'll be doing something no one else has been able to do."

"We have the power of subpena, Mr. Gove. They'll either come willingly or they will be compelled to come."

Gove shrugged.

"Well, I suppose orders are orders."

When Gove had gone, Doctor Foster met briefly with Lawson, Hayes and Doyle.

"I want to thank you gentlemen for your fine attitude and your offers of cooperation," Doctor Foster said when the interview ended. "We'll see a great deal of each other during the next few weeks, and I am certain our relations will be most pleasant."

CHAPTER X

UNCLE SAM ASKS QUESTIONS

The investigating committee opened its first session in the State House of Representatives Feb. 9, 1914, with a reading of the empowering resolution.

"You have heard the resolution," Chairman Foster said. "If either side of this controversy wishes to be represented by counsel the committee would like to have those gentlemen indicate the counsel that will represent them."

J. C. Osgood, head of the Victor-American Fuel Co., addressed Dr. Foster:

"Mr. Chairman, the coal operators have no general organization and we have no general attorney representing all the operators. The three largest corporations have gotten the service of Fred Herrington, of the Colorado Fuel & Iron Co., Mr. F. E. Gove of the Victor-American Fuel Co., Mr. J. V. Sickman of the Rocky Mountain Fuel Co., and Mr. J. C. Northcutt is general attorney for the three companies, and if any other operators have counsel here I do not know them. Senator Hayden is joint attorney with Mr. Northcutt as general counsel for the three companies."

Dr. Foster nodded, and recognized Professor Brewster who informed the committee that the United Mine Workers would be represented by Horace N. Hawkins, Edward P. Costigan, and himself. General Chase added his voice.

"I desire to state that it may be important that the military organization of the State of Colorado be represented, and we will be represented by Major Edward Boughton and Captain W. C. Danks," General Chase said.

The committee moved slowly. It was on strange ground and in a strange field. John Lawson fidgeted in his seat while Russell D. George, the state geologist, gave the committee the necessary background on coal resources and the extent of development in the state. James Dalrymple, chief state coal mine inspector, told the committee of the work in his office. He testified there were so many accidents in Colorado mines and such a heavy loss of life that his office was unable to perform all of its duties because of lack of sufficient personnel.

When Labor Commissioner Brake was called he speared the coal operators for the first time, contending they dominated the state politically and failed to obey state laws.

"Don't they have any fair elections?" Representative Sutherland asked.

Commissioner Brake smiled thinly and stared at Judge Northcutt a moment before he answered.

"You couldn't get anybody that is not directly interested in this country to think that you ever had a fair election for 20 years."

Mr. Herrington jumped to his feet.

"I rise to protect the dignity of the state," he cried. "I think this witness has gone far enough on suspicion, and if he has any facts, this committee are entitled to know them, but I don't believe that every court, every other officer of this state, has been delinquent in its duty, and this is the only officer who has done his duty. And I rise, not for this case, but for the fair name of the state."

"The committee is ready to protect the State of Colorado in whatever rights Colorado may have," Chairman Foster replied sharply.

The union leaders and their friends were convinced they were having a day in court, while the mine operators looked upon the hearings as merely obstructions to be hurdled and quickly forgotten. There was no meeting of the minds, no honest intention of presenting facts with a view to arriving at a solution. Fully a dozen witnesses were heard before John Lawson was called to the stand. As he walked up the center aisle of the chamber in response to a call, several coal company officials leaned forward in their chairs. This was the man who had caused them so much trouble. A number of them had never seen him before though they knew of his work and something of his mettle.

Professor Brewster drew from Lawson the entire union story of the strike and the events leading up to it. Lawson answered each question, slowly and deliberately. He was perfectly at ease even though he sat in the midst of men who had done everything they could think of to intimidate him, to ruin him, and to drive him from the country. The members of the committee refrained from questions. They seemed anxious for Lawson to tell his story as he would, not simply in brief answers to questions from attorneys.

"You tell the story of conditions in Las Animas and Huerfano counties, Mr. Lawson," Chairman Foster said, interrupting Professor Brewster.

"I'll be glad to," Lawson replied. "The miners in that field have not had their political, social, religious or industrial liberty for many years. In fact ever since they started to dig coal there about thirty-five years ago. Quite naturally they have become restless. As a result of this they struck in 1884, in 1894, again in 1903, and they were compelled to strike again in 1913. Each time large bodies of thugs have been imported. We hear a great deal about the imported agitator, but large bodies of thugs have been imported, men from every walk of life, and men of bad reputation, and these men were given deputy sheriff's commissions. These men were turned loose on the miners and their families, permitted to walk up and down the streets of Trinidad, Walsenburg, Aguilar[3]—I will take Aguilar back; Aguilar was not such a safe place for them in days gone by—and if they didn't like the cut of your hair they might take a six-shooter and hit you over the head and point to the hole between the hills and tell you to go."

Lawson told a story of terrorism and intimidation. Once, when he fumbled for a term, Mr. Herrington called out:

"Gunmen—you might as well call them all the names."

Lawson nodded solemnly.

"Gunmen is the proper term," he replied.

Representative Byrnes wanted to know if the miners had imported guns or machine guns.

"Did you buy guns or ammunition or did you buy machine guns?" he asked.

"No, we didn't; we had an idea that we were going to get a couple of machine guns without buying them. We knew the companies were importing machine guns into the field."

Lawson remained on the stand all the second day. Costigan asked most of the questions for the United Mine Workers. Arrests of scores of persons were recited in detail as were stories of assaults, beatings, and other intimidations.

On cross examination by Judge Northcutt and Herrington, the operators sought to delve into union business, but Lawson was adroit. He was an organizer, not the secretary. He didn't have any information on union finances because he was not the treasurer. He answered coolly, and gave none of the information desired by the operators for future use. Other witnesses followed him to the stand in quick succession.

John Wennberg told the committee he was forced to discharge miners because they were union men while he was foreman in the Bowen and Hastings mines. A Pueblo hardware merchant testified that a Walsenburg merchant purchased guns from him, mostly thirty-thirty caliber carbines, and that the

[3] A small mining community mid-way between Trinidad and Walsenburg.

guns were picked out by Adolf Germer, a union organizer, who accompanied the Walsenburg merchant to the Pueblo store. The most choice bit of testimony came on the third day when A. C. Felts, superintendent of the Baldwin-Felts Detective Agency, took the stand. He readily admitted hiring guards on orders from the coal companies, adding that he knew little or nothing of the characters of the men he engaged.

"These men were merely referred to and sent to the mine superintendents who had the privilege of putting them to work or dropping them as they saw fit," Felts explained. "They worked under the jurisdiction of competent men."

Members of the congressional committee took turns quizzing Felts. They drew from him admissions that most of his regular men came from West Virginia and that they had taken part in fights to break coal strikes in that state.

Deftly, Chairman Foster turned the questioning from men to guns.

"Let me ask you this, Mr. Felts: Who owns this gun, this rapid-fire gun, these guns that have been brought into the State of Colorado? Who owns them now?"

"I presume I can only answer you on information."

Felts then went on to say he had obtained the first rapid-fire gun from his brother, T. L. Felts, head of the detective agency, in West Virginia along with a quantity of ammunition, and that the coal operators paid for the express and later for the gun. The actual payments, he said, were made by W. C. Babcock, vice-president of The Rocky Mountain Fuel Co.

"When you thought it was necessary to bring in rapid-fire guns and ammunition, then they gave you money for it; is that the situation?" Chairman Foster asked.

"They paid for such guns as I bought," Felts replied.

He admitted bringing in four machine guns, and that more might have been imported.

"Suppose your employment should terminate tomorrow," Representative Evans said. "Would you take these guns away with you when you left here?"

"I would leave the guns here."

"You claim, then, no ownership in the guns?"

"No, sir, no ownership."

Felts insisted he could not tell the investigators where the machine guns were located in the southern field although he expressed belief that "the militia have control of some of them."

The 34-year-old Felts, an agency man for more than 13 years, had a bad time of it when he was cross-examined by Costigan.

A Harvard graduate, who had long been known as a political liberal, Costigan was well launched on a career that was to carry him to the United States Senate. A slender man of medium height, Costigan's dark face had an ascetic quality. He was polite to the point of courtliness, but behind the pleasant manner was an intellectual rapier that sought relentlessly for the weak spot in an opponent's guard.

He forced Felts to admit that several of the imported gunmen had been tried for various criminal offenses in West Virginia; that a drunken Baldwin-Felts detective had caused trouble in Lafayette, and that there were eight machine guns mounted at mines in the northern field alone.

"Mr. Felts, were you ever personally tried on a criminal charge?" Costigan asked blandly.

The detective bristled.

"What, when and where?"

"That is what I am trying to find out."

"The rule is, has he ever been convicted of a crime," Judge Northcutt interposed. "The mere charging is not even a reflection."

Costigan returned to the attack.

"Have you ever been convicted of a crime?"

"I do not recollect of any charge," Felts said in a low voice.

"Have you ever been charged?"

"I would prefer the gentleman would say when and where."

"I do not happen to know," Costigan said smilingly. "I am asking you in the light of some information—let me say in West Virginia, for the purpose of refreshing your recollection . . . "

"I possibly have, but I have never been guilty of any criminal charge. I was never convicted."

"Have you ever been tried?" Representative Sutherland asked.

"Yes, sir; a number of times."

"Were you ever tried—I am speaking now, for robbing a paymaster?"

Felts squirmed and glanced at the coal company attorneys. Then he answered:

"I want to say there was a case where one of our clients was robbed and the paid counsel for the United Mine Workers and the district attorney who had formerly been their counsel induced an imbecile, a man who was weak in body and mind, and who had formerly been a charge of the county in which he lived, to go before the grand jury and swear that I was the man. My bond was signed by the president of the company, and by other citizens representing an aggregate wealth of over $175,000,000. I was tried, I was prosecuted by the paid counsel of the United Mine Workers, and I was acquitted in six minutes before a jury of 12 honest men, and in a court, the honesty and integrity of which has never been questioned. One more effort on their part to get rid of a man in another way outside of the assassin route."

Several witnesses pictured the militia, the guards, and the Baldwin-Felts as cruel tyrants and oppressors; others painted the strikers and their leaders as anarchists who sought to overthrow lawful government.

While Costigan carried most of the burden for the union in the hearings, Horace Hawkins was not idle. He filed an original suit in the Colorado Supreme Court Feb. 13 in an effort to effect Mother Jones' release from Mt. San Rafael Hospital. This action, coupled with the testimony against them in the hearings, angered militia officers in Trinidad. They raided the Starkville tent colony, confiscated papers of witnesses, and wrecked a number of tents. Leaders of several of the colonies thought Lawson should return to the southern field immediately, but he knew a major attack would not be made on a colony while the committee was in the state. He stayed on in Denver to hear the testimony of such men as Osgood and Welborn.

Perhaps the clearest and most explicit statement of coal company policy and attitude toward working men was given by Osgood in a frank dissertation in which he declared he never would do business with the United Mine Workers of America.

"I don't want any business relations with it, and I am not going to have any business relations with them," Osgood said, shaking his head from side to side. He took the union demands one by one.

"We feel there is no justification for the payment of an increase in wages at this time," he said. "We put an eight-hour day into effect March 5, 1913, five months before the demand was made. Why that demand was made I have no knowledge, except that I suppose it was there for foreign consumption. I would like to go a little further into this matter of an eight-hour day. I have always been opposed to it, and I know a great many just as strongly opposed to it. In the first place I don't think a coal miner ever did work eight hours. No man likes his liberty restricted in this way; in the second place, it is particularly a seasonable business.[4]

"I have always been against the eight-hour day, and I have made repeated efforts to have it killed.

"A bill was introduced into the Legislature for an eight-hour day, which by the Legislature was amended—I think the credit went to Senator Simon Guggenheim[5] but I want to take it for myself—and it was made to include in that bill that only an

[4] Conditions in the Coal Mines of Colorado, Hearings of the Subcommittee of the Committee on Mines and Mining, 1914. Part II, P. 401.

[5] A member of the smelting family who was active in Colorado politics. He was referred to in opposition newspapers as $enator $imon Guggenheim.

eight-hour day could apply where those conditions existed—where it was dangerous to life and limb. The labor men opposed the law. I endeavored to persuade all of our men to abide by it; the law made the laborer responsible, and not the company which was not in a position to prevent him from working. I don't know how long that law lasted—a year or two—and then a law was passed which eliminated that feature, at the instigation of labor leaders. Under our referendum law of Colorado it was referred, which made it inoperative until it was passed by the people.

"I made such efforts as I could, in accordance with my views, to prevent the enactment of the law; but when it was unavoidable, I yielded to it and obeyed the law."

When Welborn went to the stand, he was a pleasant witness as long as coal company attorneys did the questioning. He stiffened as soon as Professor Brewster began the cross-examination. He readily admitted that he personally purchased eight machine guns and ordered them set up around C. F. & I. Co. mines in the southern field. The guns took the place of many guards, he said.

Welborn insisted his miners were well paid and that there was no dissatisfaction among them that was not artificially induced by outside agitators. On the question of who owned the C. F. & I. Company's 36 million dollars worth of outstanding stock, Welborn was very hazy. He did not know whether John D. Rockefeller or John D. Jr. owned a majority of the stock or not, although the younger Rockefeller was a director of the C. F. & I. Most of the directors, he said, lived in New York. In response to a series of questions, Welborn said he saw nothing illogical in the C. F. & I. protests against union officials from other states advising with the miners while the coal company itself was being directed out of New York.[6]

"By the way," Professor Brewster said, "did you have a talk

---

[6] Conditions in the Coal Mines of Colorado, Hearings of a Subcommittee on Mines and Mining, 1914. Part II, Pages 485 and 618.

with Governor Ammons just before the last election, or during the campaign, about your influence in the south, those two counties (Las Animas and Huerfano), in politics?"

"Yes, Governor Ammons came to my office and talked to me about . . . "

"Just before the election? Go ahead."

"He came to me and talked about our connection with politics."

"And he wanted to know your attitude toward his candidacy, did he not?"

"No, I don't think he did; I am sure he did not."

"Did you not tell him that you were not opposed to him and would not oppose him down there?"

"Yes—I am not sure, but I should have been perfectly willing to tell him that."

"You vote down there, do you?"

"No, I do not."

"Then, when you said that, you meant your company, didn't you?"

"Yes, sir."

Asked by Professor Brewster if he thought the United Mine Workers directed miners to shoot and murder, Welborn said:

"I do not know as to that, but in my opinion I have held certain of these officers morally responsible for the murder of a great many of our men."

"Yes, I know," Professor Brewster replied. "Now, do you hold yourself morally responsible for the murders that some of your guards have committed, Mr. Welborn?"

"I know of no murders committed on the part of guards."

"You do not?"

"No, sir."

"Do you know about the shooting up on Seventh Street in Walsenburg that really afterwards caused the La Veta shooting?"

"Yes; do you know all the circumstances of that?"

"I asked if you knew?"

"I knew there was a shooting, but I am not willing to admit it was by our guards."

Governor Ammons withdrew all except 200 troops from the strike zone Feb. 27, 1914. The expense of the militia in the field had been more than the state government could bear, and, like Lawson, Governor Ammons decided to lean heavily on the theory there would be no disturbances while the congressional committee was on the ground. In six months' time, according to reports submitted to Governor Ammons by fiscal officers of the state, a total of $685,000 had been spent for guard duties at properties which yielded an aggregate return of $12,378.67 to the state treasury in annual taxes. Not all of the huge cost could be attributed to the mere fact the militia was in the field, however. One of the major reasons for the high cost was that the militia had a military organization similar to the Mexican armies of the comic pages. The field force of 695 men had been commanded by 397 officers.

Withdrawal of the major part of the troops did not relieve the state treasury as much as Governor Ammons had anticipated, however, as the heavy headquarters expense was continued. General Chase, who received a monthly salary of $400 and expense money varying from $150 to $175 a week, remained in the field as did a large number of his subordinates. One group of 12 officers continued to cost the state $5,000 a month. Major Boughton was receiving $200 a month in salary and approximately $100 a week for expenses. To add to the financial difficulties, a large number of unpaid bills came to light. Auditor Kenehan's office received hundreds of demands from private business firms and individuals for payment of bills incurred by the military. He refused to pay any of them on the ground he had never received any notification of the expenses from the military department. As the main body of militia moved out of the southern district, the congressional investigators moved their hearings from Denver to Trinidad. On March 6, 1914, while the committee was sitting in Trinidad's West Theater, holding a hearing, Horace Hawkins again sought release of Mother Jones through a petition to Las Animas County District Court for a writ of habeas corpus. It was denied.

General Chase, who was busy preparing a report for the governor, wrote in it:

"During the arguments, the court room was packed with a heterogeneous audience, the majority of which neither spoke nor understood the English language. The crowd was very unusual and could not have been attracted by any desire to hear the proceedings, which it could not understand. Without any doubt in the world, these men—Montenegrins, Greeks, Italians, Servians, and other recent arrivals from the southern countries of Europe—were present for the one purpose of participating in any riot that might be started. I discovered a conspiracy among certain Italians in the audience to kill myself, the judge advocate, who was presenting the argument, and the district judge, who had incurred the hatred of the strikers by his decisions. The conspiracy was not unusual, since I have had military information of just such plots over and over again. On each of these occasions I found it necessary to surround the courthouse with soldiers. I have always been able to enforce order and prevent riot or disperse mobs, but with all the forces at my command I could not prevent secret assassination, and assassination was impending that day."

The pompous general was not able to surround the congressional committee with soldiers when it summoned him, but he did refuse to be cross-examined.

"We cannot hear General Chase at all if he refuses to be cross-examined, as other witnesses," Chairman Foster ruled. The committee left Trinidad the same day for Denver to hear a few remaining witnesses at brief hearings in the State Capitol. Osgood, Welborn, and one or two others were recalled. Antone Langowski, young official of the Sopris union local, who testified to bombings in Sopris, was forced by Costigan to admit from the stand that he was paid $3 a day by the Colorado Fuel & Iron Company to discredit the union while he was accepting $3 a week in strike benefits. He also admitted he had traveled to Denver in the company of a C. F. & I. guard and that he had had a long talk with E. H. Weitzel, general manager of the C. F. & I., on the train enroute from Trinidad.

When the committee completed its work and left Denver for Washington, strife again broke out in the southern field. Colonel Davis and a detachment of militia destroyed the Forbes tent colony March 10, 1914, after a non-union miner, Neil Smith, was found dead on the railroad tracks between Forbes and Suffield. Sixteen strikers in the lower Forbes colony were arrested and 48 women and children in the upper colony were forced out of their tent homes.

General Chase announced that Smith had been murdered by strikers with clubs and stones, and "then the victim's body was laid on the railroad tracks to be run over, as it was, by an approaching train."

Lawson charged that Smith was drunk and had fallen on the railroad tracks in a drunken stupor.

"General Chase has been looking for an excuse for some time to destroy the Forbes colonies," Lawson said in a public statement. "The train crew saw Smith killed, but Chase refused to allow them to testify at the coroner's inquest."

The Trinidad Free Press, a union organ edited by Joe M. Scatterthwaite, cried in a headline:

"How long, Oh God, how long?"

The newspaper asked "how long must we endure the tyranny of these military poltroons and cravens?" Scatterthwaite said the trainmen—J. M. Riley, conductor; T. H. Mitchell, engineer, and J. M. Dean, brakeman—were the first persons to examine Smith's body after the train passed over it, and they found no evidence of bloody clubs or stones such as militiamen and company guards, who arrived at the scene hours later, claimed to have found.

The editor of the Free Press wrote:

"Governor Ammons, sitting on his shoulder blades in a cushioned chair, replies to complaints concerning this Forbes outrage, that he knew nothing of it—and that it will not happen again.

"Of course it will not occur again—and it does not need an anemic, spineless, truckling executive to give that assurance. The thing has been done! The tents are down. The women are in tears, the children are in hysterics, the peaceful colony is scattered. It will not be done again at Forbes. Oh, no!

"But will it be done at some other point? Will Ludlow be the next to suffer? Will the mailed fist fall on Starkville? Will these unrebuked outlaws next attack some other law-abiding band of citizens? These are questions for a kow-towing executive to answer. He does not know what the next order of the coal barons will be, but he knows that he will probably obey that command as he has sniffingly and cringingly obeyed every order that has come to him from the offices of the Colorado Fuel & Iron Company and the Victor-American Fuel Company— his masters. He does not know what his militia will do, for he is fully aware, in his puny heart, that the militia has got beyond his control.

"He knows that these desperate men of the gun and bludgeon can no more be checked and held in leash than the imps of hell. He assures the people that there will be no further outrages at Forbes, but he is powerless to say that the heavy hand will not fall on some other community. And so he keeps silent, groveling out his excuses to righteous complaints."

Three days later, Lieutenant Linderfelt and his men rode down a crowd at Ludlow station at train time, and the next morning two strikers, Johanne Demosa and Jack Gill, were shot and killed by gunmen in Oak Creek. While the disturbances agitated the strike field, Attorney Hawkins made a last move to get Mother Jones out of the Trinidad hospital. He sought a test of the famous Moyer habeas corpus case. The Supreme Court set March 16 for arguments. The day before the case was to come up, the militia suddenly released the aged organizer. A half hour before a train left Trinidad for Denver, a militia officer called on Mother Jones in her room at the hospital.

"Get up and dress, Mother," he said. "You've got just 30 minutes to catch the train for Denver. The governor wants to see you."

She hurried to get ready. An automobile, provided by the National Guard, was waiting to take her to the station. On her arrival in Denver, Mother Jones was chagrined to find a statement in the newspapers from the military department to the effect that she had given up her fight against military rule. She called the governor immediately only to find he had not asked to see her.

She stayed in Denver several days, meeting with union officials and making speeches, but by March 22 she was on her way south to Trinidad again.

CHAPTER XI

ROCKEFELLER ON THE STAND

Mother Jones worked out several plans of action on her ride south across the state. She planned to get off the train again before she reached Trinidad. The ruse had worked once and it ought to work again, but the militia were too smart for her. When the train stopped in Walsenburg, a detail came aboard and placed her under arrest. She was taken directly to the Huerfano County jail and placed in a dirty cell—the same cell, incidentally, which had held another strike prisoner, Gus Martinez, who had contracted rheumatism while in the hands of the military. He had died shortly after his release. Mother Jones was, of course, quite pleased with the cell as it would strengthen sympathy for her.

Shortly after Mother Jones was safely locked up, General Chase submitted his report to Governor Ammons. It contained 119 printed pages and carried the military's answer to most of the charges made against it. Of Mother Jones, General Chase wrote:

"She is an eccentric and peculiar figure. I make no mention of her personal history, with which we are not concerned."

This was his only allusion to the coal operators' whispers that old Mother Jones was a woman of ill repute.

"She seemed to have in an exceptional degree the faculty of stirring up the more ignorant and criminally disposed to deeds of violence and crime," General Chase's report said. "Prior to the advent of the state's troops she made a series of speeches in the strike zone, of which I have authentic and verbatim reports. These speeches are couched in coarse, vulgar and profane language, and address themselves to the lowest passions of mankind. I confidently believe that most of the murders and other acts of violent crime committed in the strike region have been inspired by this woman's incendiary utterances.

"She has returned to the strike district, not for the transaction of any business, or for any other purpose than to defy the power of the state, and, as she stated in numerous interviews, 'to establish her right to go where she pleased,' and in open defiance of the power and authority vested in the chief executive."

He referred in his report to women who had made complaints against militiamen as "women of the lower classes." In every instance, General Chase found his soldiers performed well and were "young men of good families," while the strikers were invariably referred to as "the lower and rougher elements."

"I would be derelict in my obligations if I did not emphasize the splendid conduct of the National Guard as a whole," General Chase wrote. "The errand was a patriotic one, and occasioned by a quarrel wholly impersonal and void of interest to them. The men of the guard have discharged their services well, faithfully and patiently. For all the task has been a thankless one. The only visible return for the sacrificing citizenship displayed has been the heaping of reproach and opprobrium, falsehood and scurrility, upon the shoulders of the commonwealth's defenders. It is hoped that a just and discriminating public will in the end realize the disinterested service of these champions of the state's integrity and honor, who for the present have only the consciousness of a stern and unpleasant duty well performed to console them."

The union policy committee, with a nice sense of humor, pointed out that General Chase had a nice "visible return" in the form of money, and that practically all of the officers were or should be somewhat consoled by large salaries and heavy expense accounts which were a matter of public record. After giving guard expenditures in some detail, the policy committee hurled new charges at the militiamen.

"If the investigators of the State Federation of Labor and the congressional committee have proved to you beyond a doubt that the Colorado militia is anything but patriotic and self-sacrificing, remember that General Chase says so, and, of course, you cannot doubt the word of a tyrannizer of men and an out-rager of womanhood," the statement concluded.

The word war over for the moment, Lawson went to Forbes to rebuild the colony. The land had been leased by the union and he believed the miners had fully as much right to their tent homes as other citizens had to their brick and stone structures. He had one tent erected when a detail of militia and guards arrived and tore it down. Lawson went back to the Ludlow colony. That night three militiamen and a Baldwin-Felts detective fired several shots into the Suffield colony and then fled into the darkness. On March 28, 1914, while Lawson was still in Ludlow, militia surrounded the colony and attempted to draw the inhabitants into a fight. Lawson, Fyler and Tikas restrained them.

Mother Jones remained in the Walsenburg jail 30 days, but the United Mine Workers got in several good licks at the militia and operators through the medium of letters which Mother Jones purportedly and allegedly smuggled out of the filthy jail.

"The courts of Las Animas and Huerfano counties are open and unobstructed in the transaction of business," one Mother Jones letter said, "yet Governor Ammons and his Peabody appointee, General Chase, refuse to carry me before any court, and refuse to make any charge against me. I ask the press to let the nation know of my treatment, and to say to my friends, whom, thank God, I number by the thousands in the United States and Mexico, that even my incarceration in a damp, underground dungeon will not make me give up the fight in which I am engaged for liberty and for the rights of the workingman.

"Let the nation know and especially let my friend, General Francisco Villa know, that the great United States of America, which is demanding of him that he release the traitors that he has placed in custody, is now holding Mother Jones incommunicado in an underground (sic) cell, surrounded with sewer rats, tin soldiers, and other vermin."

Early in April, the congressional committee reconvened, this time in the House of Representatives chamber in Washington, to hear John D. Rockefeller, Jr. This was the man union leaders had long pointed to as the owner of the C. F. & I. Co. and the czar of the Colorado coal industry. Now they would hear what this millionaire had to say and hear it from his own lips. The examination was made solely by the committee. There were no corporation or union attorneys to ask questions.[1]

Rockefeller testified that his family owned 40 per cent of the preferred and 40 per cent of the common stock of the C. F. & I. Co. His father, he said, owned 43 per cent of $14,450,000 worth of one bond issue of the company. Although a director, Rockefeller said he had not attended a meeting of the board of directors for 10 years, and that he did not have the "slightest idea" of who was present when the directors of the corporation were elected. He could not remember the exact date the Colorado strike had been called.

"I could refer to the exact date in this correspondence," Rockefeller said, tapping a sheaf of papers. "It was in September or October, some place along there; but the date I would not have retained."

"Do you realize that since last September this strike has been reported in the press of the country, that the Governor of Colorado has called out the militia to police the disturbed district, and that the conditions prevailing in that district were

[1] Conditions in the Coal Mines of Colorado, Hearings of a Subcommittee of the Committee on Mines and Mining, 1914. Part X, Pages 2841 to 2946.

shocking, according to such reports, and that the House of Representatives deemed it a duty to undertake this investigation?" Chairman Foster asked.

"I have been fully aware of all those facts," Rockefeller replied.

"And yet neither you, personally, nor the board of directors, have looked into the matter?"

"I cannot say as to whether the board of directors have looked into the matter or not, their meetings being held in the West."

"What action has been taken personally to find out about the trouble in Colorado?"

"This correspondence will give the whole thing."

"Personally, what have you done, outside of this, as a director?"

"I have done nothing outside of this; that is the way in which we conduct the business."

Chairman Foster glanced at his colleagues and then went on:

"What remedies have you personally suggested to end this industrial disturbance?"

"The conduct of the business is in the hands of the officers, and so long as they have our entire confidence we shall stand by them; we could not conduct the business in any other way," Rockefeller replied.

Asked by Chairman Foster if he considered himself a dummy director in the C. F. & I., Rockefeller replied:

"I do not."

"But you represent someone else and not yourself?"

"I do; because, since his retirement from business some 15 years ago, my father has given no personal attention to the conduct of any of the private businesses in which he is an investor."

Rockefeller expressed belief that 90 per cent of the miners employed by the C. F. & I. did not want to belong to a union and then admitted, under questioning, that he based his belief on reports given to him by his two Colorado officers, Welborn and Bowers. Over and over, Rockefeller repeated his contention that he had no personal knowledge of the strike, but that he had absolute confidence in his subalterns to handle it as they saw fit. Inquiries from the committee concerning the coal company's control of liquor, schools and churches brought vague replies. He did not know that high school facilities were not provided in the various company camps.

He expressed opposition to the United Mine Workers on the ground that its officers were outsiders without interest in the Colorado coal fields, and on the ground the miners should be left free—free to work for whom they chose.

"But the killing of these people, the shooting of children, and all that has been going on there for months has not been of enough importance to you to communicate with the other directors, and see if something might not be done to end that sort of thing?" Foster asked.

"We believe that the issue is not a local one in Colorado," Rockefeller replied. "It is a national issue; whether workers shall be allowed to work under such conditions as they may choose. And as part owners of the property, our interest in the laboring men of this country is so immense, so deep, so profound that we stand ready to lose every cent we put in that company rather than see the men we have employed thrown out of work and have imposed upon them conditions which are not of their seeking and which neither they nor we can see are in our interest."

Foster frowned and made Rockefeller go over his position again. The chairman's eyes gleamed.

"And you are willing to go on and let these killings take place—men losing their lives on either side, the expenditure of large sums of money, and all this disturbance of labor—rather than to go out there and see if you might do something to settle those conditions?"

"There is just one thing, Mr. Chairman," Rockefeller said, "so far as I understand it, which can be done, as things are at present, to settle this strike, and that is to unionize the camps; and our interest demands that the camps shall be open camps, that we expect to stand by the officers at any cost. It is not an accident that this is our position ... "

"And you will do that if it costs all your property and kills all your employees?" Chairman Foster interposed.

"It is a great principle," Rockefeller replied.

The capitalist's opinions were widely broadcast through the press. Bowers was filled with "boundless delight" as well he might be, and, the morning after the one-day hearing, he wrote Rockefeller from Binghamton, N. Y.[2]

"You have rendered a service for the entire country in your testimony before the congressional committee, that cannot be over-estimated for its value just at this period in our industrial history," Bowers wrote. "As the writer anticipated, these biased political wire pullers utterly failed in their attempt to trip you and every word you said simply brought out clearer and clearer your genuine American loyalty to stand against all comers, to protect every man who seeks employment in the enterprise in which you have a commanding interest in the enjoyment under the stars and stripes, of life, liberty, and the pursuit of happiness.

"I believe the hours you gave to the committee and the position you so ruggedly maintained against the assaults of Dr. Foster, will do more for the cause of millions of laboring men, than all the efforts of social reformers in many years.

"It will set thousands of faltering employers to thinking and inspire confidence and spur them to activity in opposing the schemes of political, social and religious demagogues, who are in the clutches of the union labor leaders, whose aim is to shut the open shops.

[2] U. S. Commission on Industrial Relations, 1915; Report of the Colorado Strike, P. 141.

"I cannot put into words my satisfaction, I will say boundless delight with your magnificent and unshaken stand for principle, whatever the cost may be. Now for an aggressive warfare into 1916 and beyond for the open shop."

Rockefeller's public statements that unionization of the miners was undesirable and that he stood ready to spend huge sums to defend the open shop as well as his expressions of faith in the Colorado officers of the C. F. & I. heartened Welborn and the other Colorado operators as well as Bowers.

Predictions that the strike was nearing an end were heard on every side, but in the tent colonies the miners remained steadfast. They were as unshaken as Rockefeller. The miners were resolved to fight to the bitter end. They were determined to sit in their colonies and picket the mines as long as a striker remained. There was little violence, however. The union leaders continued to hold a tight rein on their men. This task was made somewhat easier by the fact that the guards and gunmen remained sullenly in the coal camps, apparently fearful that any outbreak would react against the coal companies while the congressional investigation was under way.

So peaceful was the southern field that on April 14, 1914, Governor Ammons decided to remove the rest of the troops and rid himself of a financial burden that was fast crippling his administration. It was agreed, however, that two troops, Company A, a cavalry outfit, and Troop B were to remain in the field under the command of Major Patrick J. Hamrock. The balance of the troops entrained with General Chase and left the strike zone April 17, 1914. The brutal K. E. Linderfelt went north with them—ostensibly to be mustered out. Of the troops remaining, Company A was made up of mine guards, pit bosses, mine superintendents, mine clerks and the like, while Troop B was composed of mine guards, professional soldiers and adventurers who had chosen to remain on strike duty when the rest of the force was withdrawn. Every pretense of fairness and impartiality disappeared with the troops that went north as the soldiers who remained behind were nothing more than gunmen who were economically dependent upon the coal companies and completely subservient to the wishes of the operators.

That Company A, or Troop A as it was sometimes called, was organized with the full consent and knowledge of the C. F. & I. Co. was shown in a letter written by Bowers to Rockefeller April 18, 1914, the day after the main body of troops had left the field.

"We have reliable information that the United Mine Workers are pinched as never before for funds," his letter said in part. "Another favorable feature is the organization of a military company of one hundred volunteers at Trinidad the present week. They are to be armed by the state and drilled by military officials. Another squad is being organized at Walsenburg. These independent militiamen will be subject to orders of the sheriff of the county. As these volunteers will draw no pay from the state, this movement has the support of the Governor and other men in authority."[3]

Thus it was that the final groundwork for one of the greatest disasters of history was completed. The preliminary steps were taken in distant New York when Rockefeller asserted he stood for "a great principle," and the final steps were taken in Las Animas and Huerfano counties with the organization of ruffians into what Bowers called "independent militiamen."

[3] United States Commission on Industrial Relations, Report on the Colorado Strike, 1915. P. 125.

CHAPTER XII

THE LUDLOW MASSACRE

The Greek Easter, April 19, 1914, was a gala day in the Ludlow tent colony.

Happy, fun-loving men and women of a score of races decked themselves out in their national costumes or Sunday bests to help the Greeks celebrate the festive day. The colony was a riot of color. Outside the leased area, tiny patches of snow still dotted the prairie, but a warm sun flooded the streets of the canvas city. Laughing children played tag around the tents or danced to the lively tunes of a half dozen jovial accordion players while their elders clapped approvingly. Feasts were prepared in many of the tents, and a baseball game was planned for the afternoon.

Louie Tikas, head man of the important colony, wore a picturesque Greek costume. His round face beamed as he walked about the colony, greeting the people with a kiss and the ancient cry, "Christ is risen." A medium sized man with a shock of thick, black hair and a dark complexion, Louie spoke English with a strong accent, but he spoke it well. He had had the benefit of a college education in his native Greece, and he had long been active in the affairs of the Hellenic Society. Strikers and union officials alike loved him for his even disposition and his unfailing courage in times of distress.

Louie's beaming smile and apparent enthusiasm for the Greek
Easter were forced. A few days before, when the Catholic and
Protestant Easter had been celebrated, Louie had entered into
the festivities with genuine pleasure. There had been egg rolls
and spaghetti dinners. John Lawson and a dozen other union
officials had spent the entire day in the colony. Today John
Lawson was busy in Trinidad, and Louie was filled with foreboding. Since the departure of the main body of militia, Lieutenant Linderfelt had returned to Hastings. Some said he was
in the southern field to get his traps and pay a brief visit to
friends, but there were more disturbing reports. Louie had
heard that Linderfelt had boasted he would wipe out the Ludlow colony. The mine owners' newspaper in Trinidad was
calling almost daily for the expulsion of alien agitators whose
presence was "an offense to the community."

Even more disturbing to a man of Tikas' intelligence were
rumors circulated among anti-union groups to the effect that
the strikers planned to attack the militia volunteers now that
the main body of troops had been withdrawn. A union spy
had told Louie that mine guards were reporting to the operators
that the strikers had laid careful plans to attack the mines and
the coal camps April 20, but had deferred the attacks to April
21 because the Greek Easter celebration usually carried over into
the second day. To Louie the rumors sounded like a build up,
an excuse for another attack on the colony.

Early in the afternoon, the miners and their families trooped
to the ball field for the big game. On a pinion-clad hill a
mile distant, Lieutenant Linderfelt lay on his stomach with field
glasses pressed to his smouldering eyes. He was watching the
throng of men and women intently a half hour later when five
mounted gunmen rode out of the mouth of the canon and
straight toward the ball field. Linderfelt swung his glasses
toward another hill and saw that a machine gun was in position; then he focused them again on the plain below. The
mounted gunmen rode close to the diamond before they pulled

in their horses. Their high-powered rifles rested easily across the pommels of their saddles as they stared insolently at the crowd.

The players stopped their game and stood as though stricken, while the spectators, strung along the first and third base lines, whispered nervously. The women sat silently. Suddenly the leader of the gunmen nodded to his companions and they turned their horses away. One of the women laughed hysterically. The leader pulled up his horse and half turned in the saddle.

"Oh, that's all right," he snarled. "Have your fun today; we'll have our roast tomorrow."

The woman laughed again, shrilly, and the faces of a dozen other women creased in smiles. Gunmen were always threatening, but there was nothing to fear. The men of the colony were strong and capable. They would not let these gunmen harm the colony. That night, while the colonists were making merry in the big tent, Major Hamrock called Louie Tikas on the telephone.

"You're holding a boy in that camp against his will," Major Hamrock said. "We want him."

Tikas asked the boy's name, and then informed Major Hamrock there was no such boy in the colony.

"My information is that he is there," Major Hamrock replied sharply. "Either you deliver him to us or we'll come and get him."

When the major had hung up, Tikas called John Lawson in Trinidad and informed him of the demand.

"If we have anyone there they want, let them have him," Lawson said.

"But he is not here," Louie protested.

"Then you can't do anything about it," Lawson replied. "If Hamrock calls again just tell him you don't have the boy."

"Is martial law still in effect, John?" Louie asked. "Do they have a right to search the colony?"

"No, they don't."

"John, I am afraid something is up. This doesn't look good to me."

"Nor to me, Louie. But sit tight and don't let any of the men give offense."

John Lawson was as worried as Tikas. The responsibility rested on Lawson's shoulders alone as Hayes was out of the field. He stayed at his work in Trinidad, but never got very far from his telephone. He was near it early Monday when Tikas called a second time.

"The five gunmen who were down at the ball field yesterday are here again demanding the boy," Louie said. "I've had the colony searched, but he isn't here."

"Then you can't produce him," Lawson said. "Get rid of the gunmen as easily as possible."

Meanwhile, Major Hamrock telephoned Linderfelt and told him to bring his men down the canon. Then the major called Tikas on the telephone.

"Come over to the camp," he said, "I want to talk to you."

Louie demurred. He didn't like the tone of the major's voice. Intuition told Louie something was wrong.

"I don't want to come over to your camp," Tikas said. "I'll tell you, major, I'll meet you at the Ludlow depot."

"Very well," Major Hamrock barked, and banged the receiver.

Tikas called his camp police together.

"You men stay close around here," he said. "There is something up. I am going over to the depot to talk to Major Hamrock."

As Louie approached the depot, his alarm mounted. Militia swarmed around the place. They carried their Springfield rifles and full belts of ammunition. Major Hamrock was waiting.

"You've got that boy in your colony," Major Hamrock began. "You'd better turn him over to us."

"I tell you Major that he is not there," Louie said, gesticulating excitedly. The meeting was brief. As he talked, Louie watched the warlike preparations going on around him.

"I am going back to the colony now," he said finally. "We do not have the boy."

Major Hamrock snorted and turned on his heel. As Louie started to leave the depot, he glanced toward Water Tank Hill. The crown of the elevation was black with militia. He thought he made out a machine gun. Louie looked quickly back toward the colony. Miners were standing near the edge of the union land, looking west toward Water Tank Hill. Louie pulled two white handkerchiefs from his pockets and, holding one high in each hand, began to walk swiftly toward the colony. Before he reached the tents, he heard a bomb explode, then a second and then a third.[1] The rattle of small arms broke out and then the rat-tat-tat of a machine gun. Ducking low, Tikas broke into a run.

It was 10:01 a. m.

Louie saw his men running from the colony toward the nearby steel bridge, a strong breastworks. Bullets screamed through the tents. He made his way to the headquarters tent and called John Lawson on the telephone.

"They're firing on us," he yelled into the mouthpiece. "It looks like a big attack."

"We'll get help there as fast as possible," Lawson replied. "Hang on, and watch out for the women and children."

Tikas made a hurried trip through the colony. Machine bullets were spraying the streets and ripping the tents to shreds. The women and children had taken refuge in their underground cellars. Most of the men had scattered. A number were stretched out along the Colorado & Southern railroad tracks, returning the militia fire as best they could. Twenty minutes after the first shots were fired, Louie called Lawson again.

---

[1] Linderfelt later testified he prepared the bombs in advance to summon aid if the miners attacked the militia.

"They're going to wipe out the colony," he cried. "Bring help."

"We're coming," Lawson said grimly.

As he replaced the receiver, Lawson turned to the organizers clustered about him.

"You boys take over and keep things moving—fast. Get all the men and rifles you can possibly find. I am going to Ludlow now."

With his gun strapped to his side, Lawson was on the road to Ludlow a few minutes later. John Barlitch, the union chauffeur, drove the automobile. Peter Gorman, an organizer from Ohio, and Mike Livoda, a Colorado organizer, sat in the back seat, nervously folding and unfolding their hands.

"Keep the throttle down," Lawson directed. "We haven't a second to lose."

Opposite the Suffield colony, on the road north, Lawson ordered Barlitch to pull over and stop. He turned to Livoda.

"You drop off here and warn these people."

As Livoda stepped to the ground, the machine roared northward again.

Before they reached the Ludlow colony, they could hear the sound of steady firing. Lawson's face was grim. He reached for his gun when two men stepped out from behind an old adobe house and ran into the road in front of the car. Barlitch applied the brakes when Lawson muttered: "They're miners. Stop."

"We thought it was you, Mr. Lawson," one of the men said. "Don't stay on this road. They've got it covered with a machine gun."

Barlitch turned the car off the narrow road and cut across the prairie by a circuitous route toward the colony. The machine guns could be heard more plainly now. When they were within 150 yards of the nearest tent, Barlitch glanced at Lawson. Bullets were kicking up dirt in front of the machine.

"Stop here," Lawson commanded. "Get out and lay on the ground."

Lawson thought at first that the bullets were coming from the colony, but, as he hugged the ground, he saw they were exploding.

"Militia bullets," he said. "They are shooting at the car."

He turned on his side and called to Barlitch, who was huddled a few feet away.

"Do you think you can turn the car around?"

"I'll try, Mr. Lawson."

"Get in then."

Barlitch skidded the car around in the soft dirt and they drove swiftly back out of range. The sun was high. It was almost noon when they parked the car in the shelter of a small hill. Lawson left Barlitch with the car and took Gorman into an arroyo. They picked their way up the narrow defile until they were within a hundred yards of the tents. Lawson peeped over the edge of the arroyo. The stricken colony appeared to be deserted, but his ears caught the cries of children and the wails of women above the ugly whine of bullets.

"I guess you had better wait here, Pete," Lawson said. "I'll go on up a few yards. Two of us would make a better target."

He ran swiftly up the twisting arroyo, keeping under cover as best he could until the cleft thinned out. Then he ducked low and ran faster, zig-zagging while bullets screamed by him. At the railroad tracks he flung himself down beside ten miners who were using the railroad bed as a breastworks. They were firing, slowly and deliberately.

"Hello, Mr. Lawson," they called. "Keep down or the melish will get you."

"This looks bad," he replied between gasps for breath.

"Yes," a Greek growled. "They are going to kill us all this time."

"Where are the rest of the men? And Louie?"

"They are spread out everywhere," the Greek replied. "Every-body is fighting. We get Louie for you quick."

One of the riflemen slipped away, keeping to cover. A few minutes later Louie threw himself down beside Lawson. His face was streaked and grimy. Quickly he told Lawson of the meeting with Hamrock and of the condition of the colony. When he had finished, Lawson gripped his hand.

"We're gathering a relief force now, Louie," he said. "You have to hold them off until dark anyway. I'll be back with help by that time."

They embraced each other and Lawson, after a quick salute to the riflemen, sprinted back toward the sheltering arroyo. He found Gorman and hustled him back to the automobile.

"There is nothing we can do here now," Lawson said. "We've got to get help and get it quickly. We're going to Trinidad as fast as we can."

A cruel cross-fire from machine guns and rifles slowly cut the colony to pieces. The miners kept up a steady return fire in the hope of keeping the militia from approaching close enough for a charge. Hysterical women, screaming at the top of their voices, clutched their little ones tightly as they huddled in the underground cellars while explosive bullets burst in the streets and tents. Eleven-year-old Frank Snyder crawled from his cellar to get water for his mother when she fainted from fright. As he reached the surface, a bullet ripped through his head, killing him instantly.

There were no men in the colony with the exception of Tikas and a few aides who were doing what they could to succor women and children. The defending miners were scattered over the prairie in an effort to draw the militia fire away from the tents.

Mrs. Pearl Jolly, the wife of a striker, pinned a Red Cross badge on her waist and two others on her sleeves, and attempted to aid the women and children, but the militia kept their guns trained on her, forcing her to cover. One slug ripped through her dress and another tore the heel off her shoe before she found shelter behind a coal pile. Later in the afternoon, however, with Tikas' aid, she managed to get a number of women and children together and into a nearby arroyo. Under the shelter of the protecting shoulders, they started toward the Black Hills, low, pinion-clad elevations two miles east. Some of the women and children were only partially clad as the firing had started before they were fully dressed and they had had no opportunity to get their clothes after they went into the underground cellars.

In the hills nearby, where a group of miners had taken up positions, machine guns of the militia played over the tree-covered slopes. Charles Costa, a striker, raised up from behind a rock to look at the colony below. His wife and children were there. A bullet tore through his head and he fell back. Several of his companions crawled to him, offering aid.

"Nothing to do," Costa said. "Nothing to do. I'm dying. Sing the union song for me, boys."

Five miners, huddled close to the ground, granted Costa's wish:

> "We have fought them here for years, boys,
>   We'll fight them to the end,
>   Shouting the battle cry of union."

Costa raised his head. Blood streamed from the death wound, but he joined weakly in the chorus:

> "We whipped them in the North, boys,
>   We'll whip them in the South,
>   Shouting the battle cry of union."

The refrain died away. Costa was dead. His companions crawled away as militia bullets spattered on the rocks around them.

Hundreds of women and children cowered in the under-ground cellars through the long, terror-filled afternoon. Dogs and chickens lay dead in the colony streets. Here and there was a crumpled body.

In Trinidad, John Lawson issued appeal after appeal for volunteers to go to the aid of the colonists. Boxes of ammunition were stacked near the brickyards on the north edge of the city, and word was sent out for union men to assemble there. By late afternoon, 500 men were gathered at the appointed place. Not all of them had guns. Those who did have weapons were given ammunition. At dusk, an armed delegation was sent to induce a train crew to move the reinforcements to Ludlow as "a friendly gesture." The trainmen promised to make up a train as quickly as possible.

At Ludlow, Tikas found Mrs. Jolly bandaging a wounded child.

"Do you want to get away now?" he asked.

"No, Louie, I'll stay and help."

"Good." Louie smiled through the grime and dirt that caked his face. "We'll get the rest of the women and their kids to the arroyo. The men are running out of bullets. They cannot hold the melish away much longer."

The Greek leader and the woman moved from tent to tent, calling into the cellars for women and children. As fast as they collected a little group, they started it toward the arroyo.

"Go right down the arroyo and keep going until you get to the Black Hills," Louie ordered. "And don't stop."

A train crew abandoned a locomotive and several cars on the tracks between the colony and one machine gun. Scores of women and children escaped by using the cars as a shield.

While Tikas and Mrs. Jolly were pulling one woman and her three children from a cellar, a messenger ran into the colony and grabbed Tikas by the arm.

"The men," he said. "They want to talk to you, Louie."

Tikas went with the messenger to a group of about 40 miners. Their ammunition was almost exhausted.

"We are going to retreat, Louie," one said in Greek. "Our ammunition is gone."

"Go ahead then," Louie replied. "If you do not have bullets you cannot fight. Hurry up. I have to stay here and help the women and children. You go to the Black Hills."

"No, no, Louie. The melish will kill you."

Louie Tikas waved them toward the Black Hills.

"Do as I tell you," he shouted. "I am the head man. I give the orders."

He waved to the Greeks and ran back toward the colony. He turned once and saw them moving single file, on a fast trot, toward an arroyo, their empty guns in hand.

Major Hamrock, who boasted he was one of the best shots in Colorado, and a small band of militia were hidden in steel cars on a siding a few hundred yards from the colony. They shot at anything that moved. The machine guns on Water Tank Hill chattered continuously. The sun dipped behind the mountains and long shadows crept out across the gory plain and over the riddled tents of the prostrated colony. A wind blew lustily across the barren flats.

Shortly after 7 p. m., Lieutenant Linderfelt and a long line of militiamen rose from a protecting gully and charged toward the colony, yelling madly. They reached the first tents. A soldier lit a torch and applied it to the dry canvas of the nearest tent. Flames shot skyward. Gunmen followed the uniformed guardsmen into the edge of the colony. Torches were applied to other tents as looters ran from them, carrying such valuables as they could find. A triumphant yell went up from the attackers.

Screams of women and children filled the air. There were a few scattered shots from militia rifles. Louie Tikas, on his way to a cellar to help a woman with two children, was seized by militiamen. They hustled him to the road. A score of uniformed men surrounded the prisoner.

The Ludlow Tent Colony in April, 1914, shortly before the massacre. The big tent at the right was used as school and meeting hall.

Twisted bedsteads and charred household furnishings were all that remained of the tent home after the machine gun and the torch had completed their grim work.

A coal company guard and two militiamen wait on a loaded car for the approach of union pickets. This action photo was taken near Ludlow in 1913 by Stuart Mace, staff photographer of the Denver Times, Denver, Colo.

Thousands of miners and sympathizers attended the funeral of Louis Tikas, head man of the Ludlow Colony, who was murdered while a prisoner of the State Militia, April 20, 1914. The funeral procession is moving from the Trinidad business district to the cemetery.

"Hang the damned red neck," a soldier shouted. Others took up the cry.

"Yeah, string him up."

Two soldiers held Louie tightly by either arm. Lieutenant Linderfelt strode up and looked Louie full in the face.

"Oh, it's you, you God-damned lousy red neck."

Tikas, his face ashen gray, stared back for a moment, and then started to reply, but the words never got past his lips. With a quick motion, Linderfelt seized a Springfield rifle from a militiaman. He swung it over his head and brought it crashing down on the prisoner. The startled soldiers stepped back, releasing Louie's arm. The Greek cried out and threw up one arm. He partially caught the blow. The bone in his arm cracked and the heavy rifle struck his head.

Louie fought to keep his feet. "Linderfelt . . . Linderfelt . . . ," he muttered drunkenly, and staggered forward. Linderfelt tossed the broken Springfield aside and stared at the reeling man. Louie staggered blindly for about 10 feet and then pitched forward and was still as three shots rang out and three steel-jacketed slugs ripped into his back. A militiaman kicked the prone body and rifled the dead leader's pockets, leaving them turned inside out.

Lieutenant Linderfelt spat on the ground.

"The damned son-of-a-bitch," he snarled. "He tried to escape."

The little knot of militiamen broke up. Linderfelt turned toward the burning tent colony with a sharp order, "Come on, men." The lurid light from the burning tents disclosed another body a few feet from Tikas' still form. It was that of James Fyler, the union local secretary. He had retreated with the miners, but had returned for his family and had been captured by the militia. An explosive bullet had entered the back of his head and torn away his face.

John Lawson left Trinidad that night with his 500 volunteers. The train crew agreed to take them as far as Barnes Junction, a point two miles east of Ludlow. Riflemen, crowded on the cars, raised their voices in the union battle song as Lawson urged the trainmen to speed. When the train reached Barnes, the men unloaded swiftly.

"We'll march right to Ludlow," Lawson said. "John Wennberg will lead the way."

Wennberg, a union sub-leader, started off in the direction of the colony with the riflemen following him. Lawson brought up the rear. He had his revolver, but no rifle. Before they had marched a hundred yards, faint-hearted men started to turn back. Lawson stopped them.

"You can go back if you wish," he said. "But you can't take your gun. We need that here."

As fast as the timid turned back, Lawson took their guns away from them and handed them to braver men who had none. When the miners reached the arroyo between Barnes and Ludlow, Wennberg halted the column and called for Lawson. The two leaders stood for several minutes looking across the flats toward the tent colony. They could see the burning tents and the figures of soldiers running back and forth with torches. A voice hailed them in the darkness.

"Are you union men?"

"Yes," Lawson answered. "Come ahead."

A striker slipped out of the darkness.

"The colony is done for," he said. "There are a lot of refugees at the Bayes' place."

"Who wants to go to the Bayes' place with me to get those folks?" Lawson called out. None of the men answered.

"Then I'll go," Lawson said. A small wiry man with a carbine stepped forward.

"I'll go with you," he said.

"Very well," Lawson replied. "The rest of you stay here until we get back."

Lawson and his companion made their way without difficulty to the Frank Bayes' farm home where they found a number of hysterical women and children. They seemed to be in no immediate danger so Lawson told them to remain there until proper relief could be organized. Several strikers, who were hidden in the barn, were ordered out.

"You men get out of here right away," Lawson said. "Either join the men or go on to the Black Hills and wait there."

The tents in the colony were burning no more fiercely than the anger in John Lawson's mind when he returned to his volunteers. Outwardly he was cool and deliberate, but inside fierce hatred shook his reason. He wanted to order his men to charge the militia. He paced back and forth, deliberating the chances while the men watched him soberly. His better judgment finally prevailed. He knew the militia had been reinforced by the notorious Troop A of Trinidad. He knew, too, the deadliness of the militia guns and the inadequacy of the weapons carried by his own men. If he sent his untrained, undisciplined mob against the troops it would probably be routed and slaughtered.

He stopped his pacing and faced the men.

"We'll go to the Black Hills," he said. "We'll make camp there and organize."

The column reached the Black Hills, two miles east of Ludlow station, just at dawn. They found hundreds of Ludlow colonists scattered along the slopes, hungry, cold and terror-stricken.

In the distance, where the first shafts of sunlight were lighting up Ludlow, they saw smoke rising from the flats where the colony had stood.

CHAPTER XIII

CALL TO ARMS

Direct communication with Ludlow by telephone and telegraph was cut off during the massacre, but news of the killings and the burning swiftly reached the outside world even though the reports were meager and sketchy.

The Denver Express, in a brief story on its front page, said uniformed militia were shooting into the strikers' tents and that appeals were being sent out by the miners for aid.

"Linderfelt notified General Chase, in Denver, of the shooting at Ludlow, but said the strikers were responsible," the story concluded. It was played down, while news of the federal government's decision to send troops into Mexico against General Huerta was carried under big headlines. The Denver Times, in a dispatch from Trinidad, which was carried on Page 14 in its evening edition, said there was a battle in progress two miles from the Ludlow colony and that the "militia are fighting alone against strong odds." The story said in part:

"General Manager Murray of the Victor-American Fuel Co. received the following message from Trinidad at 12:27 this afternoon: 'Nothing new. Lots of shooting at long range.' This telephone message was sent to the armory at Trinidad by one of the soldiers at Ludlow and transmitted to Denver. At the main offices of the operators, there is no excitement. At the noon hour telegraphic reports from Trinidad gave the information that all wires, both telephone and telegraph, were down and communication was impossible with the district in and around Ludlow."

"I hardly think that the striking miners would attempt to enter upon the property at Ludlow," said Frank E. Gove, attorney for the operators. "It does not seem reasonable to me. We were not left without protection of the guard when the troops were mustered out."

In union headquarters in Denver, Ed Doyle was frantic with anxiety. Call after call from Trinidad brought conflicting stories of what had happened to the colony. The reports worsened hourly, however, and Doyle finally realized that a major catastrophe had befallen the big colony. When union headquarters in Trinidad informed him that at least 20 women and children had been slain by machine gun fire and that refugees were pouring into Trinidad, Doyle went into action. He sent a telegram to President Wilson and members of the state's congressional delegation:

"Striking miners and families shot and burned to death at Ludlow. Mine guards with machine guns riddled tents of striking miners and set fire to the colony. Four men, three women, and eleven children murdered. State not only fails to protect, but allows uniforms and ammunition of the commonwealth to be used to destroy the lives of workers and their families. We shall be compelled to call on volunteers in the name of humanity to defend these helpless people unless something is done. The colony is burned to the ground."[1]

Doyle sent other messages. He notified United Mine Worker officials throughout the nation and sent a wire to each local union in Colorado asking the members to hold themselves in readiness to defend their lives.

John D. Rockefeller was given a telegraphic report by Bowers.

"Following withdrawal of troops by order of governor an unprovoked attack upon small force of militia yesterday by 200

---

[1] The Denver Post, April 21, 1914. Page 9.

strikers," Bowers wired his chief. "Forced fighting resulting in probable loss of 10 or 15 strikers. Only one militiaman killed. Ludlow tent colony of strikers totally destroyed by burning; 200 tents; generally followed by explosions, showing ammuntion and dynamite stored in them. Expect further fighting today. Militia being reinforced. Suggest your giving this information to friendly papers."

And Rockefeller wired back:

"Telegram received. New York papers have published full details. Today's news is appearing on the ticker. We profoundly regret this further outbreak of lawlessness with accompanying loss of life."

Early reports of the death toll and the union statement that at least 195 women and children were missing seemed to be confirmed in The Rocky Mountain News Tuesday morning which listed two identified dead, Louie Tikas and Private A. Martin of Company A, Denver, and "eleven unidentified strikers and a non-combatant." Tuesday was a day of confusion as far as the general public was concerned. Militia and mine guards had blocked off the Ludlow area, and none could enter. Physicians, nurses, undertakers, including Coroner B. B. Sipe of Las Animas County, were turned back by machine gun fire. When they got close enough to the colony to see the smoking ruins, the militia fired machine gun bullets into the road in front of automobiles and dead wagons. Tourists on the main highway, unaware of trouble in the vicinity, were fired upon by the militia.

Governor Ammons first learned of the massacre through news dispatches printed in Washington where he had gone to protest against the administration's land leasing bills. He announced he would return to Colorado just as soon as he had completed his mission.

The miners of Colorado, however, didn't seem to care whether Governor Ammons ever returned. They were convinced now that the state, in league with the coal operators, planned to

exterminate union men and their families.   They determined
on a policy of defense at any cost.   Red-handed war stalked
into Southern Colorado.   Angry, furious men, armed with any
kind of a weapon they could find, poured into Trinidad and the
Ludlow district.   John Lawson directed hundreds of newcomers
to the improvised camp in the Black Hills.   The Greeks named
Pete Catsulis as Tikas' successor, and other groups named new
leaders to replace those who were either dead or missing.   When
the work of caring for the refugees was organized, Lawson hurried into Trinidad and called Denver.   He talked to his fellow
members of the policy committee and to other union leaders.
An hour later, the policy committee, together with the chieftains
of other union groups, issued a formal "Call To Arms."   Dated
April 22, 1914, it read:

"Organize the men in your community in companies of
volunteers to protect the workers of Colorado against the murder and cremation of men, women and children by armed assassins in the employ of coal corporations, serving under the
guise of state militiamen.

"Gather together for defensive purposes all arms and ammunition legally available.   Send name of leader of your company
and actual number of men enlisted at once by wire, phone or
mail to W. T. Hickey, Secretary of State Federation of Labor.

"Hold all companies subject to order.

"People having arms to spare for these defensive measures
are requested to furnish same to local companies, and, where
no company exists, send them to the State Federation of Labor.

"The state is furnishing us no protection and we must protect ourselves, our wives and children from these murderous
assassins.   We seek no quarrel with the state and we expect to
break no law; we intend to exercise our lawful right as citizens, to defend our homes and our constitutional rights."

The call was signed by John R. Lawson, John McLennan, E.
L. Doyle, John Ramsey, U. M. W. A.; E. R. Hogue, Denver
Printing Press Assistants' Union No. 14; W. T. Hickey, secre-

tary of the Colorado State Federation of Labor; T. W. Taylor
and Clarence Moorehouse, representing the Denver Trades and
Labor Assembly, and Ernest Mills, secretary of the Western
Federation of Miners.

Text of the call was printed on the front page of practically
every newspaper in Colorado. The operators charged it was a
"Call To Rebellion" rather than a call to arms, and that reports
from Ludlow were "greatly exaggerated." Mr. Gove, speaking
for the operators, said two children "may have been suffocated
as a result of an overturned stove."

Offers of armed assistance reached Denver union headquarters
from every section of the United States within a few hours,
and cash donations totaling more than $20,000 arrived by tele-
graph, mail and messenger before noon Tuesday. Denver
Italians, led by Frank Mancini, a newspaper editor, formed a
company of 100 armed men and offered their services to the
United Mine Workers. Mancini also worked out a plan to enlist
the aid of Italian organizations in every part of the mountain
region. He wired their officers:

"Over half men, women and children slaughtered are Italians.
Organize your men. Arm them. Hold them ready for call. We
may need your assistance to prevent further wholesale slaughter
of our brothers and sisters. We shall wire when we need you."

New York unions placed nurses on trains bound for Colorado. Jack Cassidy, leader of the Northern Colorado coal
miners, organized 200 men into four companies of 50 men each
at Lafayette. Another company was formed in Erie. Missouri
unions offered armed assistance as did those in Thurber, Texas,
where 500 volunteers banded together, named officers, and prepared to move north into Colorado as soon as they received a
call. The machinists' union organized and armed a company of
men in Denver. The men drilled before curious crowds in the
baseball park. The organized protests rose to an angry roar that
was heard from one end of the nation to the other when the
death toll was finally revealed. Thirteen women and children,

THE BLACK HOLE OF LUDLOW

charred almost beyond recognition, were lifted from one cellar beneath the smoking ruins of what had once been a tent home. Newspapers revised their death lists with each addition, and each time the lists grew longer.

Among the known dead were Tikas, Fyler, John Bartoloti, Frank Rubino, Charles Costa, James Costa, Mrs. Cedilano Costa, 27; her children, Onafrio Costa, six, and Lucy Costa, four; Patricia Valdez and her four children: Elvira Valdez, three months old; Eulala, eight; Mary, seven, and Rudolph, nine; Gloria Pedregone, four; Roderlo Pedregone, six, and the three children of Mrs. Mary Petrucci, Frank, six months old; Lucy, three, and Joe, four years old. There were others, such as little Frank Snyder, and Primo Larese, 18, a non-combatant, who was killed by an explosive bullet as he hiked along the highway.

The attackers admitted three dead—Steve Donovan, Carl Johnson, and Fred Dougherty—all guards employed by the Victor-American Fuel Co.

Colorado & Southern railroad trainmen pleaded with John Lawson, in a telegram sent from Rugby to Trinidad, to do what he could to get the bodies of the victims.

"Bodies of women and children exposed in the tent colony," the telegram read. "Please do something with the bodies, for God's sake, for they are human souls and deserving of decent burials."

The telegram was signed by Owen Roberts, R. C. Davis and N. Fowles. They did not know that every effort had been made to send rescuers and undertakers into the ruined colony. They did not know that machine guns still sprayed the highways. The bodies of Tikas and Fyler were lying near the ruined colony, objects of derision by gunmen and guards who prowled the outskirts and through the blackened ruins, looking for loot.

The militia, in the first reports to General Chase in Denver, charged they were attacked by the miners. Major Hamrock, in a telegram to the adjutant general, said destruction of the tents was undoubtedly caused by the overturning of a candle, lamp or stove, and that the military saw the tents were burning when they were still some distance from the colony. He said, too, that when the colony burned 20,000 rounds of ammunition exploded in John Lawson's tent.

Lawson made an immediate reply:

"It is my opinion that the first tents were fired by explosive bullets. I know that ammunition of that character has been used by the militia for I have heard the bullets explode. It is my belief that soldiers entered the colony and looted many of the tents before the destruction by fire was complete. The story that ammunition was found in my tent is a deliberate lie. There never was any ammunition in my tent. I must decline to state where the strikers secured the guns they used in the fighting. I will say, however, that I am sorry they haven't 10,000 times as many guns as they have. In that case I would tell them to use them to defend their homes, and I would go out with them. Reports have come to me that some parties today are exploding dynamite in the holes under the ruins of the tents, in order to destroy evidence of the number of women and children who lost their lives. I am positive that more non-combatants perished than will ever be known."

Cigar Makers Union No. 129 met in Denver in special meeting and, after condemning the massacre, called for impeachment of Governor Ammons, a general strike, and an assessment on all the union's members.

Congressman Keating wired Doyle:

"Apparently the federal government is helpless. Have shown your telegram to our friends in House and Senate, but while they condemn the militia they offer no working plan by which we may aid you. Will continue my efforts."

The Mine Workers distributed 20,000 circulars in Denver asking residents of the capital city to write or wire the President of the United States for help. Thousands complied.

The uproar was more than the coal operators had bargained

for. Their efforts to minimize what had happened in Southern Colorado were of no avail as the full import of the massacre dawned on the people of Colorado and the nation.

The Rocky Mountain News, which never had been particularly friendly to the strikers or their cause since its owner switched editors at the beginning of the strike in response to an Armour-transmitted demand from the Rockefellers, called on President Wilson in no uncertain terms to intervene in Colorado. William Chenery, editorial writer for the newspaper, wrote an editorial that cost him his job though the loss later proved to be a kick upstairs as he became editor of Colliers. Under the heading, "The Massacre of the Innocents," he wrote:

"The horror of the shambles at Ludlow is overwhelming. Not since the days when pitiless red men wreaked vengeance upon intruding frontiersmen and upon their women and children has this western country been stained with so foul a deed.

"The details of the massacre are horrible. Mexico offers no barbarity so base as that of the murder of defenseless women and children by the mine guards in soldiers' clothing. Like whitened sepulchres we boast of American civilization with this infamous thing at our very doors. Huerta murdered Madero, but even Huerta did not shoot an innocent little boy seeking water for his mother who lay ill. Villa is a barbarian, but in maddest excess Villa has not turned machine guns on imprisoned women and children. Where is the outlaw so far beyond the pale of human kind as to burn the tent over the heads of nursing mothers and helpless little babies?

"Out of this infamy one fact stands clear. Machine guns did the murder. The machine guns were in the hands of the mine guards, most of whom were also members of the militia. It was a private war, with the wealth of the richest man in the world behind the mine guards.

"Once and for all time the right to employ armed guards must be taken away from private individuals and corporations. To the state, and the state alone, belongs the right to maintain peace. Anything else is anarchy. Private warfare is the only sort of anarchy the world has ever known, and armed forces employed by private interests have introduced the only private wars of modern times. This practice must be stopped. If the state laws are not strong enough, then the federal government must step in. At any cost, private warfare must be destroyed.

"Who are these mine guards to whom is entrusted the sovereign right to massacre? Four of the fraternity were electrocuted recently in New York. They are the gunmen of the great cities, the offscourings of humanity whom a bitter heritage has made the wastrels of the world. Warped by the wrongs of their own upbringings, they know no justice and they care not for mercy. They are hardly human in intelligence, and not as high in the scale of human kindness as domestic animals.

"Yet they are not the guilty ones. The blood of the innocent women and children rests on the hands of those who for the greed of dollars employed such men and bought such machines of murder. The world has not been hard on these; theirs has been a gentle upbringing. Yet they reck not of human life when pecuniary interests are involved.

"The blood of the women and children, burned and shot like rats, cries aloud from the ground. The great state of Colorado has failed them. It has betrayed them. Her militia, which should have been impartial protectors of the peace, have acted as murderous gunmen. The machine guns which played in the darkness upon the homes of humble men and women, whose only crime was an effort to earn an honest living, were bought and paid for by agents of the mine owners. Explosive bullets have been used on children. Does the bloodiest page of the French Revolution approach this in hideousness?

"In the name of humanity, in the name of civilization, we have appealed to President Wilson. His ear heard the wail of the innocent, outraged and dying in Mexico. Cannot the president give heed to the sufferings of his own people?

"Think, Mr. President, of the captain of the strikers, whose truce with the gunmen was ended with his murder. Think of the fifty-one shots (sic) which were passed through the strike leader. Think of his body, which has lain exposed since his infamous killing. Then, with that vast power which has been committed to you as the executive of a great nation, attend to the misery wrought by an anarchistic lust for dollars. Without your speedy aid the poor and the needy, betrayed by the state, may be slaughtered to the last smiling babe."[2]

The newspaper also carried a statement from Lawson that infuriated the coal operators fully as much as did the editorial.

"It is unthinkable and unbelievable that there are fiends in human form that could be induced to commit these hellish acts," Lawson's statement said. "The cold-blooded murder of Tikas does not come as a surprise to the people who knew him and his work, for Linderfelt and others in the Colorado National Guard said that they would kill him the first time they got a chance. John D. Rockefeller, Jr., may ease his conscience by attending Sunday School regularly in New York, but he will never be acquitted of committing the horrible atrocities that have occurred in a country such as America, and he will be convicted at the bar of public opinion for his part in the Colorado murders."

The rage of the operators turned to genuine concern for their own welfare when the angry miners of Southern Colorado launched a counter-attack.

More than 1,000 miners, led by a dozen fierce-faced men of as many nationalities, attacked coal camps along a 40-mile front. This was to be war to the finish. There would be no quarter asked or given. It was the militia and gunmen now, or the strikers. One or the other must be wiped out. With red bandannas around their necks and sacks containing food and extra ammunition slung over their shoulders, they swept over

[2] The Rocky Mountain News, April 22, 1914.

the hills and up the narrow canons, driving militia and mine guards before them.

> "The union forever, hurrah! boys, hurrah!
> Down with the militia, to HELL with the LAW,
> We'll rally round the flag, boys, we'll rally round the flag,
> Shouting the battle cry of union."

The wild war song sounded through the hills from Walsenburg on the north to Trinidad on the south. Five hundred men from Aguilar attacked the Empire Mine property. The guards, and such women and children as were on the property, about 30 in all, retreated into the mine, leaving three dead guards outside. The mine buildings, valued at $70,000, were burned.

Unwilling to make war on women and children, the miners allowed them to come out of the mine, and then escorted them to safety while rifles were kept trained on the portal.

"Let the men come out and fight or starve inside," the miners chanted tauntingly. At the last minute they weakened and permitted Mrs. William Wittmore of Trinidad to carry food into the mine for the besieged guards.

In Berwind Canon, between Ludlow and Delagua, bands of strikers drove their opponents up the canon with a deadly fire. Two Victor-American guards fell before the first vicious charge. Three members of the notorious Troop B of the militia died in the pitched battle. Other bands of strikers moved against guards at the Rouse, Primrose, Brodhead and Royal mines. Approximately $200,000 worth of property was destroyed by fire and dynamite in the attacks.

Above the roar of flames in a half dozen canons rose a cry that chilled the guards and militiamen: "Remember Ludlow!"

Everywhere the military and their aides fell back. The main body of militia remained in Ludlow, unable to assist the coal operators in the various canons. Major Hamrock knew war when he saw it and he didn't intend to move out and expose his troops to almost certain annihilation.

"Remember Ludlow!" The war cry was heard in Denver,

too. Lieutenant Governor Fitzgarrald wrung his hands help-
lessly when General Chase and his staff demanded action.

"We haven't any money to send troops down there," Chase
roared. "Call a special session of the Legislature."

"Not me," Fitzgarrald whimpered. "I won't call one on my
own hook. Ammons is on his way home. If he wires for me to
do it I will issue the call."

The operators gathered in the governor's office for a star
chamber session with Fitzgarrald. Present were General Chase,
Frank Gove, Jesse Welborn, D. W. Brown of the Rocky Mountain Fuel Co., and a number of small operators. Newspaper
reporters were barred. At 10 p.m., as the secret conference
ended, 30 members of the Denver Chamber of Commerce, led
by President Thomas B. Stearns, marched in on the acting governor.

"We believe a crisis has been reached in the coal fields,"
Stearns said. "All troops should be ordered out at once."

"We haven't any money," Fitzgarrald replied. "We owe the
men $90,000 in back pay now. Why can't you business men help
pay these boys?"

Frank Briggs, a Denver banker, shook his fist under Fitzgarrald's nose.

"The bankers in Denver and Pueblo have taken $250,000 in
certificates for the militia," he shouted. "It's about time the
state banks do a little something."

Before the meeting ended, however, Fitzgarrald had a promise
from the businessmen that they would support a call for a
special legislative session. He, in turn, gave an order to General
Chase.

"All right, General," he said. "Get your troops out and get
down there as fast as possible."

"I'll take 600 men," the doughty general replied.

Early the next morning, while reports of bitter battles loaded
telegraph and telephone lines into Denver, Fitzgarrald received a
telegram from Governor Ammons approving the action in

calling out the militia a second time. Governor Ammons said he expected to arrive in Denver Friday. He asked that the formal legislative call be held up until his arrival as he wished to include a number of things in addition to an appropriation for the troops.

General Chase's mobilization order had an unexpected result. Part of his troops mutinied. Six members of Troop C in Denver refused to go back to Ludlow. Other guardsmen followed suit. Companies showed up at Union Station with as few as five men. Thirty-one members of Company D in Greeley, sixty miles north of Denver, were found to be "out of town" when called. Only seven members of this company responded for service. Before the troop train left for the south, General Chase called John Lawson on the long distance telephone.

"I am coming down there in the interests of peace," the adjutant general began in his pompous fashion. Lawson cut him short.

"There can be no peace when there is no justice," Lawson said. "It is a war of extermination. We now have the sinews of war, backed by guns and ammunition, and the faith, loyalty and financial help of every union man in the country.

"But a . . ." General Chase sought to interrupt.

"It is not now a question of negotiation of the settlement of our wrongs," Lawson went on. "Rockefeller has declared that he is fighting for a principle of non-recognition and that he will lose his investments in Colorado in support of his position. We propose to see it through, no matter what the cost."

"What about the strikers firing on Delagua?" Chase bawled into the telephone.

"I regret that," Lawson replied. "But these men were overwrought with the tragedy of Monday and overlooked the danger to which innocent people were placed. We are not making war against women and children, General, only against militia thugs and gunmen."

The general banged the receiver and hurried to his train. It pulled out of Denver at 12:15 p.m. with only 250 of the scheduled 600 troops aboard. Union sympathizers jeered at the soldiers, while anxious mothers and wives crowded close to the cars for farewells. The train consisted of two locomotives, three baggage cars, eight coaches and a caboose. Picked sharpshooters manned the windows. At Littleton, a few miles south of Denver, a halt was made to take aboard Battery B's three-inch guns and 550 rounds of shrapnel. Machine guns were mounted on a flat car in anticipation of resistance when the train reached the strike zone. Ed Doyle wired warnings to union offices in Florence, Walsenburg and Trinidad. He listed the time of the train's departure, the numbers on the engines, the number of troops aboard, and the amount and kind of their equipment, adding:

"Denver report says flat car with gatling gun will be placed in front of engine; also that men will detrain before reaching center of conflict. In order that these militiamen with their two additional machine guns may not repeat the horrible Ludlow massacre of women and children we urge you to watch for their approach across country from La Junta or ordinary route."

Within an hour after Doyle's message left Denver, press dispatches from Trinidad reported 1,000 armed strikers were preparing to meet the troops somewhere near Aguilar, 20 miles north of Trinidad and a few miles north of Ludlow. The dispatches said the strikers were equipped with train derailers and dynamite.

While the troop train sped south, Denver unions held special meetings in behalf of the strikers. The Denver Typographical Union, one of the oldest and strongest in the West, gathered in Horan's Hall. One hundred and four members had answered the call of President F. L. Pferdesteller. Ed Doyle was given the floor. He explained the events leading up to the Ludlow tragedy and called on the typographical men for united action. They responded by voting 82 to 22 to adopt the following resolution:

"Whereas, at the close of the congressional investigation of the Colorado coal strike, at Washington, D. C., one so-called

'Christian' gentleman and international freebooter by the well-known name of Rockefeller, Jr., has declared himself, and on behalf of those interests represented by him, in most emphatic terms, to refuse the demands of any trade unions, and fight to the bitter end the principle of recognition of labor organizations, under the cloak of 'freedom of contract of the individual' and

"Whereas, the wilful, premeditated murder of women and children in the Southern Colorado coal camps of Ludlow and vicinity, is the direct result of his open declaration to exterminate the miners' organization through the hired gunmen paid by him and his associates, whom he and his associates have clothed in the state military uniform with the acquiescence and connivance of an equally infamous un-American governor,

"Therefore, we, the members of the Denver Typographical Union, No. 49, in special meeting assembled, this 23rd day of April, 1914, do accept the challenge of the Colorado coal barons and their allied interests to the working class of this state for an open armed conflict, and herewith appropriate $500 as our first installment for the purchase of arms and ammunition in self-defense of our homes, wives and children, and our fellow-men."

One member wanted the purpose for which the $500 was appropriated stricken from the union records, but Martin Lacher, author of the resolution, had the amendment tabled by a vote of 76 to 29. The printers immediately adopted another resolution:

"Resolved, by the Denver Typographical Union No. 49, that in view of the murder of innocent women and children at Ludlow by imported gunmen, imported and clothed with authority to kill our citizens after being enlisted as members of the Colorado National Guard and the farming out of the militia to coal operators to coerce the union striking miners, we demand that Gov. Elias M. Ammons resign from office, failing in which he be impeached at a special session of the State General Assembly."

CHAPTER XIV
THE FEMININE TOUCH

The people of Southern Colorado were mourning their dead.
All Wednesday afternoon, while the bodies of Ludlow victims, which had finally been brought in from the colony, lay in state in Trinidad's Castle Hall, thousands filed by them. Some of the coffins were kept closed as their contents were charred beyond recognition. The death wail of Mexican women, a mournful cry as old as the West, and the sobs of glistening-eyed Italian, Slavic and American women shook the nerves of the hardiest among the miners who stood as sentinels by the dead. In one corner of the hall sat Pedro Valdez, his short, stocky frame convulsed with grief. His entire family, wife and children, lay in coffins in the center of the room. He had been in El Paso when the massacre occurred. Alarmed by the news dispatches, he had hurried back to Colorado to find his worst fears confirmed. He had scarcely been able to recognize his wife or any of their four children. Not far away sat Mary Petrucci, staring into space. Doctors had told the women who hovered anxiously about her that her sanity might return in time. Her three children were in coffins a few feet away.

Frank Rubino, murdered while a prisoner of the militia, was the first victim buried. The bells of Holy Trinity Catholic Church tolled Thursday, summoning the faithful to a Requiem Mass for the dead. When the flag draped coffin was carried from the big stone church, hundreds fell in line behind the hearse and followed the body to its last resting place in the shadow of the hills where Rubino had toiled and died.

The women and children, too, were buried from Holy Trinity Church. Huge, horse-drawn drays carried the white coffins to the church and away again. One long box contained the wife of Costa who had died with the union song on his lips. Against her cold breast was a young striker who had never had an opportunity to nurse it. The drays made crude hearses, but some dignity was provided by the teamsters who wore high silk hats and long black coats. Thousands marched in the funeral procession, black bands pinned on their sleeves. Tikas' body led the procession and then was returned to the undertaking establishment to await the arrival of a priest of the Greek church.

General Chase, with his troops separated into two sections and traveling on two trains as a special precaution, arrived in the strike zone the morning after the mass funerals. He detrained his men at several points between Monson and Rugby before 10 a.m. and within an hour was sending dispatches to Trinidad and Denver announcing his men were in action. The various strike leaders disagreed in a last minute council of war the night before and less than 400 strikers occupied positions in the hills near Rugby and Monson. The main body of miners, about 1,000 strong, were encamped on a mesa in the Black Hills east of Ludlow where there was a good spring of water and a highly defensive terrain. Opposite them, near Ludlow Station, three quarters of a mile distant, were troops and guards under Major Hamrock and Lieutenant Linderfelt.

General Chase put out his cavalry as soon as all his troops were detrained. The strikers maintained their positions in the hills. The cavalry galloped up and down along the front of the foothills on futile scouting expeditions. When one small band of strikers fired on the mounted soldiers, the troopers abandoned their horses and crawled through the underbrush as though anticipating a heavy engagement. The miners hurled taunts at the "tin soldiers" and withdrew into the protecting hills. However, there were minor skirmishes in a dozen places as the day wore on. Reports from the war zone were sketchy and on the whole inaccurate. There was no general leadership among the miners and telegraph and telephone wires were down in most places.

General Chase concentrated on a display of force. He sent his field guns through Monson and other little communities. For the benefit of the Denver newspapers, he announced he had routed 1,000 entrenched strikers from Bunker Hill. The mythical body simply dissolved in front of his army and no shots were fired.

Lieutenant Governor Fitzgarrald tried to get in touch with General Chase at noon, but was unable to get a message through to the doughty old warrior. The adjutant general's Denver office reported it could not establish communications with the field force. Failure of General Chase to telegraph an official report alarmed Fitzgarrald. His alarm mounted when 5,000 Wyoming miners announced they were in possession of arms, organized, and ready to march into Colorado.

"They can't do that," Fitzgarrald declared. "I'll appeal to the federal government. They can't cross our state line. I won't have it."

He decided he had best try and arrange a truce until Governor Ammons could arrive and take over the reins. He summoned Jesse Welborn and the union attorney, Horace Hawkins. After a short parley, Hawkins agreed to stop the miners providing the militia and gunmen would refrain from acts of violence until there could be further discussions. Welborn, at Fitzgarrald's insistence, agreed. The lieutenant governor reached for his telephone and called the union physician in Trinidad, Dr. Ben B. Beshoar.

"Doctor," Fitzgarrald said, "Mr. Welborn and Mr. Hawkins are here and we have agreed on a truce. All of the miners know you and have confidence in you so I wonder if you would get the word of this truce to them?"

"You say you have agreed on a truce and you want me to send word to the miners?"

"Yes, that's it, Doctor."

"Fitzgarrald, I wouldn't believe you on your oath," the physician replied.

The lieutenant governor purpled and turned the telephone over to Hawkins who quickly explained the situation. The physician then agreed to send out word of the truce.

Governor Ammons reached Denver late that night. A huge crowd awaited him at Union Station, but it was disappointed. He got off the train at Derby, a few miles north of Denver, where he was met by President Stearns of the Chamber of Commerce and Fred P. Johnson, Colorado representative of Chicago packing interests. They whisked him by back roads into the city and to the State Capitol. Governor Ammons conferred immediately with Fitzgarrald, Attorney General Farrar, and a number of other advisers who constituted his kitchen cabinet. Newspaper reporters were barred. Later they were called in, and Governor Ammons made a statement in which he indorsed the truce action taken by Fitzgarrald.

"I am going ahead with the call for a special session," Governor Ammons said. "Nothing except the payment of the troops and other matters pertaining to the strike and its possible settlement will go into the call."

Governor Ammons' face was drawn. He was nervous and distraught. On the morrow he must face a mass meeting of the Women's Peace Association which had issued a call for a thousand women to gather at the State Capitol at 10 a.m. Saturday. Mrs. Anna Steele, widow of Robert W. Steele, a former chief justice of the Colorado Supreme Court, would lead them.

While Governor Ammons was giving his statement to the reporters, their newspapers were receiving dispatches from the southern field of increased firing in the hills. The truce message had been sent out, but it had not been possible to contact all of the guerrilla bands. The Chandler coal camp, it was reported, had been captured by strikers and the buildings looted. One man had been killed and a second wounded, the dispatches said.

Another dispatch, this time from General Chase, recounted his activities of the day in glowing terms and announced he would name a military board of inquiry to make an investigation of the Ludlow massacre.

"I intend to make the most thorough examination that can be made," General Chase's announcement said. "I am going to get at the truth of this matter. The truce will be respected in every detail, but if the strikers start anything we will clean out every one of their colonies in the district."

General Chase did not know that a few hours earlier 300 strikers, rifles over their shoulders and red bandannas around their necks, had marched into Trinidad from Lawson's stronghold in the Black Hills. As they marched in the north end of town Captain Randolph and his militia company hastily marched out the south end. Approximately 30 businessmen, who had been hostile to the union, left town with the militia. Sheriff Gresham, with a large number of deputies, barricaded the courthouse and prepared for a possible siege.

Long before the scheduled hour, members of the Women's Peace Association gathered in force in the rotunda of the State Capitol. There were smartly-dressed women, housewives with babies in their arms, women in furs, and women in calico. Promptly at 10 a.m., Mrs. Steele and Mrs. Anna Lafferty, president of the association, mounted the steps leading to the second floor and held up their hands.

"Women of Denver," Mrs. Lafferty cried: "We are gathered here today on serious business. We are not here to take sides in this terrible trouble between the strikers and the operators, but we are here to demand of the governor that he take steps to bring this civil war to an end. We are not accusing anyone, but we want action at once. Let us stay here until we get it."

"We'll stay," the women shouted. "We'll stay."

"Let us be quiet and dignified in presenting our demands," Mrs. Lafferty urged. "We want to act with credit to the women of the state. Let us go forward with the quietness of despair."

Led by Mrs. Steele, the women pushed toward the governor's office. The executive's messenger stopped them at the door.

"Governor Ammons wants you to go to the House of Representatives' chamber," the messenger said. "You can't all get into these offices."

"Will the governor come up there?" Mrs. Steele asked. The messenger was evasive, and the women blocked the doorway until positive assurance was given. Once in the House of Representatives, the women sang "America." A woman cried out as the song died away, "Remember the women and children of Ludlow."

When the governor failed to appear, the women became impatient. Mrs. Lafferty named Mrs. Stuart D. Walling, Mrs. Evangeline Heartz, Mrs. Helen Ring Robinson, and Mrs. H. T. Herlinger, a housewife with a baby in her arms, as a committee to get the governor. As the committee left the chamber, the women sang "The Battle Hymn of the Republic."

Governor Ammons kept the committee waiting half an hour. He sent for the chief of police. Two plain clothesmen and several uniformed officers arrived to protect him.

"Why are those men allowed to go into the governor's office while we are kept waiting?" Mrs. Robinson demanded.

"They are officers of the law," the messenger replied.

"And we are citizens," Mrs. Robinson retorted. "You tell that governor we want to see him and we want to see him right now."

A minute or two later, the committee was ushered inside. Governor Ammons was seated at his desk with Fitzgarrald at his side. Two uniformed patrolmen stood behind him.

"Governor Ammons," Mrs. Robinson said, "we are here simply to escort you to the house chamber above and to ask your immediate presence there. The women wish to present some resolutions to you."

Governor Ammons cleared his throat.

"Can't you present the resolutions now?" he asked. "I have important matters to attend to, ladies. I have just received word that there is fighting going on at three mines in the strike district. The attorney for the mine workers is waiting to confer with me. There are steps which must be taken immediately to prevent loss of life. I have no time to listen to resolutions."

"We, too, represent those who are desirous of preventing loss of life," Mrs. Robinson replied sharply. "Governor Ammons, as the state's chief executive you owe it to the women of Colorado to appear before them. We were assured before we retired upstairs that you would come up."

Lieutenant Fitzgarrald's walrus-like moustache began to move up and down rapidly. He jumped to his feet and waved his arms.

"Good God," he yelled. "There's firing going on down there. The governor will join you when the firing is stopped."

"I only have until noon to arrange these important matters," Governor Ammons said. "Can't you wait until then?"

The committee members placed their hands on their hips and delivered an ultimatum.

"We'll give you just five minutes."

With a hopeless wave of his hand, Governor Ammons arose and started toward the door with the committee following. Fitzgarrald and the police officers trailed along.

The throng of women shouted when Governor Ammons entered the chamber, but quieted quickly when Mrs. Lafferty rose to speak.

"Governor Ammons," she said, "we are here to demand that this dreadful warfare in Southern Colorado cease at once. I am pleased to introduce to you Mrs. Steele."

The women stood up and waved their handkerchiefs, gloves, and pocketbooks. Mrs. Steele addressed the chief executive in a firm voice:

"In the name of humanity and the women of Colorado, we demand immediate intervention of United States troops. We demand the immediate withdrawal of the state troops and the arrests of Major Hamrock and Lieutenant Linderfelt. Governor Ammons, I am assured that a telegram which was given out as sent by Representative Taylor from Washington was not the correct telegram which was sent by him. The first telegram stated that the congressional delegation had called upon President Wilson and the cabinet and that federal aid was out of the question. The second telegram, which I am assured was the true one, stated that President Wilson and his cabinet gave much consideration to the question of intervention, but that nothing could be done unless the governor, Governor Ammons, requested aid. We therefore ask you, here and now, to write out a telegram to President Wilson, asking for aid, and that Mrs. Lafferty then appoint a committee to see that the telegram is immediately sent off."

Governor Ammons colored and squirmed in his seat. The women screamed their approval as Mrs. Steele handed a telegram form to the executive. Governor Ammons shook his head and stood up.

"Ladies," he said, "while in Washington I took up the matter of federal intervention with the president. It wasn't the first time. Early last winter, when affairs here reached a crisis, I made inquiries as to the possibility of intervention in case the state should be unable to handle this situation, and was given very discouraging reports. When I left for Washington a week ago Tuesday, I went in the fullest confidence there would be no more trouble in the strike district. By the time I had reached there the Mexican situation was very acute. President Wilson and the cabinet were engrossed in consideration of it.

"Then I got word of the trouble out here. Not until last Tuesday night did I get anything very definite. At that time I could not see the president, but I took it up with members of the investigating committee sent out here from Congress, and also with our own congressional committee. When the situation became so acute, I left for Denver. On the road I received a telegram stating that the congressional delegation from this state had interviewed the president and that there was no hope of federal intervention. That is the telegram which was given out. If it was not correct, I want to know it. Before going any further, I would like to telegraph to Washington and find out what is correct. It will take only a few hours, and if you will adjourn until tomorrow morning . . ."

Shouts of protest drowned out the governor's words.

Governor Ammons looked around, his face haggard, and then spoke again:

"I was assured when I came up here that you were going to help me. God knows I need help. I don't need anything else. I have used up what little ability I have to serve this state and to bring about an adjustment in this matter. I have had only a few hours to get in touch with the situation. I am trying to organize a committee to go down south and make an investigation to get the facts. When we know the facts then we can act, and no one will demand a more speedy punishment of the guilty parties if they are found than I will.

"I didn't go to bed last night until two o'clock, when I tried to get a little sleep. But I couldn't sleep at all and got up at five. Since I went into office I have spent on an average of sixteen hours a day at my desk. And I am willing to spend every hour of every day of the coming weeks in an effort to adjust this matter without further bloodshed. Will you give me a chance? I ask you as good citizens, to give me your help and support. Give me an opportunity, an opportunity. I can't do anything unless I have public sentiment back of me."

A man in the gallery shouted something at the governor and Mrs. Lafferty called back, "This is a woman's meeting. Keep still." Governor Ammons started to talk again: "I suggest you postpone action until . . ."

"We'll stay here until the governor sends the telegram," the women cried.

"When the governor quibbles it is time to stop," Mrs. Lafferty told the throng. Governor Ammons gave her a nasty look, jumped down a step of the rostrum and headed toward a side door. The members of the special committee followed him to his office where they announced to his force they planned to camp until he took action. Inside, Governor Ammons dictated a telegram to Washington.

Addressed to President Woodrow Wilson, the telegram read:

"Conflicting reports as to action of cabinet meeting yesterday morning have reached here. What I would be greatly obliged to know is, if we cannot control situation in Southern Colorado coal fields, can we have federal troops?"

When they learned of the telegram, Mrs. Steele and Mrs. Lafferty said they would sit in the governor's waiting room until a reply was received. Mrs. Robinson came down to replace Mrs. Lafferty a short time later and the women's president went upstairs to the House chamber to ask her flock to be patient.

"It will only be a few hours at the most," she said. "The women of Southern Colorado have been waiting for peace and justice for many months. We can wait a little while longer."

The women sang songs and listened with rapt attention while wives and sweethearts of strikers described the Ludlow Massacre. Not all of them were as accurate as they might have been.

Governor Ammons received an answer promptly. President Wilson had the Mexican crisis to worry about and was not anxious to have the job of policing Colorado. With his customary diplomacy, President Wilson refused to commit himself on the subject of troops.

"He wants us to ask him outright for troops," Fitzgarrald said. "You can see that."

"Yes, that is what he wants," Governor Ammons replied. He turned his head slightly toward the doorway leading to the outside corridor. He could hear the strains of a militant song in the House chamber.

"They're still up there," he said slowly.

Fitzgarrald nodded.

"It looks as though we'll have to ask the president for aid," Governor Ammons said finally.

At 9:15 p.m., he dispatched a formal request to Washington: "The situation has passed beyond the ability of the state to control. This domestic violence is the result of an industrial controversy between interstate organizations with headquarters outside the State of Colorado. I therefore, urgently request that you send forthwith to Ludlow, Colorado, and to such other portions of the state as the commanding officer may deem necessary, not less than one battalion of infantry and one troop of cavalry."

A few minutes later, Governor Ammons issued a call to the Legislature to convene May 4 in special session to clean up a million dollars worth of National Guard obligations.

CHAPTER XV

REQUIEMS AND REPRISALS

While Governor Ammons was busy with the women and Washington, John Lawson worked feverishly to keep the victorious Trinidad miners under control. He established a new colony just east of Trinidad on the site of the former militia camp, and made arrangements to feed the men and police the town proper. Armed patrols were kept moving up and down the streets. Reporters from Denver newspapers insisted Lawson make a statement as they were convinced he contemplated an offensive against the coal companies even though the federal government had been asked for aid.

"We understand you're going back to the hills," they said. "If that is true, what are you going to do? Attack the coal camps or the militia?"

"There isn't much to be said right now," Lawson replied evasively. "I suppose you know we are constantly receiving offers of men, arms, ammunition and money from different parts of Colorado and from other states. However, I think we should be humble in victory, and I will gladly meet with General Chase or anyone else to talk over plans for preventing further bloodshed. I want peace, but I insist upon peace with justice."

The statement reached General Chase's ears a short time later and he telephoned from Ludlow for a meeting. Lawson, with McLennan, Frank Miner and Robert Bolton, rode to Ludlow in an automobile carrying an American flag. General Chase, oddly enough, received them cordially. His gruff manner was gone for the time being at least. He escorted them to the freight room of the Ludlow station where a meeting was held. Soldiers crowded around the station, but this time they were merely curious. General Chase, in the school of bitter experience, had learned at last that the strikers had guns, courage and unlimited backing. He didn't intend to step over the line if he could possibly help it. The men were closeted only a short time before they reached a tentative agreement. The militia would remain in their camp at Ludlow and they would recognize Ludlow as their southern boundary line. Trinidad was to remain in possession of the strikers for the time being.

When Lawson and his three colleagues returned to Trinidad, they found wild rejoicing. The streets were crowded with swarthy men armed with carbines and with women dressed in bright calicoes and hand-embroidered shawls. A contingent of 30 heavily-armed Greeks had just walked in from Raton, N. M., across the mountains to reinforce the miners' garrison. Another band of Greeks, all carrying high-powered rifles, had arrived from Fremont County. The union army was growing by the hour. The city police were helpless, although in truth there was no need for their services as the patrols of strikers kept order in the town. The police did make one trip to Castle Hall to order that arms be moved out of the building. A strange cry sounded and from every quarter men came running—desperate men who had nothing to lose except their precious arms. The police bowed themselves out and returned to City Hall. Parades and impromptu song fests were held, but the citizens of the town were not molested or interfered with as they went about their business.

Down at the principal undertaking establishment, a group of strikers and their wives knelt in prayer by the bier of Louis Tikas. There was rejoicing in the streets, but the dead were not forgotten.

While the miners celebrated the seizure of Trinidad and the awakening of a state and nation, members of the Denver Chamber of Commerce met and voted a boycott of the Denver Times and the Rocky Mountain News because of the manner in which they had handled strike stories since the massacre. As the boycott went into effect, the two newspapers printed lists of those who had sent in stop orders. To one such list, the Times added a personal paragraph:

"Mr. Frank McDonough, Sr., a lawyer in the McPhee Bldg., informs us that he wishes to cancel his subscription to The Times, but will continue as a subscriber to The News 'under compulsion' as he needs a morning newspaper. Mr. McDonough is mistaken. We have ourselves cancelled his subscription to The News, since we do not desire any compulsory subscribers."

The News carried another list, adding at the end of the column, "Mr. J. Foster Symes requests that we cancel The Times, but continue the News except on Sunday. We have cancelled all."

The Colorado Fuel & Iron Co. entered into the spirit of the thing by filing a $500,000 libel suit against The News, a suit that never was prosecuted.

Governor Ammons named a committee consisting of Chief Justice George W. Musser, Appellate Judge King, MP Capp, Norton Montgomery, and the Rev. Allen Tanner to investigate the strike, but neither the public nor the miners accepted this action as indicative of good faith on the executive's part.

Lawson left Trinidad early Sunday for Denver to confer with the new investigating committee and to attend a mass meeting at the State Capitol. Before he left the southern coal city, he forbade the use of the customary band in the Tikas funeral which was set for the next morning.

"A band might cause trouble," he said. "March quietly in the procession. Louis would want it that way."

President Wilson was scheduled to rule the day of the funeral on whether federal troops would be sent to Colorado and there must be no overt act upon the part of the miners. Lawson had the largest body in Trinidad, and the guerilla bands still in the hills were quiet. By 2 p.m. the next day, more than 5,000 men and women were gathered on the grounds outside of the State Capitol.[1] A steady rain, driven by a strong wind, drenched the shivering crowd. They broke into cheers, however, when the United Mine Workers of America, led by an American flag and the flag of Ludlow, the flag that had floated over the colony only a week before, came marching up the hill from the down-town business section. A band crashed into the stirring union song. The demonstrators bared their heads to the rain and sang fervently:

> "The union forever, hurrah! boys, hurrah!
> Down with the gunmen, and up with the law,
> For we're coming Colorado, we're coming all the way,
> Shouting the battle cry of union."

Jesse Vetter, a member of the machinists' union, climbed to a high step on the capitol building entrance and raised his arms. The crowd fell silent. He began to speak, slowly and distinctly. Then the crowd alternately cheered and cried imprecations as he demanded the impeachment of Governor Ammons and Lieu-tenant Governor Fitzgarrald, the arrests of Major Hamrock and Lieutenant Linderfelt on charges of murder, the immediate seizure by the state of all coal lands, and a repudiation of the National Guard debt of $1,000,000.

"Are you ready for the question?" Vetter shouted.

A roar was his answer.

"Now," he cried, and cheers burst from the crowd, swelling until they echoed far downtown. Hats and umbrellas were tossed into the air. Charles Ahlstrom, a union leader, introduced George Creel, a newspaper writer who was soon to serve as chief propagandist for the United States during the World War.

"The martyred men, women and children of Ludlow did not die in vain," Creel told the throng. "They have written with

[1] Denver Express, April 27, 1914; The Rocky Mountain News, April 27, 1914.

their blood upon the wall of the world. Those like the Rockefellers, who profess Christ in public and crucify Him privately,
have been unmasked, and never again will the patter of prayers
be permitted to excuse Judas' greed. Patriotism is robbed of
power to befool, for the love and union of 26 nationalities at
Ludlow have shown us that brotherhood is a finer, better word.
Private ownership of natural resources and public utilities is seen
as a thing that corrupts officials, poisons the law, and makes
murderers, and we will have no more of it.

"These, then, are Ludlow's challenges to those who sit in the
seats of the mighty, wrapping the flag around their profits,
putting their assassins in the country's uniforms, buying law and
legislators, and crying out against class prejudice, even while
they draw class lines with a bayonet's point.

"But is there not a message from those graves to you your-
selves, oh brothers, in all callings? The blood of children is on
the hands of Rockefeller, Osgood and Ammons, but can we
count ourselves entirely free from blame? Is it not true that the
massacre was made possible by the failure of labor to appreciate
labor's strength? Who does not know that it is in the power of
the workers to prevent every industrial crime and economic injustice by united action? You, whose energies turn the wheels
of life, have mastery in your grasp by the exercise of no greater
violence than the putting down of tools, not by groups, but as
a class.

"Look at the solidarity of capitalism! Mark the unity with
which coal companies, railroads, banks and merchants have
worked throughout the strike. Are we less intelligent? Let this
solemn occasion mark regret for past failures and stern resolve
for future unity. March as an army, toilers, and fear no defeat.

"Drag down such traitors as Ammons and Fitzgarrald, banish your Welborns and your Osgoods, jail Chase, Hamrock and
Linderfelt on the charge of murder, and pursue the Stearnses
and Johnsons into obscurity with your loathing.

"Take back the privileges that have been bribed and stolen,

and let the people provide for the people. The instinct of self-preservation demands it. If the miners are crushed today, it means that Chase and his murderers will be used to crush you tomorrow. The life of the race demands it. When the sordid shopkeepers of the Chamber of Commerce condone the slaughter of babes out of regard for dirty dollars, when women withdraw from a society because it is so vulgar as to cry out against the Ludlow horror, when the operators print that the strikers made no effort to save their women and children, when men in uniform find fun in murder and torture, it shows a society far on its road to rot.

"Gather, unite, and advance! Destroy the evil, the unclean, the sordid, and the unjust. Bring about a government that is a working partnership with the people. Water your own deserts, harness your own streams, operate your own machines, and make this great wonder state one where there is every opportunity for the worker, but no room for the parasite.

"By your might and your right, bring to pass the brotherhood for which Christ died. Transform Colorado into a haven for the oppressed of the world, rising into happiness under a law based upon love and equal justice.

"It is the command of Ludlow's living dead."

There was a moment's silence as Creel's voice died away. Then a roar broke from the crowd. Other speakers followed Creel, but he had stolen the show. Shorthand reporters, sent by the coal operators to get transcripts, hurried away. John M. O'Neill, editor of the miners' magazine, attacked Ammons savagely. Ed Doyle, his Irish brogue more pronounced than ever in his excitement, warned that the miners were "far from licked."

"The Ludlow massacre was premeditated and John D. Rockefeller is the man responsible," he cried. "His statements before Congress will prove that I tell the truth. I denounce the real governor of this state, the man who has been behind Ammons, the tool of the coal companies. I denounce Fred P. Johnson, the stockyard's boss and the man who backed the militia in the

killing of women and babies. I denounce the mine guards wearing the uniforms of the militia, Hamrock and Linderfelt."

While Doyle was speaking, Mother Jones reached the capitol
from Union Station. She had just arrived from Washington
after an interview with the Foster committee. The crowd
screamed its approval when she appeared. Doyle jumped down
and assisted her up the steps. She took off her bonnet and threw
up a clenched fist in welcome.

"Here I am again, boys, just back from Washington, and you
aren't licked by a whole lot," she said. "Washington is aroused
and there is help coming. Just keep your heads level and don't
do anything to disgrace the state. The state is all right. It is
just a few fools at the head of things that are bad. Not all of
the militia is bad. There is one man in it that is a gentleman. I
knew him in Trinidad. He's Colonel Verdeckburg. I told President Wilson all about him.

"Don't commit any depredations. We'll make some laws to
put the Colorado Fuel & Iron Co. out of business, and Mr.
Rockefeller who's probably teaching his Sunday School class
right now. We'll get some regular men for state officers next
time. You've had your lesson. I found this governor thing of
yours in Washington trying to save some trees. I told him, 'God
Almighty, save the people and let the trees alone. Back there
you have murder of women and children and here you are pray-
ing for the trees.'

"Go home, boys. Mind me now and keep cool. Stay out of
the saloons, save your money, and when I want you I'll call
you."

Unknown to those attending the mass meeting, war was flam-
ing across Southern Colorado again. Armed strikers attacked the
Victor-American's Chandler mine six miles south of Canon City
and captured the property after a desperate battle with guards.
One guard, Charles King, was killed. Another guard, Charles
Velow, lost both arms when a bullet struck the weapon he was
firing and it exploded. Preliminary dispatches indicated the

death toll might exceed thirty. Five hundred vigilantes were sworn in Canon City, and an appeal for aid went to Governor Ammons. He immediately ordered Chase to proceed to Canon City with 200 troops. Former Governor Peabody announced the Chandler property had been dynamited by the attackers. The defeated guards said the miners advanced under a flag of truce and then opened fire.

Despite the excitement near Canon City, Trinidad remained quiet with 600 fighting men resting on their arms in camp. They were restless, however, as Coroner Sipe had announced that Tikas had been shot several times in the back.

In Washington, Representative Keating, Senators Shafroth and Thomas, Doctor Foster and Secretary of Labor Wilson went to the White House to see the President. There was a pile of telegrams from Colorado, all asking for troops, on his desk. The President was deeply affected by the massacre and the threat of additional fighting. He assured the delegation he would consult with his cabinet and reach a decision Monday on Governor Ammons' request for troops.

Louie Tikas was buried Monday morning. The street outside of the mortuary was crowded with Greeks and miners of more than 20 other nationalities. Before the appointed time for the Mass for the dead, four Greeks with carbines on their shoulders forced their way through the crowd and marched into the undertaker's chapel. They halted in a line at the rear of the room. For a moment or two, they stared toward the body of Tikas. Then they lifted their hats and muttered an oath to "avenge Louie's death." That done, they pounded four times on the floor with their carbines, turned and left the chapel.

The body of Tikas lay before an altar on which were branched candles, holding high, burning tapers. The Greek priest, with Peter Catsulis, the new leader of the Greek colony, serving as the acolyte, intoned the Mass.

Three times the priest kissed the cheeks of the dead leader.

Three times he anointed the brow with wine. Three times he sprinkled dust on the dead man's face, while Catsulis swung the brass censer and wailed dolefully.

"Jesus give a place in Heaven to Louis Tikas," chanted the priest in the Greek tongue.

"Jesus give a place in Heaven to Louis. Bring life from the grave." Solemnly, the dark-faced fighting men in the chapel repeated the words of the priest.

"Jesus, if Louis has any enemies, may they forget their hostility," chanted Catsulis.

The tapers burned low. The place was dim with incense. The priest chanted on, his iron-gray hair and flowing beard in somber contrast with his resplendent vestments. This was the funeral of the man beloved by all he had led and served. But a handful of women were present, and no arms were carried to remind those who watched that a cruel industrial war was in progress. Orderly, reverent, deeply religious, was the service. When the body was carried from the chapel, 500 Greeks followed in line after the hearse. The American colors, draped in crepe, were lifted, and in utter silence the cortege moved along the streets, past the headquarters of the United Mine Workers of America, and on over the hill to the Knights of Pythias cemetery. Thousands of persons walked in the funeral that day, but there were no disorders of any kind.

Farther north, in the Canon City district, General Chase and his 200 troopers, after a fast trip from Ludlow, recaptured the Chandler mine without firing a shot. The gallant soldiers found the mine buildings and houses undamaged, former Governor Peabody to the contrary. The strikers withdrew into the hills before the soldiers arrived. The Denver Times said the recapture showed that reports of fatalities, disseminated in Denver by the operators, were "greatly exaggerated." The one guard was the only fatality. Although only 16 of the 50 guards who had been stationed at the Chandler before the battle were accounted for, General Chase found the others were hiding in the hills. The adjutant general heaved a sigh of relief. He had had a stomach full of this war. The strikers fought hard, they were elusive, and all he got out of the battles was condemnation from the public. General Chase's relief was short-lived, however, for when he telephoned Governor Ammons to report his victory at the Chandler Mine, he learned fighting had broken out elsewhere in Southern Colorado, and that a serious battle was raging near Louisville in the northern coal field.

"We have to do something quickly," Governor Ammons said. "The whole state is in rebellion."

He ordered the distraught Chase to send militiamen north to Louisville at once.

"I'll have 110 men on a train north in no time," General Chase said. "Our troops in Ludlow will take care of the new fighting down here. I'll send them to Walsenburg."

Fighting had broken out in Louisville at 2 a.m. after company-owned machine guns mounted at The Rocky Mountain Fuel Company's Hecla Mine had swept the streets of the town. The miners had armed and surrounded the coal property. The women and children, fearing a repetition of the Ludlow massacre, fled to Denver and adjoining towns. Vigilantes were organized in Boulder later in the day and classes at the University of Colorado were disrupted. Sheriff Buster made his way to the Hecla and went into the stockade. He soon found he couldn't get out again as the firing was too heavy. Fifty Baldwin-Felts left Denver in automobiles to reinforce the Hecla guards, while the unions sent guns and ammunition. William Hickey, secretary of the State Federation of Labor and one of the signers of the Call to Arms, and Jack Carter, an official of the Marshall union local, were seized by Baldwin-Felts detectives on the outskirts of Denver as they sped north with an automobile-load of guns and ammunition. The two men were jailed in Denver and held for several hours.

The firing continued in Louisville until late in the day when the militia arrived. More than 20,000 shots had been exchanged.

Six men had been wounded, two of them fatally. As the militia detrained, a huge crowd gathered to watch. The troopers lined up and fired two volleys over the heads of the onlookers. The streets cleared as though by magic. The troops then occupied the town and mine property.

"There was not the slightest intimation from either side that there would be trouble," John O'Connor, leader of the Louisville strikers, told militia officers and newspapermen. "I can account for the shooting only by the fact that the operators were trying to intimidate us. We were unarmed and having a meeting in the union hall when the guards commenced shooting. We put our women and children in cellars and rushed to protect ourselves."

"That's a lie," said Walter Belk, Baldwin-Felts head of the mine guards. "The strikers fired first from Louisville. We were forced to return their fire."

The new fighting in Walsenburg, it soon developed, was much more deadly. Guards at the Walsen mine swept the city with machine guns. George Bock, a 40-year-old striker, was found dead in his home on Seventh Street, not far from the mine property, his body riddled by machine gun bullets. Mike Lenzini, a non-combatant, was killed, and Henry Lloyd, another non-combatant, was fatally wounded.

The strikers entrenched themselves on the hogback, a long pinon-covered hill near the edge of town, and prepared for the coming of troops from Ludlow. Meanwhile, Governor Ammons issued a manifesto calling on all peace officers of the state to arrest any man found carrying arms. In the war zones, the sheriffs remained barricaded in their courthouses and ignored the governor's plea. At wit's end, Governor Ammons finally called John Lawson in Trinidad.[2]

"Have you heard of the Louisville shooting?" Governor Ammons asked.

[2] Denver Post, April 28, 1914.

Three of the outstanding figures in the coal strike of 1913-1914 were John R. Lawson, left, international organizer for the United Mine Workers; Mother Jones, and Horace N. Hawkins, attorney for the union.

A section of Forbes after coal miners attacked the camp in retaliation for the massacre. Between the rails is the body of a mine guard. In the background, smoke rises from the burning mine property.

Typical state militiamen in camp on the east edge of Trinidad show their fighting faces and weapons for the benefit of newspaper photographers. Note the two field pieces at the left.

Miners such as those above, armed with nondescript guns, many of which were antiques, guarded the tent colonies from gunmen and participated in attacks on company coal camps after the Ludlow massacre.

"Yes, I heard about it," Lawson replied, "but I don't know how it started though it is my understanding mine guards turned machine guns on the town."

"This has got to stop," Governor Ammons said. "I'll give you one hour to stop all this shooting."

Lawson laughed into the telephone.

"The truce is in effect here, Governor," he said. "There hasn't been a shot fired in Trinidad. We are doing everything we can to keep order, but I can't promise to stop trouble every place in the state. Besides, don't blame the miners until you get the facts. There has been too much of that already."

"The men have got to lay down their arms and go to their homes," Governor Ammons said.

"Their homes?" Lawson asked incredulously. "Their homes were in the Ludlow and Forbes colonies destroyed by your militia. Now the only homes they have are in the rifle pits. Just because the mine guards try to start new battles don't try to place the odium on the miners, Governor. I doubt if the miners are aggressors anywhere—not after what I have seen of the guards and a lot of the militia. And don't forget, Governor, our miners will shoot in self-defense and they have a perfect right to do so."

John Lawson stayed on in Trinidad, observing the truce with General Chase to the letter. His men were restless and nervous. They wanted to march to Walsenburg, where the miners on the hogback were engaged against a strong force of guards and militia equipped with machine guns and small cannon. Interest shifted to this front, and then back to Las Animas County again when an even bigger battle broke out at Forbes. Two hundred miners gathered on the hills above the camp on the east, south and west sides just at dawn. The mine guards and strike breakers occupied the north hill with a machine gun.

The miners began to close in slowly shortly after the sun lit up the slopes. The machine gun chattered. Greek riflemen returned the fire. The line moved slowly forward and again the machine gun spoke and then was silent. The guards worked frantically with it, but it was leaded. The miners sensed what had happened and the order was given: "Charge."

The strikers ran forward up the slope with the cry, "Remember Ludlow!"

Others charged down from their positions on to the camp with wild yells. The guards in the camp dropped to their knees and fired slowly. The Greeks used the Balkan system. Part sprinted toward the camp while part knelt and fired. Then the runners stopped and fired while the other riflemen charged toward the enemy.

"Remember Ludlow!"

The blood-curdling cry panicked the guards. They began to move back. Their slow retreat quickly turned into a rout and they fled, leaving their dead in the streets. A number of Japanese ran into the boarding house and barricaded the doors.

"Come out and surrender," a miner yelled. The answer was a shot. A torch was applied to the building and the miners waited grimly for the Japanese to come out. They never did.

Eleven guards were dead in the street. Nine others were captured.

"Put them to death," a miner called out. A leader turned and slapped the man who made the suggestion.

"We're not militiamen," the leader snarled. "We don't put our prisoners to death."

The guards were marched off to the hills.

The torch was applied to the mine tipple, the post office and other mine buildings which were at some distance from the mine opening. A fortune in mules went up in flames. Some 40 women and children, families of strike breakers, were taken into the mine by the superintendent for safety.

When the battle ended, the miners formed a line in the center of the street and marched out of the burning camp, singing:

"The union forever, hurrah, boys, hurrah!
Down with the militia, to hell with the law,
For we're coming Colorado, we're coming all the way,
Shouting the battle cry of union."

A miner turned as the song ended and shook his carbine at the smoking ruins of the camp. "Remember Ludlow," he bellowed. "Remember Ludlow."

The strikers had lost four men. When their column reached the Majestic Mine, the leaders ordered the captured guards turned loose.

"You fellows get the hell out of this state and stay out," a burly coal miner told them. "Next time we won't take prisoners."

"We promise," the guards replied.

Although the troops were only six miles away in Ludlow, they refused to leave their camp despite frantic pleas from the Forbes superintendent.[3]

---

[3] Many union men interpreted this refusal as indicative that the militia had come to fear the strikers. However, the Ludlow soldiers were undoubtedly justified in refusing to leave camp in view of the truce. Lawson's Trinidad miners were held in their camp.

CHAPTER XVI
FEDERAL TROOPS

President Wilson moved swiftly when he finally decided to send federal troops to Colorado. In a formal proclamation, he ordered that all violence and disorder cease.

"Whereas, the governor of Colorado has represented that domestic violence exists in said state which the authorities of said state are unable to suppress; and has represented that it is impossible to convene the Legislature of the state in time to meet the present emergency," the proclamation said in part, "Now therefore, I, Woodrow Wilson, president of the United States, do hereby admonish all good citizens of the United States and all persons within the jurisdiction and territory of the United States against aiding, countenancing, abetting or taking part in such unlawful proceedings, and I do hereby warn all persons, engaged in or connected with said domestic violence and obstruction of the laws to disperse and retire peaceably to their respective abodes on or before the thirtieth day of April, instant."

Citizens of Trinidad publicly thanked God for the proclamation, while those in Walsenburg dodged stray bullets and hoped for an end to the battle on the hogback. Major P. P. Lester of the militia was dead and three troopers were wounded. The miners admitted one dead. When the strikers, who were under the command of Don MacGregor, former Denver Express reporter, withdrew and ended the battle, the death toll stood at 12. Ten of the dead were coal company guards who had participated in assaults on the miners' positions.

Denver newspapers blamed Governor Ammons for the battle, contending the miners were merely occupying the hogback to keep an eye on the militia and that the battle would not have occurred had not the governor ordered the militia to "clean the strikers off that hill." The militia charged that Major Lester was killed while wearing a Red Cross badge and attending a wounded man. The miners said he was actively engaged in the fighting when he went down.

The first contingent of federal troops, 175 men under command of Major McClure, reached Denver from Fort Russell, Wyo., April 29, at 3 a.m. and, after a brief stop over, continued south toward Trinidad. The second squadron of the Fifth Cavalry, under Major William A. Holbrook of the Tenth Cavalry, left Fort Leavenworth, Kan., about the same time, bound for Trinidad. President Wilson asked withdrawal of the militia from the trouble zone and this Governor Ammons agreed to do.

General Chase hurried to Denver from Louisville and threatened to resign. In an angry conference with Governor Ammons, the adjutant general contended federal troops were not needed. "I can handle this," he said. "My men are good soldiers. We can take care of this trouble. I should not be surprised if every National Guard officer resigned."

"The federal troops are on the way now," Governor Ammons replied. "We'll have to withdraw until these troubles can be worked out by the Legislature."

In New York City, Upton Sinclair, the novelist, picketed the Rockefeller offices. With a number of women, who wore mourning bands around their arms, he paraded up and down in front of No. 26 Broadway.[1] Business practically suspended in lower Broadway when the demonstration began, but police soon cleared the sidewalks. Sinclair and the four women were arrest-

[1] Denver Express, April 29, 1914, P. 1.

ed, but eight other mourners took their places and paraded back and forth. The second group was not molested by the police. Among the eight was Mrs. Sinclair, who was escorted by George Sterling, the California poet. At the Tombs Court, where he was taken with his four companions, Sinclair bitterly denounced Rockefeller.

"This is the first time," Sinclair said, "that a protest in the matter of human rights has been carried directly to headquarters. Usually some employed superintendent is singled out as a scapegoat. We want to register our protest where the dividends are paid."

Mr. Rockefeller's secretary, C. O. Heydt, told newspaper reporters that no statement would be made by No. 26 Broadway.

"Mr. Rockefeller knows nothing about the demonstration that has been going on in front of the building," Mr. Heydt said, adding:

"And he will ignore it."

Back in Colorado, Lawson ordered the miners to lay aside their weapons.

"There will be no resistance to the federal troops on the part of the miners," he declared. "We expect to restore the colonies and if the federal troops prohibit this course we will immediately carry a protest to President Wilson. We expect to be permitted free access to any of the coal towns, and the right to talk to strike breakers."

Lawson was on hand with the Trinidad miners April 30, 1914, to greet the federal cavalrymen when they pulled into the city at 8 a.m. The miners cheered as the train came to a stop. There was no cheer from the operators, but they had a representative on hand to greet the troops. William Murray, general manager of the Victor-American Fuel Co. and the only coal company official who had remained in Las Animas County through the "Ten Days War" was the first man to extend a hand to Major Holbrook when the officer stepped from the train. Murray gave the impression he was an official city welcomer.

With Acting Mayor Max Kahn of Trinidad lending nervous assistance, Murray deftly steered Major Holbrook into a waiting Colorado Fuel & Iron Co. automobile. As the three men drove off, the miners thought of the adjutant general's first ride in a C. F. & I. automobile and the way the operators had taken over the militia. Murray drove Major Holbrook by the miners' colony east of town and hospitably offered use of a Trinidad building to the federal troops.

The federal soldiers did not immediately detrain. They leaned from their coach windows and chatted with the strikers in friendly fashion. Chris Mihele, a Greek war veteran and a member of F Company, talked with fellow countrymen who stood along the tracks. The Greek miners laughed and joked with Mihele, and told him stories of their own war.

"And where are the state's tin soldiers?" Mihele called gaily. "We would like to look them over."

When Major Holbrook returned to the train, he was buttonholed by newspaper reporters who told him what they knew of the strike and conditions in the field. As a result of the talks, Major Holbrook announced he would not use any proffered buildings in the city, but would quarter his men at the fair grounds, a mile and a half north and east of the business section. At 10:30 a.m. he met with a number of union leaders—John Lawson, Armando Pellizarri, Robert Bolton and "General" John Brown who was in active command of the strikers' Trinidad colony. At the conclusion of the conference, Major Holbrook called in the newspaper writers again.

"The federal troops will be absolutely neutral," he said. "We'll make no distinction between strikers, militia or mine guards. The representatives of the strikers expressed themselves as very willing to give all assistance in their power toward bringing about a normal condition of affairs. After talking with these men I am sending Captain Smith, C. C. Smith, boys, and a troop of 65 men to Walsenburg to take charge of the situation in Huerfano County. One thing more, I have given the strikers permission to rebuild their tent colonies."

The strikers were elated at the decision for Governor Ammons, while admitting the strikers had a right to tent homes, had refused to sanction reconstruction of either the Ludlow or Forbes colonies.

Willingness of the miners to take steps toward peace was in sharp contrast to the attitude of some of the operators. Newspaper reporters found Frank Gove, the coal company spokesman, in General Chase's private office in the State Capitol. Mr. Gove made another of his many declarations of war.

"You will never get a statement from the operators agreeing to any sort of a truce," Gove said angrily. "The coal operators will fight the miners until every last one of them is in jail."

"Are you the real commander-in-chief of the militia?" a reporter asked impudently.

Gove rocked back and forth on his heels and glared, but made no answer. Another reporter asked about a rumored break between Governor Ammons and General Chase.

"Chase has a right to be sore," Gove snapped. "Federal troops here reflect on the ability of the Colorado National Guard to handle the situation. I don't know of any break between the governor and Chase, but Chase is sore."

When asked what business he was transacting in the adjutant general's private office, Gove turned on his heel and went into the inner room, slamming the door behind him.

The sore spot in the militia organization was the failure of a military commission's report to come to light. Boughton, Danks and Van Cise had completed their work, that was certain, as the special commission, named by General Chase after the massacre, was no longer sitting and the three officers had left the southern coal field. General Chase said he hadn't seen the report. There were widespread rumors that the findings would whitewash the militia, but severely condemn the gunmen em-

ployed by the coal operators. Newspapers demanded the report
and were refused. Private citizens asked Governor Ammons to
release it to the public, and were told it had not reached his
office. After a great deal of secret maneuvering, quiet hand-
shakes and little deals by the newspapermen, the report found
its way into the public prints. General Chase roared with anger,
but he could not deny its authenticity as he knew that at least
two members of the military commission would not permit a denial to go unchallenged.

The commission of militia officers placed the blame for strike
battles on the coal operators, and found Lieutenant Linderfelt
guilty of breaking a Springfield rifle over Tikas' head.

"He (Tikas), Fyler, and an unidentified striker were shot to
death while prisoners of the military," the report said. "We
find that the colony was looted by participants and spectators
in the battle."

The report also found that the soldiers deliberately spread
the fire in the colony by pouring oil on the tents and applying
torches, and that Linderfelt was largely responsible for the an-
tagonism existing in the coal fields because of his wholly "tact-
less treatment of mine guards and strikers." It also found that
Tikas sought to prevent the battle, that the militia brought
up reinforcements before the first shot was fired, and that Hamrock trained a machine gun on the colony and fired a volley
into the tents "to test his range."

On the other side of the ledger, the report blamed the Greeks
for firing the first shot and charged that a slain militiaman
was mutilated.

"The immediate cause of the battle was an attack upon the
soldiers by the Greek inhabitants of the tent colony who mis-
interpreted a movement of troops on a neighboring hill," the
report said. It also charged that 15,000 rounds of ammunition
were exploded in John Lawson's tent during the fire. In conclusion, it recommended the establishment of a state constabulary, and further investigations by both the state and fed-

eral governments. The dapper Major Boughton urged against re-establishment of the Ludlow colony.

The report confirmed most of the charges made by the miners even though it attempted to whitewash the militia's role in the Ludlow tragedy. While the report was heatedly debated in every part of the state, Governor Ammons withdrew his militia from Southern Colorado in compliance with President Wilson's request. The state troops in Walsenburg, however, did not get away without a clash with the federal soldiers. Six militiamen were arrested by the federals and charged with looting a Seventh Street saloon. The federals recovered 50 bottles of whisky, 25 boxes of cigars, and a number of other articles which had been stolen from the establishment.

In Washington, Chairman Foster, at the direction of the President, asked the operators to enter into negotiations looking toward a settlement of the strike. Led by Rockefeller's company, 19 corporations promptly refused to enter into negotiations with the United Mine Workers of America. Rockefeller referred Doctor Foster to the Colorado officers of his company. The C. F. & I. Co. officials, together with the officials of allied coal companies, met immediately in Denver and drafted a reply to the congressional committee chairman:

"Answering your telegram of last night addressed to Mr. John D. Rockefeller, Jr., and referred to Colorado mine owners for reply: When on April 16 the governor withdrew all except a small detachment of militia from the field, law, order and quiet prevailed in this state. There were employed by the operators of coal mines more than 10,000 apparently contented men. On the morning of April 20, the striking miners in the Ludlow tent colony, two miles from the nearest coal mine, placed their women and children in what they considered places of safety and made an armed attack upon the militia encamped nearby. During the battle the tent colony was destroyed by fire. Next day the bodies of two women and eleven children were discovered in a hole under a tent, where the strikers had

placed them when the attack began. They had all been suffocated. None of these children and no woman was killed by
rifle fire, nor did the soldiers know or have any reason to
suspect the presence of non-combatants where the strikers had
concealed them.

"On April 23, Lawson, international board member, United
Mine Workers of America, and the leader of the strikers, in a
published interview, asserted that a war of extermination would
thenceforth be conducted by the strikers, and Doyle, secretary
of the United Mine Workers, by wire, instructed the officials
of local unions to watch for the approach of the militia, which
had been again ordered back into the field. The meaning and
purpose of such language was obvious.

"Since that time, the strikers, in bands varying from 56 to
400, have attacked the town of Delagua from the hills, and
killed three men. They have dynamited and burned the buildings and equipment of the Empire, Southwestern and Green
Canon mines at Aguilar. They have driven men, women and
children into the Empire mine and sealed the entrance with
explosives. After the declaration of a truce, agreed to between
the governor and Hawkins, mine worker attorney, they drove
the postmaster and others away from the Sunnyside mine and
took possession of it, as well as the Pictou mine."

The letter went on at length, reciting the many battles in
the southern field and the fighting around the Hecla mine near
Louisville, concluding with the statement:

"We cannot enter into negotiations of any character with
the officers or agents of the United Mine Workers of America,
who alone are responsible for the terrible reign of disorder
and bloodshed which has disgraced this state."

President Wilson brushed all other matters aside and set out
to end the strike. He ordered additional troops sent into Colorado from Fort Oglethorpe, Ga., and Fort Robinson, Neb., and
Chairman Foster, at President Wilson's direction, again wired
Rockefeller, asking him to use his influence to end the strike.

At the same time, Secretary of Labor Wilson, also acting under instructions from the President, named Hymel Davies, president of the Kentucky Mine Operators' Association, and W. R. Fairley, a member of the miners' organization in Alabama, as special mediators. Secretary of State William Jennings Bryan announced that complications with foreign governments were imminent as a result of the killing of their nationals in the coal fields.

A request from Major Holbrook that the miners turn over all their arms to the government caused Lawson to summon a mass meeting of the miners in Trinidad to vote on the question. The meeting was abandoned at the last minute because of a cold, drizzly rain. A week later, after a number of parleys with the federal officers and after assurances that the coal operators would turn in their rifles and machine guns, union headquarters issued a bulletin to the miners:

"You are hereby officially requested and advised to turn over to the military officers of the United States Army all firearms and ammunition in your possession or under your control beginning at 10 o'clock a. m., May 9. You will bring all firearms and ammunition to Beshoars Tent Colony, close to San Rafael Hospital, and receipt will be given to you by the United States army officers in charge and authorized to receive same."

A total of 725 guns, most of which were handed over by residents of Trinidad and not strikers, was given into the custody of the federal troops. Still others were surrendered in other towns of the coal district.

A half dozen public and private investigations of the Ludlow massacre and the Ten Days War were undertaken in Denver and Southern Colorado. A committee of women, composed of Mrs. Lee Campion, Mrs. Evangeline Heartz and Mrs. Lafferty, toured the strike field and interviewed both strikers and mine guards, while the National Guard announced it was proceeding with plans for court martials. When the Legislature

met in special session, there was a strong demand for impeachment of Governor Ammons and Lieutenant Governor Fitzgarrald. At the outset, an executive session was engineered
by Senators W. H. (Billy) Adams and Samuel J. Burris. The
legislators yelled at each other while the public peeked in windows opening on to the corridor. Senator Burris moved that
only the payment of strike bills be considered by the Legislature, but the executive meeting, after a great deal of wrangling,
was adjourned without concrete action. The Rocky Mountain
News immediately charged that the C. F. & I. Co. again had
control of the assembly.

Governor Ammons demanded authority to compel arbitration of strikes. This move on the executive's part came to
naught when Attorney General Fred Farrar ruled that such
legislation could not be considered under the terms of Governor Ammons' call. Only five bills were introduced. They
provided for restrictions on sales of firearms in strike districts,
establishment of a state constabulary, restrictions on saloons in
troubled areas, and an appropriation to cover expenses of the
militia.

While the legislators argued, the Law and Order League
of Women, composed of Denver's "Sacred Thirty-six" met and
expressed sympathy for Governor Ammons and the militia "in
their great ordeal" and denounced "vicious people and a prejudiced and inaccurate press corrupted either by money or by
the influence of the labor vote." Mrs. W. W. Grant, Jr., Mrs.
Helen Grenfell, Mrs. William V. Hodges, and a number of
other women concluded their meeting with a formal resolution decrying anarchy. This support and articles in the Chicago
Herald-Record, signed by Jesse Welborn, blaming the union
for strike deaths heartened the operators and their representatives in the Legislature. Governor Ammons increased his demand for militia money from $800,000 to an even million
dollars. This measure, and bills to give the governor authority
to restrict saloons and the sales of firearms, were passed. How-

ever, Governor Ammons suffered one set back when the constabulary bill, which was a pet measure, was killed. Before the session closed, President Wilson rebuked Governor Ammons in a telegram:

"Am disturbed to hear of the probability of the adjournment of your legislature and feel bound to remind you that my constitutional obligations with regard to maintenance of order in Colorado are not to be indefinitely continued by the inaction of the State Legislature. The federal forces are there only until the state has time and opportunity to resume complete sovereignty and control in the matter. I cannot conceive that the state is willing to forego her sovereignty or to throw herself entirely upon the government of the United States and I am quite clear that she has no constitutional right to do so when it is within the power of her legislature to take effective action."

With the passage of the appropriation bill, Governor Ammons quickly informed President Wilson that the state would be able to maintain order as soon as new bonds could be issued. Meanwhile, the military court martials opened at the State Rifle Range near Golden, a few miles west of Denver, with Captain Edward Smith serving as judge advocate. Captain Danks had refused to take any part in the proceedings as had a number of other National Guard officers after they had been told by their superiors:

"We've got to take care of these men of ours. We've got to vaccinate them so no court in the land can touch them at some future date. A man's life can't be put in jeopardy twice in the courts and we'll take care of these boys."

Sixty-two charges of murder, looting, arson and larceny were prepared. Although invited, United Mine Worker officials refused to appear before the military court on the ground that it was nothing more than a carefully arranged whitewash. Major Hamrock was the first to be tried. The charges against him were murder and arson. He was promptly acquitted. A score of National Guard witnesses were placed on the stand. Lieutenant Linderfelt was tried for the murder of Louie Tikas. He was released with a light reprimand for striking a prisoner.

Perhaps the most important result of the trials, all of which ended in acquittals, was the release by General Chase of the rosters of Troops A and B. The general's own record showed that in Troop A there were 71 employes of the C. F. & I. Co., 50 Victor-American Fuel Co. workers, and one employe of the Rocky Mountain Fuel Co. Of the total enlistment of 130 men in the two troops, 122 were coal company employes.

A union contention was borne out in the testimony of Sergt. P. N. Cullen of Troop B who told the military court that the troops had planned to attack the colony. On the day before the massacre, he testified, he had refused to place his men in skirmish formation on Water Tank Hill while the strikers' ball game was in progress at the edge of the colony.

As soon as the court-martials, which were as farcical as the union had expected, were concluded, General Chase and Major Boughton went on tour to explain "the real facts of the mine war" to the people of the United States. Major Boughton took himself to New York and No. 26 Broadway for a talk with Rockefeller. The capitalist also felt explanations were in order, but instead of making one night stands he hired a publicity man to do the job for him. He selected Ivy L. Lee, whom he borrowed from President Rea of the Pennsylvania Railroad.

Lee was well qualified for the job Rockefeller wanted done. A former reporter for several large newspapers, Lee had served for many years as publicity agent for corporations and such organizations as that of the anthracite coal operators. It was decided Mr. Lee should obtain information from a committee of Colorado coal operators and issue a series of bulletins entitled, "Facts Concerning the Struggle in Colorado for Industrial Freedom." In addition, at Lee's own suggestion and with Rockefeller's acquiescence, he drew up a letter from Governor Ammons to the President of the United States and a second one to the governors of the various states "setting forth the situation as

Governor Ammons saw it." The letter was drafted, but not used.

A clever, finished workman, Lee turned out polished, well written bulletins for his operator-employers, but, unfortunately, he relied upon them for correct information. In one bulletin,[2] he discussed the salaries and expense accounts of United Mine Worker officials, saying:

"Frank J. Hayes, nine weeks salary, $4,052.92; Frank J. Hayes, nine weeks' expenses, $1,667.20; total for salary and expenses, $5,720.12. Frank J. Hayes was thus paid over $90 a day; at the rate of over $32,000 a year. For just the same period of nine weeks, John McLennan received for salary $2,683.65 and for expenses $1,496.55, or $66 a day. John R. Lawson received for nine weeks salary $1,772.40. Mother Jones, whose sole duty was to agitate, received $2,668.62 salary for the same period; $42 a day."

There were hurried conferences at No. 26 Broadway when the United Mine Workers opened their books and showed conclusively that Hayes' figures were for a year instead of nine weeks; that McLennan was paid a salary of $2,400 a year, and that all the rest, including Lawson, received the magnificent salary of $4 a day. Mother Jones wasn't paid a cent during jail terms, a policy that showed the United Mine Workers were more economy minded than gallant. Lee was forced to admit he had not checked the figures supplied him by Jesse Welborn and other Colorado coal operators. Welborn announced he would just as soon believe his set of figures as any other. It was weeks before the Lee bulletins were corrected. The union retaliated by issuing a series of bulletins of its own, and mailing them to newspapers and periodicals throughout the country.

Ben B. Lindsey, judge of Denver's juvenile court, went East with affidavits of Ludlow survivors to see if he could con-

[2] Facts Concerning the Struggle in Colorado for Industrial Freedom, Series 1, 1914.

vince Washington of the seriousness of the Colorado situation.
Judge Lindsey was in great favor with liberal circles in Colorado and had earned himself a favorable reputation on the
juvenile bench. He had not yet advanced his companionate
marriage theory and, in fact, had just taken a bride to himself
in the prosaic manner of his fathers. The bride, a charming
young woman, went East with him. It was her honeymoon,
but the fact that they were a legally married couple, very
much in love, did not save her husband from the loose tongues
of the coal operators. They used the same tactics against Judge
Lindsey that they had used against Mother Jones, intimating
that the diminutive jurist was a Don Juan who had left Denver
for a few days to pursue an amorous quest. They didn't mention that Judge Lindsey was accompanied East by a bride and
something of a crowd—Mrs. Jolly, Mrs. Thomas and her two
children, and the massacre-shocked Mrs. Petrucci, whose three
children had died at Ludlow. The women and two children
were in charge of Mrs. Edward P. Costigan. On their arrival
in Washington, Judge Lindsey discussed Colorado's troubles
with a number of representatives and then went to the White
House with the women. President Wilson received them cordially, and bounced the Thomas children on his knee while
stories of Ludlow and operator oppression were told. Judge
Lindsey argued that sovereignty of the state had broken down,
and that the federal government should compel the coal operators to arbitrate.[3]

"Judge Lindsey, I think this is a very important question with
reference to all the people, and I want you to know that myself
and others connected with the administration have done and
want to do all we can within our legal rights to bring about
peace and order in Colorado," President Wilson said as the interview ended.

Judge Lindsey spoke that night in Rifles Armory before a mass

[3] An interesting argument in the light of the 1941 dispute between the
United Mine Workers and the administration over the right of miners in cap-
tive coal mines to strike.

meeting arranged by Mrs. Medill McCormick, a relative of John D. Rockefeller by marriage, and then went on to New York to see John D. Jr. himself. He did not succeed. Rockefeller was out to the Colorado jurist.

President Wilson's mediators were ignored by the coal operators as other mediators had been ignored before them, and the strike dragged on into the summer of 1914. John Lawson re-established his tent colonies and the miners held firm. With warm weather, work in the mines slackened and there were no serious clashes. Various investigators made their reports, but they contributed little to the record and served no purpose. The general public knew the strike was still in effect, but that was about all. The newspapers displayed little interest and, in fact, there was little for them to print. Miners and their families sitting stolidly in their tents awaiting victory, and operators sitting in their Denver offices awaiting capitulation on the part of their workers were not good copy. It took beatings, blazing colonies and pitched battles to place the strike on the front pages.

Rockefeller was convinced by now, however, that he would have to take some step to alleviate conditions in Colorado. He conceived the idea of making an investigation of industrial conditions through the Rockefeller Foundation. He held a conference with W. L. Mackenzie King of Ottawa, Canada, former labor minister of the dominion, and suggested he take charge of the inquiry. On Aug. 1, 1914, Rockefeller wrote to King, who had not yet joined the Foundation:

"As you have doubtless learned from the newspapers the situation in the coal mines of Colorado is quiet. Practically all of the mines are in operation, the output being seventy or eighty per cent of normal, but quite all that present business conditions will absorb. Practically all of the men who are needed are obtainable. On the other hand, tent colonies are maintained, in which some 1,500 to 2,000 strikers still reside.[4]

[4] Records of the United Mine Workers show benefits were being paid to support 24,000 miners and their dependents.

The tent colonies are a constant menace to peace and are only held in subjection by the presence of federal troops. If the latter were withdrawn, doubtless these unoccupied men, many of them, we believe, paid by the union to continue the disturbances, would renew active hostilities. I wrote Mr. Welborn, the president of the fuel company, a few days ago, inquiring what the present status was of the various committees or individuals appointed to undertake to terminate the industrial warfare. A copy of his interesting reply I enclose herewith.

"There would seem to be but two ways in which a permanent condition of peace can be restored. First, by the calling off of the strike by the United Mine Workers. That this is likely to happen in the near future we have no definite reason to believe, unless the financial resources of the union are so depleted as a result of their industrial conflicts in several states that they cannot much longer continue to support the striking miners. Secondly, by developing some organization in the mining camps which will assure to the employee the opportunity for collective bargaining, for easy and constant conferences with reference to any matters of difference or grievance which may come up, and any other advantages which may be derived from membership in the union."[5]

Mr. King, harried by the outbreak of war between England and Germany, supplied Mr. Rockefeller with a rough draft of a labor plan a few days later and advised how advantage might be taken of the war situation to defeat the aspirations of the workers. Mr. King wrote in part:[6]

"Having regard to the more cordial relations between labor and capital which, it is hoped, the Foundation may be able to effect, it would be fortunate, indeed, if you could, out of the changed conditions which this European war is certain to produce, find a means of restoring industrial peace in the United

[5] U. S. Commission on Industrial Relations, Report on the Colorado Strike, 1914. P. 158.
[6] U. S. Commission on Industrial Relations, Report on the Colorado Strike, 1915. P. 161.

States in industries such as coal and fuel where there is a certainty of direct hearing. It may be that among those who are embarrassing the situation, there are many foreigners who may feel compelled to return to Europe, and that may prove an immediate factor of importance. Looking at the ultimate, rather than the immediate effect, there is, speaking generally, going to be a large amount of unemployment as a consequence of this war, and once the war is over, thousands of men and their families in the Old World are going to seek future employment here in the New. In certain industries it is going to be easy for employers to find all the labor they desire, and unions will be confronted with a new problem. Recognition, simply for the sake of recognition, is going to be seen to be less pressing as an immediate end than that of maintaining standards, already existing, and employes may rightly come to regard as their friends and allies companies and corporations large enough and fair enough to desire to maintain those standards of their own accord. For the unions to take a different view will certainly mean to lose the substance of fair conditions while wasting resources in fighting for the shadow of recognition. Here, it seems to me, lies a possible avenue of approach towards restoring normal conditions in Colorado."

Welborn was not at all pleased when the King plan was presented to him. He expressed belief it would work in many cases of differences, but added:

"It seems to me, however, that the adoption at this time by the Colorado operators of such a plan as Mr. King suggests would weaken us with our men; would tend to strengthen the organization with our employees not now members of it, and would, in the mind of the public, be an admission on our part, that a weakness, the existence of which we had previously denied, was being corrected."[7]

[7] U. S. Commission on Industrial Relations, Report on the Colorado Strike, 1914. P. 158.

Welborn's letter kept discussions of possible improvements to an exchange of letters until Sept. 7, 1914, when President Wilson's conciliators prepared a plan which he submitted to the operators for adjustment of the strike. Drafted by Mr. Davies and Mr. Fairley, the plan proposed a truce of three years, re-employment of all miners not guilty of law violations, strict adherence to the mining laws of the state, posting of wages, rules and regulations, the establishment of a grievance commit-tee at each mine, and the naming of a commission of three members by the President of the United States to serve as a court of final appeal. Claim for contractual relations was to be waived, and there were to be no picketing or mine guards. Expenses of the federal commission would be borne by the operators and employees on a fifty-fifty basis.

In his accompanying letter, President Wilson said:

"I hope that you will consider it as if you were acting for the whole country, and I beg that you will regard it as urged upon your acceptance by myself with very deep earnestness. This is a time, I am sure you will feel, when everything should be done that is possible for me to do to see that all untoward and threatening circumstances of every sort are taken out of the life of the people of the United States."

The United Mine Worker policy committee met and discussed the proposal carefully. John R. Lawson and Ed Doyle flatly refused to approve it. The plan was put before the miners at a special convention in Trinidad Sept. 15, and they accepted it by an almost unanimous vote. The operators, however, re-jected it. The particular objection, according to statements released by the operators, was to the proposal to establish a federal commission for three years. Such a commission, they said, would interfere with the private conduct of business. The operators also refused to consider re-employment of strikers who had been so much as accused of acts of violence on the ground that to do so would force the discharge of men who had risked death or injury during the strike by remaining in the mines.

Public opinion was behind Mr. Wilson, a fact Rockefeller and the coal barons recognized. Rockefeller, however, through Murphy, had laid the ground work for the rejection in a letter to Welborn the day after the proposed peace plan was published. The letter said in part:

"The fact that the President of the United States has suggested a plan of settlement and has given it out to the public produces a delicate situation which we have no doubt you gentlemen in the West will handle in the same careful and diplomatic way in which you have handled the whole situation thus far, avoiding on the one hand any entanglement with the labor union and on the other an attitude which would arouse a hostile public opinion. We are, of course, greatly interested, and if you think we can be of any service in helping you to prepare a reply we shall be most happy to collaborate on any draft of one which you may send us."

The letter, though couched in polite phrases, was nothing more than an order and the Colorado officers of the company took it as such. A few days later, a change in tone came from No. 26 Broadway. Rockefeller's staff was impressed with the favorable public reaction to President Wilson's proposal. Murphy sent Welborn a bundle of newspaper clippings with the comment:

"I am impressed with the frequency with which they make the point that the parties should either accept the President's plan or suggest some other. It seems to me clear that public opinion will demand either the acceptance of the President's proposition or some constructive suggestion from the operators. A mere refusal to do anything would be disastrous."[8]

---

[8] U. S. Commission on Industrial Relations, Report on the Colorado Strike, 1915. P. 174.

CHAPTER XVII
THE STRIKE ENDS

With the Colorado Fuel & Iron Co. as the moving spirit, the coal operators of Colorado launched a daring campaign to punish the strike leaders even while President Wilson was bending every effort to end the conflict and bring peace to the state. In Huerfano County, Sheriff Farr and his deputies suddenly swooped on union offices and arrested scores of minor officials of the United Mine Workers. Similar raids were staged by law enforcement officers of Las Animas and other coal producing counties. Jails, already packed to overflowing with militia prisoners who were held when the troops left the field, received new quotas. Attorney General Fred Farrar, moving in the open more than at any time since the inception of the strike, arranged for a grand jury investigation in Trinidad. The time-honored coal county custom of handpicking a jury was followed. The jurors chosen for the investigation were deputy sheriffs, coal company employes, or persons who relied upon coal company patronage for their livelihood. With Farrar directing it, the jury worked swiftly. Its report to Judge A. W. McHendrie had many earmarks of a coal company bulletin.

"The evidence produced before us clearly shows that the crimes under consideration were committed by armed mobs, acting in pursuance of well-defined, carefully matured plans, having for their object the destruction of property and human life," the report said in part. "These mobs were composed of members of the United Mine Workers of America and their known sympathizers. An even more significant fact is that the organization in question through its chief officers in this state, bought and paid for and furnished to its members the arms and ammunition used, organized and led the mobs and directed the execution of various crimes. It also appears that the members of these mobs, when injured in the course of their criminal enterprises, were cared for and secreted by the officers of the organization, and at its expense.

"It is also a matter of common knowledge shared by members of this grand jury with other residents of this county, that the funds for the prosecution of this organized insurrection are derived from assessments levied upon laboring men, members of the organization in other states, and from voluntary contributions from members of labor organizations and charitable persons throughout the United States. From the systematic representation of the facts by the United Mine Workers of America, and by a portion of the press of this state, it is reasonable to suppose that these contributions were made in the mistaken belief that they were to be used for the subsistence of persons rendered destitute by unemployment due to the strike. The evident fact is, however, that they were largely used in the purchase of firearms and ammunition to be used by the strikers in a campaign of violence, designed to secure compliance with their demands through terror induced by the destruction of life and property."

Accompanying the report were indictments of 124 labor leaders in Las Animas County. High on the list was the name of John R. Lawson, against whom 19 indictments were lodged. Fourteen of the indictments against Lawson were for murder, two for assault with intent to kill, one for arson and two for conspiracy in restraint of trade.

Lawson was not surprised by the indictments. He knew the power of the coal operators in the Kingdom of Las Animas, but he had confidence that an innocent man could not long be deprived of his liberty or his reputation.

"We'll fight, just as we have always fought," he told his fellow officials. "I have long expected something like this for I have always known nothing was too base or too corrupt for our operator friends. They would stoop to anything. My opinion of grand juries and courts will go up when they return true bills against the operators who turned machine guns on innocent, unprotected women and children, and sent their imported thugs to abuse and murder honest men."

The murder indictments specifically charged that John Lawson killed John Nimmo, a guard who fell near the Ludlow colony Oct. 25, 1913, while Lawson was moving women and children to an arroyo to protect them from the fire of mine guards. There were no grand jury indictments against coal operators in any of the counties, but the number against strikers mounted as other juries, working under the supervision of coal company attorneys, carried out operator orders to punish the union leaders. While the operators were busy arranging criminal charges against the strikers, they were not idle on another front. A state election was approaching.

The Democrats ignored Governor Ammons and nominated Thomas Patterson for governor. Industrial freedom promised to be the issue of the campaign. The operators sought ways and means of avoiding this issue. Their brain department found an answer in prohibition. Evangelist Billy Sunday was brought to Colorado to fight Demon Rum and bring religion to the state. The men who had bought machine guns and imported thugs provided the funds for Sunday's revivals. Not once during his stay in Colorado did the dynamic Billy Sunday so much as mention the 24,000 men, women and children huddled in tents on the edge of the hills, nor did he once denounce industrial greed. He based his pleas on the theory that booze was the source of all poverty and distress. Morning, noon and night he attacked the liquor evil. The coal barons reached deeper and deeper into their pockets to aid him. The word went out that candidates for office must be dry. The industrial issue began to dim before the trumped up one of prohibition.

The Republican candidate for governor was George A. Carlson, an obscure lawyer who seemingly came out of nowhere. He had nothing to say about the strike or industrial problems. He was concerned with the liquor evil. As an individual, Mr. Carlson had an ingrown love for prohibition, and as a candidate he was a consistent foe of rum and the devil. The coal operators were behind Carlson to a man. They were just as united in their support of Attorney General Farrar who had proven his sterling worth by his handling of grand juries and the bringing of indictments against strikers.

On election day, 150 coal company employes served as election workers. The strike and its blood inspired issues were submerged, and both Carlson and Farrar were victorious. Coal company political tactics had worked once again. Welborn didn't waste any time sending off a report to Rockefeller.

"According to figures received today, which are practically complete, the plurality of Carlson, Republican candidate for governor, over Patterson, is approximately 33,000," Welborn wrote. "The plurality of Farrar, Democratic candidate for attorney general, over his next opponent, the Republican, is almost 38,000. Farrar is the present incumbent in the office to which he has just been elected, and has been about the only reliable force for law and order in the Statehouse. His re-election serves to emphasize the sentiment in favor of law and order, expressed in the election of the main part of the Republican ticket. Mr. Farrar has been actively engaged for several months in connection with the work of grand juries in the various coal counties where indictments have been brought against those who participated in the rioting."[1]

[1] U. S. Commission on Industrial Relations, Report on the Colorado Strike, by George P. West. Washington, 1915; P. 20.

In addition to the election and persecution campaigns, the operators sought to purge their own ranks. Employes who had dropped idle remarks that might be construed as unfavorable or at least unsympathetic to the coal companies were subjected to careful investigations. No report was too small for attention. In the case of the C. F. & I., every detail was reported to No. 26 Broadway, to the same Rockefeller who had told the congressional committee that he could not be familiar with details of the business in Colorado and that he had to leave it in the hands of his Colorado officers. Even the ministers in company-dominated camps and towns came in for attention. In a letter to New York about a clergyman in a closed camp and about the Rev. Daniel McCorkle, pastor of a small church in Sunrise, Wyo., 300 miles from the Southern Colorado coal fields, Welborn told Starr J. Murphy:

"At the time of the Ludlow affair, the minister was very outspoken in his criticism of the coal companies, but seemed to regret his action when informed of the facts concerning that disturbance. He has socialistic tendencies, however, and I have been informed that his wife is a Greek, yet they may both be perfectly honest . . . We have thought some of changing the minister at Sunrise, but have refrained from taking a course that would be unfair to him, or would indicate a prejudice against him because of what may have been simply indiscreet statements in connection with the Ludlow outbreak."[2]

Late in November, when Governor Ammons had little more than a month to remain in office, the legislative investigating committee headed by Senator S. J. Burris, made a belated report which contained little more than a recommendation that the governor use his powers firmly when the federal troops were withdrawn. And Governor Ammons, bewildered, betrayed by trusted advisers, and heartily sick of the whole business, filed

[2] U. S. Commission on Industrial Relations, Report on the Colorado Strike, by George P. West. Washington, 1915; P. 55.

it away without so much as a comment for public consumption. The report didn't particularly matter, however, as the strike was nearing a close. The treasury was near exhaustion and the international board was eager for a speedy settlement. The 450,000 members in the coal producing states couldn't match dollars with the Croesus of No. 26 Broadway. They were strong in spirit, but short of cash, and they knew they had to bring the Colorado struggle to a close at any cost. They had waited two months for President Wilson to take some action on the operators' refusal to consider his proposed settlement. In desperation, the international board asked President Wilson to suggest that the federal government take over the coal mines and operate them. President Wilson said this could not be done, and expressed regret that the operators had refused to consider his settlement plan. The United Mine Workers then asked him to make his position known through a public statement. President Wilson agreed and on Dec. 1, 1914, issued the following statement:

"The strike of the miners in Colorado, which has now lasted for 12 months, has attracted the attention of the whole country and has been accompanied by many distressing and tragical circumstances. The mediation of the Government of the United States was offered early in the struggle, but the operators of the mines were unwilling to avail themselves of it or to act upon the suggestions made in the interest of peace by representatives of the Department of Labor authorized by statute to serve in such cases. It became necessary to send Federal troops to the district affected by the strike in order to preserve the peace; but their presence could of itself accomplish nothing affirmative. After long waiting, therefore, and the disappointment of many hopes of accommodation, I ventured, after taking counsel with representatives of the government who had been on the field and made themselves thoroughly familiar with all the circumstances of the case, to propose a plan of pending agreement upon such terms and arrangements as might be made the basis for permanently satisfactory relations between them. The plan seemed to me obviously fair and sensible. The striking miners promptly accepted it; but the mine owners rejected it, saying in response to my earnest appeal that they objected to its most essential features—namely, the proposed arrangements by which differences might be settled by reference to a commission appointed by the President of the United States. I think the country regretted their decision and was disappointed that they should have taken so uncompromising a position. I have waited and hoped for a change in their attitude, but now fear that there will be none. And yet I do not feel that I am at liberty to do nothing in the presence of circumstances so serious and distressing. Merely to withdraw the federal troops and leave the situation to clear and settle itself would seem to me to be doing something less than my duty after all that has occurred. I have therefore determined to appoint the commission contemplated in the plan of temporary settlement, notwithstanding the rejection of the plan by the mine operators, and thus at least to create the instrumentality by which like troubles and disputes may be amicably and honorably settled in the future, in the hope, the very earnest and sincere hope, that both parties may see it to be not merely to their own best interest but also a duty which they owe to the communities they serve and to the Nation itself to make use of this instrumentality of peace and render strife of the kind which has threatened the order and prosperity of the great State of Colorado a thing of the past, impossible of repetition so long as everything that is done is done in good temper and with the genuine purpose to do justice and observe every public as well as every private obligation.

"The Hon. Seth Low, of New York; Mr. Charles W. Mills, of Philadelphia; and Mr. Patrick Gilday, of Clearfield, Pa., have most generously and unselfishly consented, at my request, to serve as members of the commission. I owe to these gentlemen my own warm thanks not only, but also, I believe, the thanks of their fellow citizens throughout the nation. They will

place themselves at the service alike of the miners and the operators of the mines in Colorado in case controversy between them
should in the future develop circumstances, which render mediation the obvious way of peace and just settlement."

Copies of the President's statement were sent by the United
Mine Workers headquarters in Indianapolis to each local in
Colorado along with a statement that the long strike would be
brought to an end.

"In view of this urgent request, coming as it does from the
Chief Executive of the Nation, we deem it the part of wisdom
to accept his suggestion and to terminate the strike," the official
statement said. "In our opinion, to wage the strike further
would not mean additional gain to our members. In taking this
position and in terminating this strike, which has lasted for a
period of almost five years in the northern coal fields and for
more than 14 months in the southern fields of Colorado, we
believe we are doing the best thing possible for the men on
strike, who have suffered so long that justice might be done.

"All lovers of liberty and believers in fair play between man
and man must admire the heroic struggle of the Colorado miners
against the great wealth and influence of Rockefeller and his
associates. We believe that our people have not died in vain, and
that the battle they have waged against such tremendous odds
has aroused the conscience of the Nation, and that out of the
martyrdom of our people will come the dawn of a better day
for the suffering miners and their families . . . We have made
every overture of peace since the beginning of this struggle.
We recognize no surrender and shall continue to propagate the
principles of our humanitarian movement throughout the coal
fields of Colorado. We advise all men to seek their former
places in the mines, and to those who are refused employment
we shall render assistance to the best of our ability and shall
provide every legal protection to those of our members who
are being prosecuted by the hirelings of organized greed."

The miners were ordered to meet in Denver Dec. 7, 1914, to make final arrangements for closing the strike.

John Lawson, as a member of the international board and the Colorado policy committee, aided in drafting the statement to the various locals. He remained in Denver after it was sent out to arrange the final meeting and to attend the sessions of the U. S. Commission on Industrial Relations which began an inquiry into the strike Dec. 2, with Frank P. Walsh as chairman.[3]

The 51-year-old Walsh was a two-fisted investigator who never courted the truth—he went after it with a rapid fire gun. A native of St. Louis, Mr. Walsh had been a railroad water boy, a court stenographer and finally a lawyer. He had served as a member of the Kansas City Tenement Association, president of the Kansas City Board of Civil Service and on the Board of Public Welfare of Kansas City, a parole board which he had established. Men either liked Frank Walsh very much, or disliked him intensely. The corporations hated him for his progressive legislation in Missouri where he had forced through measures to provide pensions for widowed mothers, shorter work days for women, and similar legislation.

The Saturday Evening Post described him as a man with a houseful of children who "accepts no retainers for permanent legal services; has the largest law library in the West relating to trial practice; is hard as nails; does not drink; is a handball player, a swimmer, and an enthusiastic walker; reads law books for fun; arbitrates disputes as a pastime—and is not happy when he is not fighting for something he thinks is right."

Other publications took an entirely different view of Frank Walsh. The New York World always spoke of him contemptuously as "an expert in mare's nests," while the Louisville Evening Post delighted in calling him a mischief maker and demagog who "ought to be allowed to pursue his search of useless information from the privacy of his own law office."

[3] U. S. Commission on Industrial Relations, 1915. Vol. 8.

Dante Barton, writing in Harper's Weekly, found that men trusted Walsh implicitly "unless they distrust him." The Colorado operators and their supporters, including General Chase and the militia, both disliked and distrusted Chairman Walsh.

When the Commission convened in Denver, Walsh wasted no time getting into action. The Foster Committee on Mines and Mining had already covered much of the ground and its reports and transcripts were available to the Commission. Chairman Walsh began his investigation with an interrogation of Governor Ammons.[4]

The governor reviewed his efforts to get the operators and miners into conference during the early days of the strike and the subsequent calling out of the militia. He blamed the press for his difficulties.

"You wish to go into the attitude of the public press?" Chairman Walsh asked.

"Just one or two sentences on this," Governor Ammons replied. "The greatest difficulty I had was the absolute misrepresentation of everything in the public press; and we were powerless either to correct it or to get the facts stated to the public. And the public excitement was simply tremendous here, and even an appeal to arms, couched in crafty language that could not be prosecuted, but was understood just as well as though made in the most violent language in the world, was published by our leading papers, and apparently everything was done to excite the public."

Chairman Walsh did not keep Governor Ammons on the stand long as it was apparent the executive had little to contribute and sought only to explain and justify his own role. In rapid succession, Walsh called J. C. Osgood, Governor Carlson, Mine Inspector Dalrymple, Thomas Patterson, John McLennan and Welborn to the stand. He spent a lot of time with Welborn, questioning him closely on every phase of C. F. & I. Co. activity. He drew from Welborn admissions that there had not

[4] All quotations from Commission's reports.

been a single personal injury suit filed against the company in Huerfano County in 20 years, and that the company had purchased thousands of dollars worth of machine guns, rifles and ammunition. Chairman Walsh was adroit. He led Welborn by roundabout paths to the questions at point. Every subject was covered.

"You know that a statute has been in effect in this state since 1905 with reference to blacklisting?" Walsh asked.

"I am not familiar with that," Welborn replied, "but we are not engaged in the practice of blacklisting, and we are never bothered by that."

"It is unlawful for an employer to blacklist employees or notify other employers of blacklisted employees. You are familiar with it in a general way?"

"Yes."

"Does your company keep a list or catalogue of persons that used to be employed, which you circulate among your own mines?"

"No, not as you stated it," Welborn replied. "In connection with the employment of our men, something of a description of the employee is made and his reasons for leaving our employment are given when he does leave. If he has left because he is an objectionable workman at one mine, he is apt to be an objectionable workman at other of our properties, and we so inform our men." (sic)

Chairman Walsh smiled thinly.

"Are men placed upon the list who have been discharged for the reason they have disturbed the peace of other workmen, or are agitators?" he asked.

"I do not know," Welborn said. "I should say if they had been very objectionable, no matter what the character of the disturbance was, it has been so recorded."

By Dec. 10, 1914, the great strike was ended. Hundreds of miners were without employment or a place to go. Some

clung to their tents for a time, while still others drifted out
of the state as had the victims of the 1903 and other strikes.
Some finally found their way back into the mines. It was a
dark day for the men and women who had fought so long and
endured so many hardships. Many predicted it would be 10
years before another attempt at unionization could be made. The
operators appeared to be once more complete and undisputed
masters of the state. Miners who had played prominent parts
in the strike were virtual outlaws in the eyes of the coal operators. Not a single leader could get a job. They had fought
a tooth and claw battle with the operators, and they knew
they could not expect pity now that the conflict was over.

The Rockefellers, however, were badly battered. They had
suffered heavy financial losses and had incurred more public
enmity than they liked to think about. On the records of investigating committees was spread much damaging and revealing
testimony. Practices which had long produced extra revenue
were subjects of public condemnation and censure. The operations of the companies were no longer secrets or objects of mere
suspicion and gossip. Everyone knew how their businesses were
conducted and how their business practices conflicted with state
laws and the public welfare. From No. 26 Broadway went out
an order for company executives to avoid conflict with the workers (this order apparently, in the light of later developments,
was not concerned with prosecutions of strike leaders). There
must be no disturbances of any kind. John D. Rockefeller, Jr.,
would be called to the stand as soon as the Commission on Industrial Relations returned to the East. Peace must be maintained at all costs. Rockefeller wrote Welborn that "our feeling here is that, the strike having been terminated, it will be
the wish of all those connected with the fuel company to introduce as rapidly as may seem expedient the various progressive
steps in such a plan as your further thought will suggest, looking toward the prevention of a possible recurrence at any time

in the future of the disorder and loss on every hand which has resulted from the recent strike."

David Griffiths, a former state coal mine inspector, was named to act as an intermediary between the company and its employes in a further effort to work out differences. Back of the steps toward a more cordial relationship with employees was fear of public opinion and the novel suggestion of W. L. Mackenzie King that the Rockefellers establish a union of their own to deal with their employes.

CHAPTER XVIII

NO. 26 BROADWAY

Late in January, 1915, John Lawson and other Colorado labor leaders went to New York to attend further sessions of the Commission on Industrial Relations. Chairman Walsh called the commission to order at 10 a. m., Jan. 25, in a municipal building provided by the city for the hearing.

"Will the house please be in order, and will the audience maintain as perfect order as possible?" he boomed in a big voice. "Mr. Rockefeller."

John Lawson's eyes followed the capitalist to the stand. Here, then, was the man who pulled the strings that made all the little Welborns, Bowers, Weitzels, Farrs and Linderfelts dance. Here before his eyes for the first time was the real ruler of the Kingdoms of Las Animas and Huerfano. He clenched and unclenched his muscular hands nervously. Conflicting emotions forced him to take his eyes away from the men on the stand. Lawson fought to regain his composure. He could think of nothing at the moment except the innocents who had died. The indictments hanging over his own head were forgotten for the moment.

Vaguely, Lawson heard Walsh ask the routine questions. "Your name, please?" and "What is your business, Mr. Rockefeller?" Lawson's temples pounded and his thoughts raced back across the years—years packed with intimidations, persecutions, misery, want, brutal beatings, deportations, incarcerations and murder.

Rockefeller read a prepared statement. The veins stood out in John Lawson's head as the capitalist concluded with the statement:

"If, with the responsibilities I have and the opportunities given me, I am able to contribute toward promoting the well being of my fellow man through the lessening of injustice and the alleviation of human suffering, I shall feel that it has been possible to realize the highest purpose of my life."

Fine words these—polished words—but they did not bring back the dead from their poor graves nor did they place food in the mouths of hungry children. They did not dismiss framed indictments for murder, nor banish the spectre of the hangman's noose from the minds of hundreds of innocent men. Lawson's lips curled in a sneer. He leaned forward better to hear the testimony.

"What is your attitude toward permitting union organizers who are not employed by your corporation to address employes and otherwise carry on their work without interference," Chairman Walsh asked softly.

Rockefeller hesitated a moment. Then he answered:

"I have never had occasion to take any attitude on that subject, because, as I have pointed out, it is a matter which has been left with the executive officers."

"Can you conceive of effective protest against abuses in a large industry where it is without organization on the part of the employes?"

"There again, Mr. Chairman, that is a practical question to which my lack of practical experience makes it impossible for me to reply."

Chairman Walsh pressed the capitalist hard on every phase of the Colorado Fuel & Iron Co., from its financial dealings to its work standards. Lawson's contemptuous sneer changed to open-mouthed amazement as he heard the owner of a vast industry admit complete ignorance of working conditions and pay.

"Have you given consideration to the number of hours a day a man can work at laborious employment and maintain physical efficiency?" Chairman Walsh asked.

"I have not," Rockefeller replied.

"Have you made a study of the cost of living? What a living wage ought to be in the various states of the Union where you have large industrial holdings?"

"I have not, Mr. Chairman. I should think that would be a very interesting study, but I fancy that would be even a longer study than the effort to solve the industrial problems, but I have not had the opportunity nor have I the experience to fit me to undertake such a study."

To most of the questions, Rockefeller replied he was without knowledge. He had not read anything in the newspapers and he did not know how his business was conducted in Colorado. A foe of liquor, Rockefeller did not know that he was in the liquor business through maintenance of saloons in coal camps. He also testified he had never heard of his loyal servant, Sheriff Jefferson Farr of Huerfano County.

Rockefeller, after two days on the stand, was followed by Ivy Lee, R. Fulton Cutting, Dr. Charles E. Eliot, a member of three Rockefeller Foundation boards; John Hays Hammond, the engineer, and finally John R. Lawson.

The coal miner from the West carried himself with as much assurance as John D. Rockefeller, Jr., and the other captains of industry who had preceded him to the stand. There were no indications of diffidence or fright.

"What is your name?" Chairman Walsh began.

"John R. Lawson."

He answered the routine questions about his residence, occupation and past work in a full, strong voice. In his hand he held a paper.

"Is there anything in the testimony of Mr. Rockefeller that you wish to comment upon?" Chairman Walsh asked.

"Yes, Mr. Chairman, there are several things I would like to comment on," Lawson replied, raising his voice. "I would like to comment on some testimony given before this Commission and perhaps before the congressional hearing. I have with me a brief document that I have prepared, and I should like, with your permission, to read it into the record."

"Do you desire to read it at this time?"

"Yes."

"You may proceed."

"I would like to state, Mr. Chairman, that in giving testimony before this Commission at this time relating to the foundation fund and the Colorado situation that I hope I do it without any malice and with the most kindly feeling. I sincerely hope it will be taken that way."

He lifted the paper and read:

"The Commission on Industrial Relations was created to inquire into the underlying causes of industrial unrest. Speaking for the many thousands of men, women and children who suffered through the recent coal strike in Colorado, I say to your honorable body that you can well afford to let the testimony of John D. Rockefeller, Jr., bring your investigation to an end. Out of this mouth came a reason for every discontent that agitates the laboring class in the United States today, and if remedies are provided for the injustices that he disclosed a long step will be taken away from industrial disturbance.

"For more than 10 years he has been director of the powerful Colorado Fuel & Iron Co., vested with what is virtually the power of life and death over 12,000 men and their families, for the isolated nature of the coal mining industry lends itself to an absolutism unknown in other activities. This power, let it be pointed out, came to him by no healthful process of struggle and achievement, but entirely through the fact that he was the son of his father. His huge control of men and money was, in effect, a gift that marked the attainment of his majority.

"In those first days, when he might have been expected to possess a certain enthusiasm in his vast responsibilities, Colorado was shaken by the coal strike of 1903-04. It is a matter of undisputed record that a mercenary militia, paid openly by the mine operators, crushed this strike by the bold violation of every known constitutional right that the citizen was thought to possess. Men were herded in bull pens like cattle, homes were shattered, the writ of habeas corpus suspended, hundreds were loaded on cars and dumped into the desert without food or water, others were driven over the snow of the mountain ranges, a governor elected by 15,000 majority was unseated[1], a man never voted on for that office was made governor, and when there came a thing called peace, the black-list gave 6,000 coal miners choice between starvation or exile. The Colorado Fuel & Iron Co. organized and led the attack on the liberties of free men, and yet you heard from Mr. Rockefeller's own lips that he never inquired into the causes of the strike, the conduct of his executives, or the fate of those who lost. So little interest did he take in the affair, so faint was the impression it made upon him, that he could not even answer your questions as to its larger facts.

"To take the place of the banished workers, thousands were imported, and the extent of the company's dragnet for new material may be judged from the fact that over 30 languages and dialects have been spoken in the mines since 1904.

"Ten years pass, and in 1913 Colorado is once more pushed to the verge of bankruptcy by another strike. Many strike breakers of 1903, reaching the limit of human endurance, followed the example of those whose places they had taken, choosing hunger and cold in tents on the mountain sides and plains

[1] Alva Adams (D) was unseated and was succeeded by James H. Peabody who immediately resigned in favor of Jesse McDonald (R).

in preference to a continuance of unbearable conditions in the mines. By actual count, the union was supporting 21,508 men, women and children in various colonies in January, 1914.

"What course did Mr. Rockefeller pursue in connection with this upheaval of employees? His duty was clear, for he is on record with this admission, 'I think it is the duty of every director to ascertain the conditions as far as he can, and if there are abuses, to right them.' Putting their justice to one side, the fact remains that we claimed many abuses and cited them specifically.

"The statute law of Colorado ordered a semimonthly pay day, checkweighmen so that we might not be cheated, the right to form unions, the eight-hour day, and payment in cash—not scrip. We charged that the Colorado Fuel & Iron Co. had violated these and other laws, and in addition we told of evil housing conditions, high rents, company store extortions, saloon environment, armed guards, and the denial of freedom in speech, education, religion and politics. When 12,000 men back up such claims by taking their wives and children into wind-swept tents, surely they would seem to be deserving of consideration.

"Yet upon the stand, throughout three whole days this week, John D. Rockefeller, Jr., insisted that he was absolutely ignorant of every detail of the strike. He stated he had not received reports on labor conditions, he could not tell within several thousands how many men worked for him in Colorado, he did not know what wages they received, or what rents they paid; he had never considered what the proper length of a working day should be, he did not know what constituted a living wage, and, most amazing of all, he had never even read the list of grievances that the strikers filed with the governor of Colorado and gave to the world through the press. He did not know whether or not 50 per cent of his employes worked 12 hours a day, and when asked whether or not he considered 12 hours a day in front of a blast furnace to be a hardship he answered he was not familiar enough with the work to judge. He did not know how many of his employes worked seven days a week the year around, but judged it would be a hardship, yet when asked what part of a year could be worked under such conditions without hardship, refused to approximate an opinion.[2]

"He knew that there was a system by which injured men or their families were compensated, but he did not know what the system was, and when a list was read showing the beggarly amounts paid to cripples, mangled miners, he would say nothing but that they were matters a board of directors could not pass upon. He did not know that his company's control of the courts had resulted in a condition where not one damage suit had been filed against it in years, and he did not know that men were treated like criminals for daring to mention unionism. He could not even define collective bargaining, nor had he ever made the slightest study of the great union or its principles against which the Colorado Fuel & Iron Co. threw its power and its millions. He expressed himself in favor of unions and then proceeded to negative this belief by refusing to answer affirmatively a number of questions that bore upon the manner in which unionization could be achieved. Asked whether he would vote to discharge an executive officer if it should be proved that he spent money to corrupt the electorate, he answered, 'I would want to know the conditions.' He did not know what the capitalization was of the subcompany that operates the mine stores or what it paid on the investment.

"He did not know that the company built special buildings for saloons, charging high rental, or that church meetings were compelled to be held near saloons, and that in some cases saloons were in close contact with the schools. He knew that the company had maintained a sociological department, but he did not know what its activities were, nor was he aware that his officials dictated the appointments of our preachers and school teachers, and exercised the right of discharge if they offended by criticism.

[2] Detailed reports regarding Colorado operations were sent to J. Starr Murphy, Rockefeller's attorney, at No. 26 Broadway.

As an excuse for this amazing lack of knowledge, he insisted that the board of directors had placed control of such matters in the hands of J. F. Welborn and L. M. Bowers and held them responsible for wise and just administration of labor affairs. He admitted that, aside from these two, he had knowledge of no others who would be responsible for labor conditions.

"On the witness stand, L. M. Bowers, who gave his residence as Binghamton, N. Y., stated that he was concerned only with the finances of the Colorado Fuel & Iron Co. and knew nothing of labor conditions. J. F. Welborn admitted that until his election to the presidency he had been connected with the sales department, always in Denver, and that it was not his habit to visit the mines. They pointed to E. H. Weitzel as the man in charge of labor conditions and Weitzel stated that while he did not visit all the camps 'frequently' he got to them as often as he could.

"What has been Rockefeller's attitude to this development? Has he, in spite of his own lack of knowledge, instituted any investigation to determine whether Welborn and Bowers, his trusted executives, are equally ignorant and indifferent? I invite him to point to one single admission that would show the slightest activity in this direction or the least intent to summon these men before the board of directors to give an account of their stewardship. His answer was, 'I have not had the opportunity.' Fourteen months, thousands of men, women and children suffered on the mountain sides and prairie, and two months have gone since we called off the strike as a result of President Wilson's proposal, and yet he has not had the opportunity for a personal investigation. His excuse for his lack of knowledge and his failures is that he is 'too busy.' What is his business? He explained it by stating that 'I spend a large part of my time in directing, with others, the various foundations which my father has established and in giving time to questions of investment.' I beg you to contrast his attitude with that of Henry Ford, a man who has built up his tremendous business with his own hands, and who follows every detail in its huge ramifications, and yet who finds the time to take a deep personal interest in every one of the 18,000 workers in his employ.

"In reply to this, he spoke of the rich returns given by Ford business as compared with the beggarly returns of the Colorado Fuel & Iron Co. He complained that his father had only received $371,000 on all his stock, which was but a three and a half percent interest on the cash investment. It was only under questioning that he confessed that his father had received $8,889,000 from his bonds; that the assets of the company were $23,000,000 in excess of liabilities; and that this item did not take in an appreciation in property values of some $19,000,000. Nor did he mention the vast holdings that the Colorado Fuel & Iron Co. refuses to develop, keeping it idle while the population increase adds to its value.

"Let me say to you in this connection—and I have spent a large part of my life in direct contact with the Colorado Fuel & Iron Co.—that whatever appearance of poverty clings to the company it is not due to anything but its own stupid and corrupt policy. Had it taken the money it spent in controlling officials and the electorate, in purchasing machine guns, the employment of gunmen, and in crushing the aspirations of human beings, and spent it in wages and the improvement of working conditions, they would have had rich returns in increased productivity. Henry Ford's 15 per cent wage increase, it will be noted, was followed by a 30 per cent increase in efficiency.

"These, Messrs. Commissioners—this record of indifference respecting human life and human happiness—are vital causes of industrial discontent. An employer who is never seen, and whose power over us is handed down from man to man until there is a chain that no individual can climb; our lives and our liberties passed over as a birthday gift or by will; our energies and our futures capitalized by financiers in distant cities; our masters too often men who have not seen us, who care nothing for us, and will not, or cannot, hear the cry of our despair.

"There is another cause of industrial discontent, and, this too, flows from the Rockefeller source. This is the wilful attempt that is being made to substitute philanthropy for justice. There is not one of these foundations now spreading their millions over the world in showy generosity that does not draw those millions from some form of commercial injustice. It is not their money that these lords of commercialized virtue are spending, but the withheld wages of the American working class.

"I sat in this room and heard Mr. Rockefeller read the list of activities that his foundation felt calculated to 'promote the well-being of mankind'—an international health commission to extend to foreign countries and peoples the work of eradicating the hookworm, 10 millions for the bureau of municipal research, a retreat for migratory birds in Louisiana, $100,000 for the American Academy in Rome, the promotion of medical education and health in China, 34 millions for the University of Chicago, one million for the Belgians, $20,000 a year for widows' pensions in New York, the investigation of vice conditions, and 34 millions for a general education board. A wave of horror swept over me during that reading, and I say to you that the same wave is now rushing over the entire working class in the United States. Health for China, a refuge for birds, food for the Belgians, pensions for New York widows, university training for the elect, and never a thought of a dollar for the thousands of men, women and children who starved in Colorado, for the widows robbed of husbands, children of their fathers, by law-violating conditions in the mines, or for the glaring illiteracy of the coal camps.

"There are thousands of Mr. Rockefeller's ex-employees in Colorado today who wish to God they were in Belgium to be fed or birds to be cared for tenderly.

"As if this were not enough, labor is now informed that this foundation has appropriated $1,000,000 for the purpose of doing what this Commission was appointed to do. An industrial-relations division has been formed to find out why we are discontented. Who, let it be asked, are the directors of this foundation out of which comes this investigation? The two Rockefellers; their professional advisers, Murphy, Gates, Green and Heydt; their secretaries, Flexner and Rose, on the Rockefeller payroll; and three others, Eliot, Hepburn and Judson, who furnish an outward semblance of independence. The same control that has directed the affairs of the Colorado Fuel & Iron Co., the same voice that declared through young Rockefeller that the defeat of the union in Colorado was a great American principle; for which he was willing to sacrifice his money and the lives of his workers; and they ask the laboring class to believe that what they feel as coal company directors they will not feel as directors of the foundation.

"And who is the man chosen to conduct this million dollar investigation into industrial unrest? One Mackenzie King, an alien, whose contribution to the industrial problem is a law that prescribes a jail sentence for the worker who dares to lay down his tools. If labor had any doubt as to his real intent, that doubt was removed by the letter read at this hearing. Under date of Aug. 6, 1914, Mackenzie King wrote to John D. Rockefeller."

Slowly, in a clear voice, Lawson read the letter King had written suggesting conditions arising from the European war might provide a solution to the industrial problem.

"The same thought was stated by President Welborn in a letter to Director McClement when he expressed pleasure over a two-foot fall of snow in Colorado, exclaiming, 'This ought to make a good many of the strikers who are living in tents provided by the organization seek the comfortable houses and employment at the mine.'

"Even were the source of the investigation less objectionable, what bearing can it possibly have on existing conditions? Mr. Rockefeller himself admitted that the Mackenzie King investigation will probably take many years. What is labor to do in the meantime? What is Colorado going to do? In response to this, Mr. Rockefeller says that 'the problem now is for all concerned to develop increasing good will.' Labor has been crushed by machine guns and hired soldiery; men, women and children have died; homes have been ruined and futures blighted; new thousands have been imported for another decade of exploitation; and we are to let bygones be bygones.

"Mr. Rockefeller, Sr., is quoted as saying that God must be brought to New York. In Colorado there is a suffering multitude that asks only for a little of the spirit of the Christ who died for human brotherhood. The causes of industrial unrest, Mr. Chairman, and Mr. Commissioners, are not to be removed by promises of endless investigations or by a sudden willingness to hold conferences. They lie in the treatment of men, not as chattels to be disposed of by deed and will; not in absentee landlordism, in the theft of natural resources, or indifference to the necessities and aspirations of those who toil in the dark for the benefit of those in the light. Nor will Mr. Rockefeller's proposal for the election of men in coal camps meet the needs of collective bargaining. This is in truth the shadow and not the substance, for men so elected, unless backed by an organization wider even than state lines will be utterly helpless in the hands of those who have sanctioned past grievances.

"In theory, at least, Mr. Rockefeller agrees to the principle of unionism. All that remains is to give his theory purpose and effect, something that cannot be done by simple expressions of good will or suddenly expressed desires for meetings. The United Mine Workers of America is the one organization that represents labor in this great industry. It has been in existence for 25 years. It has a present membership of more than

400,000 and enjoys contractual relations with employers in 17 states. It has kept these contracts inviolate.

"With these facts held clearly in mind, I insist that Mr. Rockefeller cannot give effect to his new point of view except with the cooperation of the United Mine Workers of America. By official conference with the executives of this organization, action should be taken to guarantee the enforcement of the mining and labor laws long violated in Colorado and the establishment of the principle of collective bargaining.

"Press reports give great publicity to meetings that are alleged to have been arranged between Mr. Rockefeller and the United Mine Workers' officials. Let me say on that subject that our one desire is for lasting industrial peace. We rejoice that after all these years Mr. Rockefeller is at last disposed to consider and confer with the workers his company officials have despised, ignored and endeavored to crush.

"We welcome any and every conference, but these meetings should be official and purposeful, not mere social visits designed to give the utterly false impression that industrial war has had no more vital cause than a failure on Mr. Rockefeller's part to shake hands. So far as possible, the remedies must be equal and be as real as our great wrongs."

Lawson's voice died away and he raised his head. A ripple of applause brought Chairman Walsh to his feet.

"We must have perfect order, please," he said sharply. "Mr. Lawson, does the machinery for securing representation by the men in the management of the Colorado Fuel & Iron Co., as outlined by Mr. Rockefeller, and now being put into effect in Colorado, constitute an effective basis for collective bargaining?"

"No, Mr. Chairman. It does not."

"Why not?"

"Because it leaves the men at the mercy of the employer as before."

At Chairman Walsh's request, Lawson gave the Commission the history of the United Mine Workers and his own case history beginning with his work in the mines of Pennsylvania as a boy of eight. Lawson introduced voluminous records to show the heavy death toll in Colorado mines and the reasons for tragedies that had claimed the lives of hundreds of men.

When the commission adjourned for the day, Rockefeller asked Lawson and Doyle to his offices at No. 26 Broadway. They debated a few minutes and then accepted. It was a strange meeting. The slight Rockefeller and the husky miners shook hands. Their backgrounds and their view points were as far apart as the poles. The one was perfectly at home in the fine office; the other two were more accustomed to the drab camps and the grim dangers of the coal mines.

Rockefeller questioned them on their opinion of his industrial plan, and both men reiterated the United Mine Workers position that it would not prove satisfactory. When they parted, the three men shook hands. As they left Rockefeller's office, Doyle could not contain himself.

"He looks human," he whispered to Lawson. "I'll bet if we could work him on the face of his Walsen mine for a week, fill him up on beans and sowbelly and get him good and grimy we could give him a card."

Lawson laughed; "Yes, I think we could at that."

When he returned to the stand the next day, Lawson renewed his attack on Rockefeller and his fellow coal operators. The Commission questioned him closely regarding the call to arms issued after Ludlow.

"The operators have used every subterfuge," Lawson said. "They have not failed to make statements that are not true concerning miners who were their former employes. And when they state that that call[3] is a violation of any law I want to deny the fact, and I want to ask the question, if you will permit it, to point out to me wherein that message is any vio-

[3] Mr. Lawson referred to the "Call to Arms" issued by the Policy Committee after the Ludlow massacre.

lation of Colorado law. I deny there is a violation of law in that message."

He refused to answer questions concerning arming of the miners because of the indictments pending against himself and hundreds of others in Colorado.

Lawson was excused at the end of his second day on the stand. Many witnesses followed him, including Amos Pinchot, John Mitchell, former head of the U.M.W.A., and former members of the Ludlow tent colony. The Commission moved gradually from the strike into a study of the Rockefeller Foundation. Andrew Carnegie, Rep. Charles A. Lindbergh of Minnesota, J. P. Morgan and finally the aging John D. Rockefeller, Sr., gave their views on the great foundations. The elder Rockefeller's testimony was brief. Like his son, he contended that he knew little of conditions in Colorado coal mines, but that he was willing for his workers to be organized in a union.

CHAPTER XIX

PERSECUTION

Coal company prestige was at a low ebb in February, 1915.
Publication of correspondence between the various operators
and between the executives of the Colorado Fuel & Iron Co.,
which had been subpenaed by the federal investigators and incorporated in the record for the general public, had proven
many of the charges made by the United Mine Workers during
the strike. Damaging admissions by witnesses had established
that Colorado was not a free state, but rather an industrial
kingdom ruled by political hangerson who winked at their constitutional duties and took their orders from the coal barons.
Despite their precarious position, it was obvious that the coal
operators were prepared to make one more effort to destroy
unionism in Colorado. A firm grip must be kept on the coal
counties. The sources of rich dividends must be protected. The
labor leaders, the men who had dared challenge the long established regime of wealth and monopoly, must be driven from
the state, jailed or even put to death. The white heat of adverse
public opinion would cool, and iron-handed control could be
resumed. The civil governments of Colorado, dominated by
money, still were available to carry out such a program. Men
like John Lawson were the backbone of the union movement
in the state. If they could be put out of the way, unionism

would collapse from lack of leadership. Fear would paralyze those who remained.

The last of the federal troops were leaving and the coal counties were free from the danger of armed conflict. The battle ground would be moved now from such fields as Ludlow to the courtrooms where company judges, company prosecutors and controlled juries offered better prospects of success for the coal oligarchy.

Lawson was not afraid, but his mind and soul were troubled. His ways were the direct ways of the coal miner, of the men who toiled to produce wealth. The courtroom world of whereas and wherefore was foreign to his nature. The first move in his behalf was a petition by Hawkins and Costigan for dismissal of the grand jury indictments on the ground that the jury had been hand-picked. District Judge Charles C. Butler of Denver, one of the few jurists in the state who had never asked for or received coal company beneficences, sat in Trinidad and ruled that Attorney General Farrar would have to answer the charge. The state immediately withdrew the indictments.

Lawson was jubilant, but the coal operators were not to be deterred. They went back into District Court in Trinidad Feb. 15 and filed a direct information charging John Lawson, Bernardo Coccio, Pete Catsulis, John Barulich, Don MacGregor, Tom Parrott, Robert Smith, Bartola Dolce, Charles Hines, Felix Sippi and Tom Ward with the murder of the guard, John Nimmo. The information was signed by James H. Wilson, a deputy sheriff who had participated in the fights near Ludlow. Lawson was released on his own cognizance and ordered to report March 3. The others named in the information were not arrested.

The Legislature was sitting in Denver and George Carlson, the avowed enemy of rum and the devil, was occupying the governor's office. While Hawkins and Costigan mapped plans for Lawson's defense, the Legislature passed a measure authorizing an increase from one to two in the number of judges in the Third Judicial District, which embraced Las Animas County. The governor was given authority to name a judge to serve until a regular election could be held.

"The coal companies are back of this scheme," Hawkins told Lawson, "and you'll see that I am right. It is a tricky move."

Governor Carlson, as soon as he had signed the bill, named Granby Hillyer of Lamar, Colo., a coal company attorney, as judge for the district. The General Assembly, known to the state as the Tainted Twentieth and as a fair rival for the ignoble honors previously conferred on the Robber Seventh and the Slinking Seventeenth, had made it possible for Governor Carlson to pick an ideal man for the task ahead. The governor would have had a difficult task finding a more biased man as far as unions were concerned. Hillyer had served several of the large coal companies in early cases against striking miners and had made public statements condemning the strike and its leaders, particularly John Lawson. What is more, he was a law partner of Frank West, deputy attorney general, who was selected by Farrar to handle strike prosecutions.

The first man to go to trial before Judge Hillyer was Louis Zancanelli, the little coal miner who had long been held on a charge of murdering the Baldwin-Felts detective, Belcher, on the streets of Trinidad. Robert Uhlich, a vice president of the State Federation of Labor, who was also charged with murder, was scheduled to be tried immediately after Zancanelli.

Zancanelli's defense was an alibi. He testified two men were seen running from the scene of the Belcher killing. The inference was the two men were the murderers. A hung jury resulted. Judge Hillyer immediately ordered a second trial and Judge Jesse G. Northcutt, attorney for the C. F. & I. Co., the Victor-American Fuel Co., and the Rocky Mountain Fuel Co., appeared in the case as a special prosecutor to assist West.

There can be no doubt that the coal operators sincerely believed Zancanelli was the slayer. Most certainly Belcher had been most foully slain, and it was equally certain that some striker had fired the well placed bullet. Zancanelli had been in the immediate vicinity, and it was known he shared the popular opinion that removal of the Baldwin-Felts detective would be a civic improvement. The coal operators erred, however, in their assumption that the killing of Belcher was the work of the United Mine Workers as an organization. While it may be granted that the murderer had the benefit of expert advice, particularly in regard to Belcher's body armor, and the assistance of well wishers who crowded around the detective at the fateful moment to shield the assassin, the killing was not an all-union affair.

The coal operators saw in Zancanelli a dupe and behind him they conjured up John Lawson and the United Mine Workers leadership. The little miner must be convicted if the leaders were to be reached in the courts. Judge Hillyer ordred the jurors drawn from an open venire instead of from the jury box required by state law. The company-controlled sheriff of Las Animas County provided the venire, and C. F. &. I. Co. guards were employed as bailiffs of the court. When the jury was finally chosen, it consisted of men who frankly admitted they were prejudiced against Zancanelli and the strikers. One juror, who was known to have made a wager on the outcome of the trial, was allowed by Judge Hillyer to remain despite the presentation of affidavits concerning the wager. Zancanelli was speedily convicted of first degree murder and sentenced to life imprisonment at hard labor.

In behalf of Lawson, Uhlich, and the remaining miners—162 men named in 42 informations—Hawkins sought a change of venue. The petition was denied and the same day the accused miners pleaded not guilty to the charges against them. Attorney General Farrar, after taking as much credit as he could in the newspapers for the Zancanelli conviction, asked a severance in the case of Lawson and secured it over Hawkins' objection. Bob Uhlich was scheduled to go to trial first.

"I want you to do something about Uhlich," Lawson told Hawkins. "He can't go to trial now. The man is sick. Months of confinement have taken his health. Someone else will have to go to trial first."

Hawkins stared at the big man.

"Do you know who goes to trial before this corporation set up if Uhlich goes over?"

"No, I don't, but I don't see what difference it makes."

"You'll go to trial if Uhlich doesn't."

Lawson's face was calm. He shrugged his shoulders in the manner of his Italian and Greek friends.

"I'll go to trial then," he said. "Uhlich is too sick."

There was no difficulty about getting the Uhlich trial set over. The coal company attorneys wanted Lawson as speedily as possible. He was the kingpin and his conviction would serve as an example to other labor leaders. The corporation attorneys didn't particularly care about the others. They wanted John Lawson.

Hawkins, through the medium of affidavits, again sought to disqualify Judge Hillyer, to quash the open venire and to disqualify the sheriff. A bill of particulars was sought and denied. It was impossible to tell if Lawson was accused of actually committing the murder or conspiring to commit it if a murder had actually occurred. The trial, one of the strangest in the history of American jurisprudence, opened in Las Animas County courthouse April 21, 1915. In outward appearance it was commonplace, with the state doing nothing more than calling a citizen before the bar of justice to establish guilt or innocence of a charged crime. In reality it was more than that. The State of Colorado was merely providing the setting for a contest between a labor leader, John R. Lawson, and a capitalist in far away New York, John D. Rockefeller, Jr. It was as if the guiding genius of the Colorado Fuel & Iron Co. had the mysterious power of multi-location. It sat on the bench in the person of Judge Hillyer and frowned down upon the courtroom. It

sat at the prosecutor's table in the person of Deputy Attorney
General West and glared at Lawson. It was in the venire, carefully selected by the Las Animas County sheriff.

Lawson paid little attention to the examination of the veniremen. During brief recesses he was silent and stared at the floor.
His wife was in California, but she was in his every thought.
Since the day their home in New Castle had been dynamited
long years before, Mrs. Lawson had not been well. Only a few
months ago she had been near death. Then she had rallied and
he had sent her to California to stay with one of her sisters.

Hawkins and Costigan did not notice Lawson's preoccupa-
tion. They had a hard battle on their hands and every second
of their time was devoted to it. They questioned veniremen
hour after hour. The sheriff's office had not placed a single
Italian, Greek or Mexican resident on the venire although these
racial groups made up a large part of the population.

The opening statement for the prosecution was made by Norton Montgomery, an assistant attorney general.

"We will show that John R. Lawson, an officer of the United
Mine Workers of America, imported arms and ammunition into
the Ludlow tent colony," he said. "We will show that Lawson
was in charge of the colony and was giving directions to the
strikers on that Oct. 25, 1913, when John Nimmo was shot
and killed while performing his duty. We will show that the
strikers attacked the deputies and that John Nimmo was killed
in the ensuing battle."

Hawkins waived his opening statement and the state began
presentation of its case. Charles and Ralph Tafoya, both company gunmen, testified they saw strikers running from the
tent colony toward the cut where deputies were stationed. Coroner Roy Campbell and Dr. Perry Jaffa, the county physician,
testified that the bullet that killed Nimmo entered the side of
his leg, a few inches below the hip. Then Lieutenant Linderfelt took the stand. Lawson stared at the military officer and
gunman. He always thought of Linderfelt by the strikers' name

for him—Linderfelt the Butcher. This was the man who had clubbed Louie Tikas that tragic night of April 20; this was the man who terrorized men, women and children for many months. Now he was here on the stand to deliver a last thrust. Linderfelt was in a sullen mood. He answered questions slowly, deliberately, as though feeling his way.

"I was half way between Chicosa and the section house, at a ruined building south of Ramey, when I heard firing in the direction of Ludlow," Linderfelt related. "There was two men with me, and we spurred up our horses and got on the hill and saw that there was a fight going on over in the direction of Water Tank Hill, so we spurred up our horses down the road as far as Ramey, passing the saloon when we were fired on."

His voice droned on and on. Lawson closed his eyes. He had heard the events of Oct. 25 told over and over again, but he had no personal knowledge of the fight. He only knew he had not fired a shot, had not taken part in the fighting, and had spent all of his time looking after women and children. He heard Linderfelt testify that he fired in the direction of the strikers whenever he saw anything to fire at, and that his immediate companions in the battle were Tex Aultman and Bob Hartman, gunmen imported from Texas.

Thad Sower, former broncho busting champion of the world, gave the most damaging testimony. He told the jury that he and a gunman named Wilson were with Nimmo during the fighting.

"Nimmo was a little ahead of me, running from telegraph pole to telegraph pole," Sower drawled. "When he was hit, he turned and said, 'I guess they got me, boys.' "

Sower declared he helped Nimmo back toward the deputies' position until the guard died.

"There were no shots being fired by the deputies when Nimmo was hit," he asserted.

Under cross-examination by Hawkins, Sower admitted he had been a gunman and guard in the 1903 strike, and that he went from Julesburg in Northern Colorado to Trinidad, a distance of more than 350 miles, in October, 1913, to become a guard and a deputy sheriff of Las Animas County.

A number of guards were placed on the stand by the state. Some said Nimmo was facing the miners when he was shot; others said he had his back to the miners. They could not agree on what had happened. Several who testified were forced to admit that they did not know Nimmo and never saw him until they viewed his body at Ludlow station. A Baldwin-Felts gunman, Charles Snyder, admitted he was looking for money.

"Sure, I'm out for the money," he said when Hawkins cross-examined him on his statements that he saw arms shipped to Lawson and that he heard Lawson and Mother Jones urge the strikers to fight.

"I went to Lawson and asked for money, telling him I would get it from the other side if he didn't give it to me," Snyder said in a scarcely audible voice. The man's face was covered with perspiration and he squirmed uneasily in the witness chair.

"Isn't it a fact that you tried to get money from the union and the Baldwin-Felts people at the same time?" Hawkins asked.

"Yes, it is," was the reply. "I'm out for the money."

"When you testified you heard Lawson and Mother Jones tell the strikers at Ludlow not to hesitate to fight, didn't you hear them say that under the constitution of this state and nation they had a perfect right to defend their tent homes?"

"Yes, I believe I did hear them say that, too," Snyder said in a weak voice.

"Didn't they tell the strikers their tent homes were as sacred as the palace of a millionaire?"

"Yes, I believe they did."

"Why didn't you tell that to the judge and jury?"

Snyder did not reply. Before he escaped from the stand, Hawkins had brought out that the witness had worked as a mine guard in 1911. The following year he had denounced the coal operators and the Baldwin-Felts Detective Agency, and

had hired out to the United Mine Workers as a spy. He returned to the mine owners and the Baldwin-Felts in 1913. He
also admitted he had been employed by the Mine Owners' Association to help prosecute cases against miners. Another state
witness, Charles Fanning, a guard, gave essentially the same testimony.

Hawkins and Costigan could not hide their contempt while
they questioned the two men. Mine guards were hated by union
men, despised by their own employers and disliked by the general public. Briefs could be written for the strikers and the
mine owners, but it would have required an extremely imagi-
native mind to have found a good word for the guards. They
were mercenaries, but they lacked the courage of the paid soldier
who must face a trained, well-equipped enemy to earn his
money. The guards came from the slums, the hobo jungles and
the big city underworlds to sell their warped souls to the highest
bidders. In the mining districts, guards were considered much
lower in the human scale than the strike breaker whom Jack
London had described as "a two-legged animal with a corkscrew
soul, a water-logged brain, and a backbone made of jelly and
glue."

While the Lawson trial was in progress, Trinidad was filled
with Baldwin-Felts detectives, mine guards and union spies.
The miasma of invisible government rested over the city. If
Hawkins or Costigan so much as stepped into a restroom, a
Baldwin-Felts detective followed. Tables in restaurants had to
be chosen with the utmost care as eavesdroppers and spotters
were everywhere. If two men stopped on the street to talk, a
stranger would invariably appear and fumble with a cigarette
and a match—within ear shot. Men selected their barbershops
and their cigar stands with reference to the chance of being
sleuthed. Officials of the Colorado Fuel & Iron Co. received detailed reports each night on what Lawson and his attorneys had
said or done during the day. The names of persons who went
in and out of union headquarters were reported. The coal com-

pany executives knew where the union men ate, what they ate, and who they talked to. The union spy system was fully as efficient. Its sleuths trailed C. F. & I. and state officials every hour of the day and night. Not a single detail escaped them. If Judge Northcutt took a drink of water, it was reported to Hawkins a short time later. If Northcutt talked to Judge Hillyer, the time, place, and often the import of the conversation were carried to union headquarters. Among the spies on both camps were those who sold information to both the union and the C. F. & I. The most faithful of the C. F. & I. henchmen were not above accepting union dollars for a bit of information, and there were union members who sneaked up to Judge Northcutt's office each night to give detailed reports on activities of the United Mine Workers.

CHAPTER XX
THE VERDICT

John Lawson's fight for freedom began in earnest the third day of the trial when the state concluded its case and Horace Hawkins made an opening statement to Judge Hillyer and the jury.

"We will show that neither the speeches of John Lawson nor Mother Jones were incendiary as the witnesses of the state have given the jury to infer," Hawkins said. "We will show, on the contrary, that both the defendant and Mother Jones always counselled peace and tried to allay excitement. We will show that it was only after miners had been killed during repeated attacks by mine guards that Lawson bought guns for the inhabitants of the tent colony at Ludlow. And we'll show they were purchased strictly for defense. We will prove that Oct. 25, the day Lawson is charged with having killed Nimmo, was pay day in the Ludlow Camp; that while miners were getting their union benefits shots were heard. We will prove a party of miners were fired on first by guards stationed in a section house where they have admitted much ammunition was stored. We will prove that Lawson did not leave the tent colony but once during the battle and then only to escort Anne Cameron, daughter of the mine superintendent at Hastings, out of danger. If the Court please, we will call Mrs. Elizabeth Bayes."

Mrs. Bayes, wife of a farmer near Ludlow, told of seeing the miners lined up for their benefits the afternoon of Oct. 25 as she was driving to Hastings with produce.

"There was no excitement around the camp," she said. "At Hastings I heard there was trouble and a number of men started down toward the colony. On my way back home, I met Miss Cameron and the hack driver."

John Lawson took the stand in his own defense the second day. The crowded courtroom was quiet, orderly. Judge Hillyer leaned forward. Attorney West played with a pencil as Lawson told of his movements on the afternoon of Oct. 25, and denied he left the colony except to escort Miss Cameron. Montgomery conducted the cross-examination.

"How many guns did the union buy and ship into the colony between Oct. 1 and Oct. 25?" Montgomery asked.

"I couldn't tell, because I don't know."

"Don't you know there were four or five hundred?"

"I do not know any such thing."

Montgomery was very insistent about the number of guns.

"Didn't you tell Major Lee there were 600 men in the colony and each man had a gun?"

"Positively—no," Lawson replied, raising his voice.

"You didn't have that many?"

"No."

"About how many did you have?"

"I should think over a hundred."

"Would you say three hundred?"

"I should think less."

Stung by a sneer on Montgomery's face, Lawson amplified his answer:

"I wished we had a thousand to defend our women and children the day of the massacre."

Montgomery tried to get Lawson to say he was on the firing line the day Nimmo was killed, but the big labor leader steadfastly contended he was in the colony, caring for women and children.

"Were these the same women and children you have mentioned several times?" Montgomery asked sarcastically.

"Yes," Lawson flashed back, "the same 200 women and 400 children whom the mine guards were attacking. And the same arroyo."

Mike Martino was put on the stand as a witness in rebuttal of Lawson's testimony. He had little to offer, but Hawkins' cross-examination brought out several interesting points.

"Are you working for the Colorado Fuel & Iron Co.?"

"Yes."

"When did you come to town?"

"This morning," Martino replied.

"And you called at the office of Mr. Northcutt?"

"Why shouldn't he?" Montgomery cried, leaping to his feet. "His offices are headquarters for the state's attorneys."

"Is this a confession?" Hawkins asked with a smile.

Hawkins had a little of the manner of Henry Clay, the old-fashioned courtliness of ante-bellum days. He was suave and urbane in his handling of juries and witnesses. He did not browbeat. The instincts of a gentleman of the old school guided his every move. Hawkins was never overawed by his opposition. The Supreme Court of the United States didn't look a bit different to him than the humblest country justice of the peace. Every question he had asked in this difficult trial had been resisted by the corporation attorneys and practically every ruling of the court had been against him, yet he held on with bulldog tenacity. His persistence in the face of great odds was reminiscent of an earlier day in a Colorado court when a judge had ordered him to sit down. Hawkins had stared back at the judge and said, "Your Honor, the only way I know how to defend my clients is on my feet." There were no tricks of manner, no bombast, and no flashy claptrap in Hawkins. He was business-like and alert to make the most of every opportunity. Costigan was equally courteous and suave, but his listeners readily recognized that a great flame burned within him. Slightly built, dark, with a fine head of black hair that showed traces of silver, the young attorney was throwing away immediate prospects of a political career by representing the miners.

"Are you going to send this fine, spendid fellow to the gallows?" Costigan asked the jury, pointing a thin finger at Lawson. Late afternoon shadows were creeping across Trinidad. The trial was drawing to a close. "I take it for granted, gentlemen, that in all the years you have lived here you have never heard of a case of this kind. The defendant is not the only one on trial. Prosecutor West has suggested that sinister influences were at work. We did not say this; the evidence indicated it. The trail of this insidious influence has been apparent. The coal company influence surrounds the court room. Baldwin-Felts detectives are standing all about here, and those interested are visiting and fraternizing at the offices of Jesse G. Northcutt, the attorney for the coal companies."

Costigan insisted that the state's entire case against Lawson rested on the testimony of two perjurors. Hawkins followed him with a final appeal to the jury.

"You couldn't hang a yellow dog, a known sheep killer, on the testimony of such men as the state has called to the stand in this case," Hawkins said quietly. "Your children's children will tell with pride of your verdict in this epochal case, and they will frame you in their hearts as men who stood like a bulwark for American liberty."

When Hawkins had finished, Montgomery analyzed the state's case and denied that the coal barons were behind the prosecution. He asked for the death penalty. Judge Hillyer turned toward the jury.

"It must appear from the evidence that the slayer of John Nimmo was the assailant and not merely shooting in defense of his life," Judge Hillyer said. "If attacked, the miners at Ludlow

were justified in returning the fire of their assailants and leaving
the colony to fight. This defendant had a right to buy arms and
send them to the colony for defensive purposes only. It is for
the jury to determine whether or not the defendant exceeded
that right. The jury can take into consideration the defendant's
reputation."

The case was placed in the hands of the jury at 9:30 p.m.,
May 1, 1915. It was Saturday night.

As the jury filed out, John Lawson looked over the packed
court room. Not a person in the audience stirred. On a bench
near the front of the room, he saw a weather-worn old couple
holding hands. These were the parents of John Nimmo. Their
tragic eyes met his, and he looked away, sick at heart for this
aged pair. Then Lawson's eyes met those of a little woman in
black, an Italian with the youth not wholly stamped from her
face. She, too, brought pity to his heart for this was Mary Petrucci, who had lost her three children in the Black Hole of Ludlow. His eyes left her and traveled on across the court room,
across row on row of swarthy faces—Italian, Slavic, Greek, Austrian—faces lined and seamed, patient and silent. Many of these
inarticulate workmen were caught in the same toils that had
ensnared John Lawson. Their trials would follow. With him
they would rise or fall. The audience stirred and workworn
women came forward with their babies.

"Will you please to kees my bambino, Mr. Lawson?"

Lawson took the little one from its mother's arms and kissed
it lightly on the cheek. Would to God that it would never have
to undergo the privations and sufferings of its parents. He
handed the baby back to the mother and turned aside. Hawkins
gripped his arm.

"Come on, John, we're going back to the hotel," Hawkins
said kindly. "If the jury finishes, we'll all be called. You need
rest."

The jury did not report that night. Early Sunday there were reports that Juror Richards was ill in bed and that a verdict would be delayed. Lawson paced back and forth in the room. He did not go out on the streets during the morning. Within him a battle was raging. An adverse verdict would probably mean convictions for scores of other men who were as innocent as himself. Then, too, he had to think about the effect on Olive. The shock might be too much for her. He was still pacing after midnight when Hawkins walked into the room.

"The jury has been locked up, John," Hawkins said. "There won't be a verdict now before noon at the earliest. Go to bed."

Lawson obeyed, and, though he did not think he could sleep, his eyes closed almost the moment he got in bed. John Lawson was tired out, mentally and physically. By morning, however, he was again in control of his nerves and outwardly was the same calm, self-assured Lawson the miners loved. He even managed a grin late in the morning when Hawkins told him that the jury had agreed on a verdict of guilty, but hadn't been able to agree on a penalty.

"I suppose most of them want to send my head to Rockefeller," he said good-naturedly.

"It isn't funny, John," Hawkins replied. "Eleven want the death penalty, if my reports are correct, and one man is holding out for life imprisonment."

"The one probably thinks life imprisonment is worse than death," Lawson said.

It was shortly after 1 p.m. when the expected call came. The jury was ready to report. Hawkins and Lawson hurried to the courtroom. It was packed with expectant men and women, many of whom had been on hand since early morning. At 2 p.m., in response to a curt direction from Judge Hillyer, J. O. Rosebrough, the jury foreman, handed the verdict to the court clerk who read in a loud voice:

"We, the members of the jury, find the defendant, John Lawson, guilty of murder as charged . . ."

Lawson smiled and glanced at Hawkins who was staring at the clerk as though fascinated. He heard the words "life imprisonment." So the lone juror had won his point.

"It's a long way to Tipperary," Lawson whispered loudly. Hawkins did not hear him. The attorney demanded that the jury be polled and, when that was done, reserved an exception and asked for 30 days in which to file a motion for a new trial.

"Granted," Judge Hillyer said, the suggestion of a smirk on his face.

"Your Honor," Hawkins said, "I would like to ask that the defendant be placed in the custody of his attorneys until the motion can be filed."

"The court will grant your request for the moment," Judge Hillyer said. "The court wants to determine if such a procedure is legal before giving a final decision."

Lawson went directly to his room in the Toltec Hotel and packed up his clothing, papers and other effects. He expected to be sent to jail immediately. The task done, he went downstairs to Hawkins' room.

"Have you got your breath yet, John?" Hawkins asked.

"I never lost it," Lawson replied. "If nobody quits until I do there will be no quitting."

"The newspaper boys want a statement. I'll have them sent up."

Lawson faced the reporters calmly.

"I'll give you a statement," he said. "The verdict verifies my statement to the Industrial Relations Committee in Denver before the committee went east. At that time I told them that John D. Rockefeller could take the life, liberty, and destroy the property of any man who opposed him. He has demonstrated that he is greater than government and higher than the law. They can put me in jail until the walls crumble, but they cannot stifle the cause for which I stand or destroy the great struggle in the interests of humanity. I shall fight for these principles as hard as I can, in jail or out, as long as I live. There is no compromise on this job. Justice and right will and must prevail in the end."

Lawson turned aside and stared out the window into the street. He had said all he could say for the moment. He heard Hawkins' voice.

"This verdict cannot stand, boys," the attorney said. "There is absolutely no evidence to sustain it."

Then the reporters were gone.

"I'm going to wire Olive now," Lawson said. "She ought to know."

"Go ahead, John. But be careful what you tell her."

"Don't worry; she has been brought up as the wife of a union man and a miner. She's gone through this struggle with me, and she'll know this is just a part of it. Thank God Fern is too young to really understand what it is all about."

The operators sprang one of their many surprises late that afternoon. The Trinidad paper, owned and controlled by Judge Northcutt, and press dispatches sent out of Trinidad, carried long stories on the conviction and equally long stories on an alleged death threat against Judge Hillyer. It was revealed (sic) by Judge Northcutt's paper[1] that an anonymous letter had been received by the jurist a week before, threatening death to himself and all persons identified with No. 26 Broadway if Lawson was convicted. Although the Trinidad Chronicle-News did not have an engraving plant, it was ready for the big story with a facsimile of the alleged letter. Reproduced throughout the country in newspapers, the letter read:

"judge hillery you had better go slow for iff you punish zancanelli lawson or any of those innocent men be punished if the law don't condemn you you will find that the worst has never come off * * * you warn all of them * * * Everyone that ever had anything to do with it * * * If there is not enough men in

[1] Trinidad Chronicle-News, May 3, 1915.

the United States they can and will come across the water * * *
If a few lose their lives the next generation will live in peace
* * * Stop, O think & pray to your God and stop our taxes is
high enough * * * I never have been in a Colorado coal mine *
no I never seen you or hawkins but I pray to my God to stop this
* * I was awaken out of my sleep to rite this warning to you of
your danger * * * I write this in the fear of God trust you will
heed it for I have heard many things but this warning should do
you now.

"Study & Pray I treat you set them right then stop our taxes.
This is for your attention & others good * * * There will be
bushwhacking as long as time it will go down one generation
after another * * * For what their fathers and grandfathers
has done * * * lippit had friends that came to his rescue and so
will zancanelli and lawson and all of them."

John Lawson roared with laughter when he read it. He
tossed the newspaper over to Hawkins.

"I've been giving the operators too much credit," he said.
"Even a child could see that this is a forgery and the purpose
behind it."

Hawkins read the letter carefully.

"Yes," he agreed. "It is a very crude attempt to divert public
attention from your conviction. Look here, the name on the
envelope is Hillyer and in the letter it is Hillery. The man
spells write two different ways in the letter and if with one f
and with two."

Judge Northcutt's newspaper was highly indignant. It gave
the Lawson conviction story a three column head and the sinister
letter a four column line, side by side. Underneath was a front
page editorial headed, "The Black Hand of Anarchy."

"Has the time come in Las Animas County when an individual selected to occupy the high and dignified position of judge
and who, in pursuance of this lawful duty, presides at the trial
of men charged by the people with violations of the law, is subjected to the threats and intimidating warnings of anonymous

blackhand letters?" the Chronicle asked. "Have the dynamiters and torch bearers and the labor agitators not yet completed their murderous work in the Trinidad coal fields and Colorado? Does the consuming passion of hatred and malice against the defenders and upholders of law and order still incite a lawless element of humanity to counsel or commit assassination? Think of it, citizens of Trinidad! What are we coming to?"

The letter and story accompanying it were a joke to others than Lawson. That night, scores of union men and citizens who had no connection with organized labor visited him at the Toltec Hotel. They laughed and joked about the clumsy letter.

"These mine guards never got close enough to our foreign miners to learn the tricks of their dialect," one miner told Lawson. "They were too busy running or skulking. The company man who wrote this letter bungled the job."

Judge Hillyer agreed that same night to release Lawson to his attorneys under bond of $20,000 pending the filing of a motion for a new trial. The bond was posted immediately. Lawson was free to leave Trinidad for the time being.

In Los Angeles, Olive told reporters:

"We'll go to him now. I have not slept since I received John's telegram. My daughter and I have not lost confidence. They never will send him to the penitentiary. The verdict will be set aside. Why, I am entirely familiar with every detail of the case. My husband was miles from where the deputy was killed that day. I am astounded over the verdict. Ten million laboring men are crying for justice for my husband. I am proud to say that the workingmen by whom he stood when they needed a leader and a friend are returning his friendship by their loyalty to him in this crisis."

John P. White, national president of the United Mine Workers, sent out a call from Cleveland, Ohio, for a special meeting of the international board to consider the Lawson case.

"Unless John Lawson is accorded fair treatment and vindicated the United Mine Workers will call another strike in

Colorado as a protest against the tyrannical conditions that prevail in the state," White announced.

From Indianapolis, Vice President Hayes delivered a withering blast at the coal operators.

"What about the massacre of women and children by subsidized militia and gunmen, the majority of whom proved to be in the employ of the coal companies?" he asked. "Not a single one of those murderers has ever been brought to trial and, furthermore, they never will be, because the coal companies will not permit it. The procedure of the courts in Southern Colorado cannot be equalled anywhere in the United States or anywhere in the civilized world. Darkest Russia is a haven of refuge compared to that region."

Protests arose on every side as the full import of the Lawson conviction sank home.

The Denver Express found the verdict "amazing and appalling." In a front page editorial, the newspaper said the answer could be found in one word: Rockefeller.

"Young Rockefeller is the man who said when he met John Lawson in New York that he had never seen a finer specimen of manhood than the Colorado strike leader," the editorial said. "He is the man who testified before the Industrial Relations Commission that we ought to work now for peace and good will.

"He is also the man who is at the bottom of the troubles in Las Animas County. What he says goes down in that corner of his kingdom. If John D. Rockefeller, Jr., would say the word, the prosecutions of such men as Lawson would stop tomorrow.

"What is the use of blinking the truth and beating about the bush?

"Lawson was tried in revenge for the strong fight he put up for his fellow-toilers against the big coal companies of this state. He was convicted as a warning to other labor leaders of what they might expect if they fought intrenched capital to a finish. The indictments hanging over the heads of hundreds of men are for the purpose of hammering down labor at the expense of the people of the state who are trying to heal instead of open strike sores. Why did Governor Carlson interfere and take these prosecutions out of the hands of the local district attorney at Trinidad? Ask a thousand men down there and they will give the same answer. He is, they say, paying a political debt to the coal companies for the support that gave him the nomination for governor. But in the end it is Colorado that foots the bill. The people of this state have paid for the strike out of their pockets. They paid in paralyzed industry, in the heavy expenses of maintaining the militia in the field, in the advanced price of coal, with the blood of women and children."

Hawkins announced he would file application for the new trial within the 30-day period on eight grounds:

1. That Granby Hillyer was disqualified from acting as judge, having been attorney for Rockefeller's Colorado Fuel & Iron Co. and allied coal companies in previous strike cases, and because of expressions of hostility toward Lawson prior to the trial.

2. Because the jury was placed in charge of bailiffs who were Rockefeller mine guards.

3. The verdict was contradictory to evidence and based upon passion and prejudice.

4. Because challenges to jurors who had demonstrated prejudice were over-ruled.

5. Because names of jurors were selected from an open venire rather than from a jury box as required by law.

6. Exclusion of proper and competent evidence, and the admission of improper and incompetent evidence.

7. Refusal of the court to permit Lawson alternate challenges to jurors who had shown prejudice, and the adoption of a system of challenging previously condemned by the Colorado Supreme Court.

Edward P. Costigan, in a statement in the Hawkins announcement, said the Lawson verdict was an overthrow of reason and law. He accused the Rockefellers of sowing the wind.

"Those who are best acquainted with Lawson know him to be an innocent man," Costigan said. "The verdict is a disgrace. Nowhere but in Southern Colorado would it be possible. The future will vindicate Lawson, and all the more because of the martyrdom with which he is unjustly threatened."

CHAPTER XXI

ORGANIZED PROTESTS

Miners, union officials and friendly men and women from every walk of life greeted John Lawson in the Union Station in Denver May 5, 1915, when he stepped off the early morning train from Trinidad. A woman ran forward, threw her arms about him, and kissed him, crying out that he was a victim of greed. A second woman, who had also broken away from the crowd, waited quietly until he approached and then shook his hand warmly.

"I hope you'll win out, Mr. Lawson," she said in a low voice. He thanked her. The welcomers swarmed around him. A burly miner seized his hand and blurted tearfully:

"It is a damned shame."

Newspaper reporters elbowed their way to him and asked for a statement.

"Well, boys, when I was in New York before the Industrial Relations Commission, John D. Rockefeller shook hands with me and remarked, 'I am sincere.' I wondered at the time what he meant. Now I know. I am confident, though, that I will eventually go free."

"Just stand around this way and smile a little," a photographer called.

"I am smiling," Lawson replied. "Just shoot any time you like."

From the station, Lawson went to union headquarters in the German-American Trust Bldg. where huge stacks of telegrams from every part of the country awaited him. He glanced over them quickly. Labor was aroused as never before in its long and turbulent history. He didn't spend much time with the messages, for he was tired. Rest was what he needed most at the moment, not kind words. He left the office and went directly to the home of his mother-in-law, Mrs. Mary Hood. There was a wire there from Olive: "Dear Jack: We haven't lost yet. Am fine." It was so like her, calm yet courageous. She would be back home in a few days to be at his side, as she had always been during his troubles.

Hawkins had stayed on in Trinidad. He had much work to do in both Las Animas and Huerfano counties as in these counties alone there were 1,155 potential indictments against strikers in the hands of the attorney general's men. In addition, Hawkins had the Lawson petition, 368 other murder indictments and informations, 191 arson cases and 100 informations charging assaults to kill, all directed against miners and members of the United Mine Workers of America.

Through affidavits, Hawkins sought to show that the Lawson jury was intimidated. Grover Hall, one of the jurors, said he believed Lawson to be innocent. On the Sunday before the verdict was returned, Hall said in his affidavit, Bailiff Frank Gooden told him that his wife was desperately ill and to "agree with the rest of the jury on a verdict of guilty."

Hall said he continued to hold out for an acquittal although he was worried about his wife and had no means of communicating with her or anyone else to learn how ill she might be. Two hours before the verdict was agreed upon, he said, Gooden looked in on the jury and said that Judge Hillyer "had ordered the jurors to be locked up in one room and given no food or drink until they agreed on a verdict." The other members of the jury, Hall's affidavit said, then berated him and said he would be responsible for their being kept without food. Hall said he then gave in and voted for a verdict of guilty "because of the threats so made, and because of intense anguish of mind, owing to the reported dangerous illness of my wife."

Hall had never served on a jury before, he said, and did not know that jurors could not be starved into verdicts.

A second affidavit, secured from Mrs. Bertha Hall, the wife, related that Zeke Martin, a deputy sheriff and labor baiter, called at her house Sunday night and insisted she was ill and needed a doctor. She finally called her own physician who told her she was all right.

"I was surprised when my husband called and told me Gooden had said I was seriously ill," she said.

Three other jurors, E. M. Forbes, Homer Canterbury and Minor Duggan, verified Hall's story in affidavits of their own.

While Hawkins was incorporating the affidavits into the Lawson petition for a new trial, the attorney general's staff secured counter affidavits and filed them with the court. Forbes, Canterbury, and three others, William Wilson, C. Spurgeon Herring and John Rosebrough, asserted they considered Gooden's threat of no food or drink as a joke and that no one on the jury took it seriously. They admitted they knew Hall's wife was supposed to be ill. Some said they heard Gooden tell Hall that his wife was sick; others said they had heard it from fellow jurors. One of the remarkable features of the counter affidavits was that they confirmed rather than contradicted those secured by Hawkins.

Hawkins also had reports of two mine guards who were present at Ludlow the day John Nimmo fell and were willing to make affidavits in John Lawson's behalf.

Meanwhile, protests against the conviction were heard in every corner of the United States. Newspapers and magazines analyzed the case and editorialized.

"Colorado law asserts itself bravely as it convicts John R. Lawson of murder in the first degree," The New York World said. "Lawson led the striking miners at Ludlow when the tent colonies in which their families lived were attacked by deputy sheriffs. The deputy sheriffs were for the most part imported gunmen, many of them on the payroll of the Colorado Fuel & Iron Co. In one of the fights that preceded the massacre of women and children at Ludlow a deputy was shot. It was not claimed that Lawson fired the shot, but as he was the chief of what the law regards as a conspiracy to commit a crime he was held responsible. This is an excellent law where law obtains. It is a very poor law in a county like Las Animas where the State of Colorado had abdicated in favor of the corporations and their murderous hirelings. Of the responsibility of the great absentee, the state itself, there can be no question. Colorado will hardly convict itself in its own courts. But it might at least forego the further infamy of punishing men for offenses that would not have been committed had Colorado done its duty."

The Cleveland Citizen found Lawson less guilty "than was John D. Rockefeller for the Ludlow massacre, but the oily plutocrat and his Colorado henchmen will not only never be tried for that horrible crime, they will never even be indicted."

The labor newspapers were more bombastic in their stinging editorials. They sent up a cry against the Rockefellers and called for an end of their rule over industry in the United States. The Masses carried a cartoon picturing John D. Rockefeller, Jr., whispering to his father in church: "Well, Pa, we've got John Lawson out of the way."

Harper's Weekly expressed belief that "enough of us will realize in time that our dollar-crazed autocrats are manufacturing rebels and fomenting rebellion."

George Creel, writing in Harper's,[1] contended:

"Upon informations filed by a coal company attorney general, the captains of a lost cause have been dragged into court to stand trial for murder before a jury of coal company retainers hand-picked by a coal company sheriff at the behest of a coal company judge who has furthermore allowed the coal com-

[1] Harper's Magazine, May 22, 1915.

panies to furnish their own paid attorneys as special prosecutors.
There is to be no cessation in the campaign of hate. The work
of extermination that United States troops kept the imported
gunmen from finishing up is now to be concluded by legal
machinery that the coal companies own and direct. Having
proved to the working class of the United States that the militia
is a strikebreaking agency, the Colorado operators are preparing
to demonstrate that the courts are a strike-punishing agency.
Evidently nothing short of a commune will satisfy their ingrown
bourbonism."

Writers and speakers of widely varying backgrounds and beliefs seemed to realize that nothing would save the union leaders
except possibly the kindling of national indignation. This avenue seemed to be the only one open as the coal barons had already
defied the President of the United States, insulted Congress,
ignored federal mediators as though they were unclean, assaulted, burned and murdered. The kingdoms of Las Animas and
Huerfano were private property by right of bribery, coercion,
the club and the machine gun. The coal counties were owned
and controlled by the coal operators, and the independent citizens in these counties were too few in number to recall corrupt
sheriffs and other officers.

Despite the criticism, Attorney General Farrar plunged ahead.
He had two scalps on his belt, those of Lawson and little Louis
Zancanelli, and he intended to have more. Zancanelli was pacing
up and down the iron-railed platform in the Trinidad jail the
afternoon Hawkins filed a petition with Judge Hillyer for his
third trial. Zancanelli crossed himself and prayed as best he
could. His lips moved and his eyes turned upward to the slate-
gray ceiling, cold and forbidding, but he had little hope. The
conviction of Lawson six days before had convinced him that he,
too, must go to prison for life. After all, he had had two trials.
In the first the jury had disagreed and in the second he had been
convicted and sentenced to life imprisonment. The appeal for a
new trial charged bias on the part of judge and jury, and asserted

Zancanelli was the victim of a case of mistaken identity. Included in the petition was an affidavit to the effect that Steve Burkhard, a Trinidad merchant and juror in the second Zancanelli trial, had made a wager on the outcome with Lee Rollins, a barber. The court had a counter-affidavit in its possession.

Over the protests of the prosecutors, who contended such an action might pave the way for questioning of every juror in each mine case, Hawkins finally obtained permission from Judge Hillyer to question Burkhard and Rollins before the court. The merchant readily admitted he had made a wager with Rollins on the first Zancanelli trial and that he had served as a juror in the second trial.

"After the first mistrial and prior to the day you were summoned you made another wager?" Hawkins asked.

"Yes, I offered to, but I don't consider it a wager."

"Did you not make the same proposition to him as on the former trial; did you not bet him two to one?"

"Yes, he accepted; but there was a proviso," Burkhard said. "If I was on the jury all bets were off."

"Were you expecting to be summoned as a juror?"

"No more than at any other time."

After he was summoned, Burkhard said, he offered to make another bet with Rollins.

"I poked my head in the door and told him it was a good chance to get his money back," Burkhard explained. "Jokingly, I offered to bet him four to one it would be a hung jury or a hung Dago."

The first bet was made, he said, at a time when the jury was out and could not know about it, and it was based upon his knowledge of jurors. He collected a shave and haircut on the first wager.

"Now, Mr. Burkhard," Hawkins said with a slight smile, "you made an affidavit regarding this affair. Do you know who drew it?"

Burkhard stiffened.

"I don't know who drew it," he said slowly. "I found it on my desk where it had been left."

Hawkins forced the merchant to admit he had gone to the office of Jesse G. Northcutt where he supplied information for preparation of the affidavit.

"Burkhard made this hung jury or hung Dago talk all right," Rollins testified. "I asked him when he was going to pay me on this last proposition and he said he wanted to wait until this case was disposed of."

Judge Hillyer refused Zancanelli a new trial, and Hawkins announced the case would be carried to the Colorado Supreme Court. With Zancanelli out of the way for the time being, the attorney general went after his third union man, Robert Uhlich, 33-year-old president of a miners' union local and a member of the sub-district United Mine Workers board, on a charge of killing Mack Powell, the striker who, while working as a cowboy, was killed near Ludlow as he sat his horse watching a battle between mine guards and strikers. Eleven others were named in the information with Uhlich, but they were not required by the state to appear.

Deputy Attorney General West opened the case with what were now regular statements. Uhlich had been seen issuing arms and ammunition to miners on Oct. 9, 1913, the day Powell was killed, and had played a role in a conspiracy to prevent operation of the coal mines.

"We expect to show that the defendant was armed with a rifle and six shooter that day, and that he later boasted of having killed Powell," West said.

In a counter statement, Hawkins charged the operators with importation of thugs and machine guns in a gigantic conspiracy to drive the miners out of their tent colonies.

"We will show that Powell was a union man in good standing and highly regarded by the strikers, and that Uhlich was not within 14 miles of the Ludlow tent colony the day Powell fell," Hawkins told the court.

Uhlich had been arrested Nov. 25, 1913, by militia on a charge of being a dangerous agitator and an alien. He was held in jail incommunicado for 25 days. At the end of that time he had managed to smuggle out a letter that told of brutal treatment. The letter was read before the State Federation of Labor and published in the press. His captors had then demanded that he issue a signed statement to the effect that General Chase and Major Boughton were not responsible for the treatment he received in jail. Bob Uhlich had refused, even when the militia baited the demand with a promise that he would be released at once. Shortly afterward, the first of several murder charges had been filed against him. The first Las Animas County grand jury failed to indict him, while the second had named him in four indictments. Uhlich was held in jail nine months. In September, 1914, he was released under $10,000 bond and the indictments were subsequently quashed when Hawkins successfully contended that the grand jury was illegally constituted. It was then that Attorney General Farrar stepped in with a direct information charging murder.

Two witnesses testified against Bob Uhlich. They were the state's star witnesses of the Lawson trial, Charles Snyder and J. R. Petty alias Pat Murphy, a confessed forger. Both men were Baldwin-Felts detectives. Hawkins placed 10 witnesses on the stand. All of them testified they had seen and talked with Bob Uhlich in Trinidad the day Powell was killed near Ludlow. It took the jury only three hours to return a verdict of not guilty. The operators had lost their first important case.

The Uhlich acquittal heartened the union leaders. They decided to carry their fight to the general public before Lawson's petition for a new trial was filed with the court. The first step was a protest meeting in Denver. Olive and Fern had returned to Denver to attend.

Before the meeting,[2] seven thousand men, women and children paraded through Denver's business section. They marched

[2] May 29, 1915.

with set faces through densely packed streets. A fife and drum corps, with a huge American flag in the center, led the way. Two hundred women, dressed in white, represented the Justice League. Fifty children, also in white, carried a monster banner bearing the words, "The Children Demand Justice for John Lawson." Then came the garment workers. A platoon of police opened the way through the streets. There were no automobiles or carriages. Everyone walked except the marshal, Benjamin F. Perry of the machinist's union, who was mounted.

At the head of the second division marched a 25-piece band followed by the tattered Ludlow flag which was carried by a stalwart Greek miner. Beside the flag bearer marched another swarthy miner, carrying a Greek flag in honor of the murdered Tikas. The railroad orders, miners and several hundred sympathetic citizens marched behind the two flags. In the third division, led by another band, marched the hosts of the Denver Trades and Labor Assembly. Union banners, interspersed with American flags, gave color to the parade. The fourth division consisted of members of the Building Trades Council—hundreds of carpenters, painters, bricklayers and other skilled workers. As the parade swept down 17th Street, coal company officials watched silently from the Denver Club. The union line did not hurl taunts, but as each group swung by, the cheer went up, "Hurrah for John Lawson."

At the corner of Lawrence and 17th streets, each division sent a mighty shout of approval up to a window in the German-American Trust Bldg., where two valiant warriors, John R. Lawson and old Mother Jones, stood, arm in arm, looking down into the street.

"Sure, boy, and they're all for you." Mother Jones beamed. "Everyone of them loves you."

The parade moved on to City Auditorium. It had originally been planned to hold the mass meeting at the State Capitol, but Governor Carlson had banned it at the last minute. Mrs. Lee Champion, president of the Justice League, opened the meeting.

"We have several speakers here," she said, "but first I want to present a charming young lady who has a few words to say to you. Miss Fern Lawson."

The crowd roared its approval when Fern, dressed in white, which contrasted sharply with her wealth of dark hair, stepped hesitantly forward. The little girl who had been thrown from her bed in New Castle years before when the Lawson home was dynamited was now a young lady of 15, known for her beauty. Her voice quavered and threatened to break as she thanked the thousands of Coloradans for what they had done for John R. Lawson and the indicted miners.

"It is not the liberty of my father alone that is in danger," she said. Her voice broke on the word "father" and she sobbed. "It is the liberty of every man, woman and child which is in danger. I thank you for my mother and myself for what you have done for my father and for us."

There were many glistening eyes in the audience as Fern fled back to her seat.

Mrs. Champion attacked the state government, the coal operators and the newspapers.

"Hundreds of indictments have been brought against miners," she said. "The operators go free though 23 persons, many of them women and children, were murdered at Ludlow. The Rocky Mountain News now asks you to forget that women and children were driven like rats into a trap and then murdered. It says the state has tried to make amends. That is an absolute untruth. Nor can the state make amends except by bringing to the bar of justice those who live by the corporations, those who are responsible for that reeking, putrid cesspool which exists in Southern Colorado. When the bankers, whom Bowers says he whipped into line, learn to consider all the people—when the chamber of commerce, which he also spanked, becomes a representative body instead of a society organization—when it becomes impossible for a governor to hire out the militia—when

those responsible for the murders at Ludlow have been brought
to justice—when all these things have happened, then, and only
then, will the state have made amends."

Mrs. Champion told the audience that authorities of the
University of Colorado were attempting to oust Professor Brewster from his position in the law school because he had espoused
the strikers' cause; that the Denver school system, at the insistence of a school board made up of relatives of Colorado Fuel &
Iron Co. officials, had denied the Justice League meeting places,
and that a vicious, lying campaign had been conducted against
every citizen who opposed C. F. & I. Co. domination.

"I have to be careful when I stand for justice or I will offend
someone at the University of Colorado," Professor Brewster said
when his turn came to speak. "I spent weeks independently investigating the strike. It was then that I first knew the man I
am now proud to call my friend, John R. Lawson. If I were to
tell you the wrongs done by the militia alone it would take
hours. Militiamen in uniform robbed strikers of the few possessions they had. I do not blame every militiaman. There were
fine men in the militia. But I want you to notice one thing.
Did you ever hear of the recent legislature, which wanted to pay
coal companies for property destroyed, suggesting the state pay
back to the miners the money which the militiamen stole from
them?"

He condemned Judge Hillyer without mentioning him by
name.

"No reputable lawyer would sit in a case in which one of the
parties had previously retained him," the law instructor said.
"Do you suppose any man employed by the miners would have
the indecency to sit as judge in a case in which an operator was
to be tried? I am a lawyer. I don't intend to abuse any court.
But I can't conceal my contempt for a man who will accept an
appointment for special purposes to try special cases."

Congressman Frank Buchanan of Illinois and Clint C. Houston, president of the Denver Trades and Labor Assembly, urged union men to stand together in their common cause for justice. The campaign to free Lawson was under way.

CHAPTER XXII
THE LAWSON STATEMENT

The true report of a legislative committee, which had investigated General Chase and the militia during the occupation of Las Animas and Huerfano counties, came to light June 16, 1915. This was the report which Governor Ammons had insisted be toned down and the committee, at his request, had issued a much milder summary of its work. The correct report provided confirmation of charges made against the military organization by the miners.

"Our investigation convinced us," the report read, "that with the exception of the medical department and the band, the entire guard is in a deplorable and totally inefficient condition. While the committee is convinced that John Chase, the adjutant general, is a brave and fearless man, the committee is nonetheless convinced that it will be impossible for the guard to ever be brought to even a moderate state of efficiency with its present adjutant general. While we find thoroughly efficient and capable officers who are extremely earnest in their support of General Chase, we find that, for the most part, the so-called Chase faction is made up of officers either personally appointed by the present adjutant general or given their official positions through his direct influence, and among these are men who, the committee feels, are totally unfit for their positions.

"Among these also are a number of officers who are nothing more or less than chairwarmers during all the time that the militia is not on active duty, and these men for the most part are drawing salaries from the State of Colorado at all times. After a careful investigation the committee believes that the adjutant general of this or any other National Guard should perform only such duties as are directed by our own statutes and the United States Army regulations, and among these laws and rules we fail to find any authorizing the adjutant general to take command of any force while in the field.

"We also find that the adjutant general is continually at loggerheads with the war department of the United States, and that many orders and rules of the war department are totally ignored by the present adjutant general. The present roster of officers contains men absolutely and totally unfit for their positions, some because of gross incompetency, one or two because of cowardice, and a number because of frequent and, in some cases, habitual drunkenness."

The various officers and their records were listed in the report. Major Boughton, Captain Thomas Linderfelt, Lieutenant A. H. Chase, Captain John R. Charlesworth, Captain F. D. Bartlett, Colonel W. A. Davis, Colonel Edward Verdeckberg, Captain Charles C. Swope and Captain Harry E. Insley were listed as incompetents.

Of Lieutenant K. E. "Monte" Linderfelt, the committee said he was "the big black spot on the guard."

The day the committee's report was released, Hawkins went into District Court in Trinidad with his petition for a new trial for John Lawson. A lengthy document, it contained the affidavits of two coal company gunmen, C. A. Kingsbury and Barton S. White, who contended they were with John Nimmo when he was shot.

Kingsbury said he was near Nimmo when the guard fell and that no other person was within sight; that the state's witnesses, who told of Nimmo's crying out when he was struck, were nowhere near the scene. Thad Sower and other state witnesses, who had testified in great detail how Nimmo had died and what he said before he died, were not witnesses to Nimmo's death, Kingsbury contended. White's affidavit substantiated Kingsbury's and both men said they had been shot at by other guards during the day, and that to their positive knowledge other guards had been forced to complain of being shot at by their comrades. Both men expressed belief that Nimmo was killed unintentionally by a coal company bullet.

"It passes understanding," the Hawkins petition said, "how any rational person could parallel these diverse statements of self-styled witnesses of the death of Nimmo without a realization that he (Lawson) was being made the victim of an interweaving of imagination and perjured testimony. The evidence has wholly failed to establish that John Nimmo was shot by any striker; but, on the contrary, it has been satisfactorily established that he was shot by one of his own party. The evidence wholly failed to establish that the defendant was in any way connected with the party accused of, but not shown to be responsible for, the shooting of John Nimmo. The evidence wholly failed to establish any malice or premeditation of any kind, nature or description, express or implied, on the part of the defendant. . . . John R. Lawson was apparently convicted for no other reason than that he was one of the outstanding leaders responsible for the great industrial strike of 1913."

Hawkins recited contradictions in the trial in detail and concluded with the argument that "we cannot believe that in the presence of the showing made in this court, or any court of Anglo-Saxon traditions, or the well-founded and recognized land marks of American law, will hesitate by prompt rejection of the jury's verdict in this case to award the defendant a new opportunity to vindicate his name and preserve his liberty, and in so doing give assurance to all men everywhere that the ancient safeguards of human rights in America continue unshaken against whatever assault."

While Judge Hillyer had the petition under consideration, the regents of the University of Colorado dropped Professor Brewster from the faculty. Dr. Livingston Farrand, president of the state university, told him, Professor Brewster said, that there had been difficulties with appropriation committees of the Legislature because of his sympathy for the miners, and that in view of his appearance before the U. S. Industrial Relations Commission as a witness, his connection with the University must end.

At almost the same moment, the U. S. War Department announced in Washington that its investigators had found the Colorado National Guard in a deplorable state of demoralization and that 12 infantry companies had been dropped from the list of recognized units. Eleven other companies had been placed on probation for 12 months, and property worth $120,000 had been ordered returned to the federal government. The order was the most stinging rebuke ever given a national guard organization by the War Department.

Judge Hillyer delayed a decision on Lawson's petition for a new trial. He also delayed decisions on Hawkins' motions in a hundred cases in Huerfano County to declare himself disqualified to sit as judge, to grant a change of venue, and to issue an abatement of the cases. In Boulder County, the state moved to press murder charges against Ed Doyle, Jack Cassidy, John O'Connor, Joe Potestio and W. T. Hickey on grounds they had participated in the Hecla Mine fighting. The cases were set for July 19. When Hillyer finally denied Hawkins' motions in several minor cases, Hawkins went to the Colorado Supreme Court and asked for an order citing Hillyer to appear before the court and show cause why he should not be disqualified from sitting in the strike cases. The justices indicated they would like to hear the motion and act the following week before they adjourned for their summer recess.

John Lawson went to Trinidad to be on hand when Hillyer acted on his petition for a new trial. As a result he was not present in the Supreme Court July 12 when Hawkins argued for a writ of prohibition against Hillyer. While the attorney stood before the black-robed justices arguing his case, Judge Hillyer sent for Lawson. The big miner went into the Trinidad court without his attorney.

"I ask you to delay action on my petition until my lawyer, Mr. Hawkins, can get here tomorrow or soon thereafter from Denver," Lawson said. He was not a lawyer, but he knew he had a right to counsel when the court acted. Judge Hillyer said a delay could not be granted. And then John Lawson knew why there could be no delay. The Supreme Court might disqualify Hillyer. He, Lawson, must be railroaded into the penitentiary before that could happen.

Attorney Fred Clark of Trinidad, who had assisted Hawkins, hurried to the courtroom. Judge Hillyer classified the motion for a new trial under eleven separate heads, discussing each. He did not call for the bailiff, Gooden, to discover for himself the truth or falsity of the charges made by Hawkins. He found the new evidence contained in the affidavits of Kingsbury and White "merely cumulative" and stated that the methods of challenging the jury, to which the defense objected, would be allowed to stand. The petition for a new trial was denied. His discourse ended, Judge Hillyer leaned over the bench and stared at Lawson.

"Have you any statement as to why sentence should not now be pronounced against you?"

Lawson looked at Clark, desperation in his eyes, and then at the forbidding judge, the corporation attorney who was about to send him to the penitentiary for the rest of his life. Lawson felt his heart beat wildly and the blood pound in his temples. Then he suddenly felt calm and cold. He felt contempt for this man who dared violate every American court tradition to carry out a campaign of vengeance. Slowly, Lawson arose. The silence in the court was oppressive. Then Lawson spoke, in clear, measured tones.

"The court has asked me what, if anything, I have to say why sentence should not now be pronounced against me.

"During argument on that very question, through which I listened, not in a personal way, but so far as possible as a citizen of our common country, I had supposed that many and unanswerable reasons supporting my view had been given to the court.

"Therefore, in the court's interest at this moment I must recognize a mere formality. It is plain that nothing I can say will change your fixed determination so far as you have the power to start me down the dark path of imprisonment for life.

"It is proper that a man so situated, especially when, as in my case, he is the victim without fault of an utterly unscrupulous persecution, should be permitted to enter his protest against injustice, however much that protest may appear weakened by its relation to individual experience.

"Fortunately, what I have to say is warranted by bigger considerations than any personal to me. So far reaching are they that I feel I have a right to ask you to hear my views with the same courtesy I have used during my trial through your rulings and remarks.

"About to be condemned by you to prison for life, I will, therefore, make answer to your question in the following way:

"First of all, in the name of the courts of my country, which I respect, I protest against your right or power to pass any judgment against me. It is undenied in this case that you were appointed to the bench this spring for the trial of myself and my associates, fresh from the employment of the very coal operators of Colorado, including the Rockefellers, who have pressed and engineered these prosecutions.

"Yourself a coal company attorney, engaged to assist as a practicing lawyer in the trial of cases arising like mine out of the industrial disturbances of 1913 and 1914, you had no right, when challenged, to sit as trial judge in the case of any striking miner.

"You were so deeply prejudiced against me that my case was a travesty on justice from the start. Notwithstanding the affidavits of reliable citizens who had sworn to your prejudice, you have persisted on the bench. Today the Supreme Court of Colorado in Denver is reviewing your conduct and yet you refuse to wait another 24 hours for the guidance of that court's decision. Such unseemly haste in the exercise of such a jurisdiction to thrust me into prison should not be passed without a protest.

"Second only to the resolution with which you hold your seat upon the bench, was the method adopted by you for selecting a jury to try me. You refused to permit the jury to be drawn from the regular jury box provided by law and you ordered an open venire.

"This method was exactly adapted to procure what none were surprised to discover: a hand-picked jury of coal company partisans. After you had removed the coroner as a summoning officer, over my protest, you selected your own instruments to pick this jury. And the jury so chosen was naturally subject to the self-same coal company influences which, with hue and cry, now seek to drive me to the penitentiary.

"It matters not that I was utterly guiltless of the charge against me. It matters not that the prosecution was forced to abandon its claim that on October 25, 1913, I fired a shot or did other than seek to avoid the violence which menaced the cause dearest to my heart.

"It matters not that it became necessary for the prosecution to invoke legal doctrines of conspiracy, which if applied impartially, would convict the leading coal operators of Colorado and the country for the deaths of men, women and children at Ludlow on April 20, 1914.

"Perhaps this seemed immaterial, because none of them have been informed against, much less tried, and none of them fear our courts or prosecuting officials.

"It matters not that the only evidence, on which the prosecution was forced to rest, was the testimony of two disreputable Baldwin-Felts detectives, employes of the coal operators' association, with whom you yourself were formerly professionally associated.

"Nothing was to be permitted to stand in the way, and it is significant that even a jury so selected refused to convict me until a bailiff selected by you, according to affidavits on file in this court, tortured a juryman with manufactured reports of the dangerous illness of the juror's wife, and as a final stroke warned the jury that under your orders the jury would have nothing further to eat until they had rendered their verdict.

"In the face of this sworn charge, which courts everywhere have held sufficient to undermine the whole structure of jury trials and to destroy the integrity of such a verdict, your bailiff has remained silent and this court impassive. May I ask whether judicial travesty is not the right description of such proceedings?

"Such practices, however astonishing to our people in general, do not surprise one who has observed our industrial history. From long experience I recognize the power of wealth, the magnitude of our industrial problems, and their effect on our existing social system. I can understand, for I have seen how men who seek a living realization for the workers of the world of the old ideals of justice and equality; who endeavor to open the eyes of their fellows to the true economic conditions that surround them as they seek their daily bread, are persecuted, defamed, and even, in exceptional cases, hounded to the gallows by those who control the wealth and privileges of our generous country.

"I have seen some masters of finance within and without this state using the full powers of government to divide the workers, to crush the hopes and aspirations in their breasts, and to extinguish the kindling light of intelligence in their souls in full realization of the fact that understanding brings the fixed desire for the higher and nobler things of life, including a dream of

equality of opportunity some day for the children of rich and
poor alike.

"And it is not overstatement to say that I am here today because, with others, I have patiently, without bitterness, yet
persistently, for years sought these things—a wider chance in
life for those who toil, a higher type of democratic citizenship
and a social system of industry which gives promise to mankind
and denies autocratic power over the lives and liberties of the
great mass of workers to the masters of millions who have
usurped government authority itself.

"Such usurpation has reached its most finished expression in
Las Animas and Huerfano counties, in this state, and those who
like myself, have continued nonetheless to worship at the ancient
altars of human liberty and justice in this country have been
marked for annihilation.

"But let no one think we have not seen through the years this
very possibility.

"In receiving sentence of life imprisonment at hard labor
from this court I can do so with the knowledge that I have
broken no law and committed no crime, unless it be that I am a
coal miner, honored by my fellow workers, with their years of
confident faith that my devotion will stand even this acid test
for the maintenance of their principles."

Lawson paused a moment and sucked in a deep breath. The
white-faced judge started to speak and then pursed his lips
grimly as Lawson went on:

"In a word, the reason this court should not pass judgment
as I see it is that by so doing it will openly violate every principle
of justice for the promotion of which our courts exist.

"Solemnly facing iron bars and prison walls, I assert my love
for justice and my faith in its ultimate triumph—not a justice
of theory, but of reality, extending to men, women and children
whose proper equality of opportunity it embraces; and with
utmost earnestness I want it understood that my one satisfaction
in my lot—separated though I be from those who are dearer to

me than life—lies in the belief that this, my undeserved experience, may help awaken others to the living wrongs in our world, calling today as definitely as in the past for remedy.

"It is a privilege and a duty even by sacrifice to advance our priceless cause. I am therefore ready to receive the sentence this court should declare itself without either authority, right or justification to impose."[1]

Lawson sat down heavily. He was not aware of the look of admiration on Attorney Clark's face, or of the fury and hatred in that of Judge Hillyer. John Lawson had merely spoken as best he could what was in his mind and heart, and he did not know he had sounded a deathless challenge to tyrannical employers and a credo for union men.

As from a distance he heard Judge Hillyer pronounce the long-expected sentence. The judge was leaving the bench. Sheriff Kane stepped up to Lawson's side and placed a hand on his big, muscular arm.

"All right, Lawson," Sheriff Kane said. "You'll have to come along with me."

Without another word of protest, Lawson rose and went with the sheriff—across the courtroom, down the steps, and into the county jail. A jailer with a ring of keys opened the door to a tiny cell. Lawson heard the door clank behind him. He sank on the hard cot and buried his head in his hands.

---

[1] John Lawson made his statement to the court without notes or advance preparation. A shorthand reporter kept a transcript of his words.

CHAPTER XXIII

FINGER ON ROCKEFELLER

John Lawson quickly settled into the routine of the riveted, boiler-plate jail. Even here, he found, there was work he could do. Little Zancanelli, often half delirious, alternately cried and stormed. Lawson found he could ease Zancanelli's mind. More than 50 other strike prisoners in the jail needed comfort and encouragement. Lawson talked to them in soothing, hopeful tones each day as they came from their tiny cells for a brief period of exercise in the filthy bull pen. Outwardly, Lawson was smiling and confident, buoying up the other prisoners with his own cheerfulness. Inwardly, he had little hope despite his great faith in ultimate justice and the abilities of Hawkins. Lawson had seen two of his friends, Fyler and Tikas, lying in the roadway where they had been shot down, and he knew that he and his friends in the jail could expect no mercy or compassion. The swaggering Linderfelt, with a deputy sheriff's commission in his pocket, was free to walk around in the bright Southern Colorado sunshine, the same sunshine that beat down upon the graves of his humble victims. Outside Lawson's cell each night, pacing up and down the corridor with a revolver in his holster, was Belk, the Baldwin-Felts detective who had killed Gerald Lippiatt. He was a deputy sheriff and clothed with the majesty of the law.

A few miles north, where many had died, were the plains of Ludlow, empty now save for the battered camp stoves and scorched bedsteads of the one-time colonists. There was one other object among the ruins of the Ludlow Colony that attracted the eyes of passersby on the nearby highway. It was a black cross, made of two rough railroad ties. It stood at the mouth of the Black Hole of Ludlow, where women and children had died horrible deaths. All of those who had died had trusted and obeyed John Lawson in life. They had followed his directions, and had looked to him for protection. They had died for him. He had teased and romped with their children; he had spent Christmas with them, given them little gifts, and had had their tiny arms around his neck. Then he had seen them lying in long rows in the morgue. Self-accusations tortured Lawson night after night as he tossed on his cell cot. If he had done this or that, perhaps the massacre would not have occurred. He found consolation in being in jail. Perhaps this was his reparation for deficiencies. The power that had taken the lives of the women and children was inflicting on him a torture worse than death. Lawson had always expected to die during the strike. He had anticipated the thrust of a knife or the bullet of a thug. The violent death had not come to him, however, and now he saw in his incarceration a means by which he was to give his life. He realized he must be patient under oppression. In no other way could he prevent a murderous outbreak which would irreparably injure the cause of unionists with the general public.

Patience was necessary to save himself and his friends from going mad with the futile, despairing rage that had animated the McNamaras and the Orchards. Lawson organized his fellow prisoners in a movement to clean up the pig-sty jail, and he organized a mock court which held trials daily and passed sentences.

"Joe Didoni is fined two cigarettes for spitting on the floor. . . ."

When Hawkins visited him at the jail and attempted to discuss plans for carrying on his fight, Lawson would not listen.

"Never mind about me, Horace. Take care of these other men first. They are far more deserving."

Hawkins had never had a man in jail say that to him before. Usually their only thought was to get out at any cost. Lawson's self-denial so inspired Hawkins that on his return to Denver he called on Olive.

"Mrs. Lawson," he said, and hesitated as though he did not know how to go on, "I am going to say something to you that I never said to a client before. I give you my word of honor that no harm shall come to your husband."

"I believe you," Olive said. "We must not allow any harm to come to him."

In Washington, the U. S. Industrial Relations Commission questioned John D. Rockefeller, Jr., once again, this time about his knowledge of the Lawson trial and his company's control of the judicial machinery in Southern Colorado.

"If it is shown that deputized gunmen, receiving your money, were witnesses against John Lawson, would you go to Colorado or endeavor to secure a new trial for him, to prevent him from spending a lifetime in prison?" Chairman Walsh asked the man of millions.

"I would do nothing to interfere with the administration of justice by the authorities," Rockefeller replied. "That is a principle for which I stand and uphold." He later amplified this statement with another:

"My opinion is that justice should be so administered as to be above suspicion; and, if in any material particular the trial of Mr. Lawson has been wanting in this respect, I, for one, should desire to see the Supreme Court of Colorado to which the appeal has been taken, closely consider every ground that may be urged and to grant a new trial should any material ground be sustained. I have no more right than any other citizen in this country to interfere with or influence the courts of justice; and questions which are so framed as to seek to put me in the position of appearing to concede that there has been wilful tampering with the courts or of stating what I am prepared to do to influence the future cause of justice, either as respect to Mr. Lawson or any other person, I cannot regard as other than improper questions, and direct reflections upon those who are charged with the administration of justice. To sinister reflections of this kind, I must decline to be a party, even by inference."

The New York Call pictured Rockefeller in a cartoon as a huge, squatting beast that crushed Lawson with a claw-like hand, and referred to the capitalist as Judge Rockefeller who "doesn't want John Lawson at liberty."

"Angel Archie" Stevenson, the man who constructed the Republican steamroller which flattened Roosevelt delegates at the Chicago convention in 1912 and made Taft the GOP nominee for president, raised his voice in Lawson's behalf.

"John R. Lawson was entitled to a fair trial before an impartial jury, and most people are of the opinion he had neither," Stevenson said in a public interview. "I don't believe John D. Rockefeller, Jr., knows the real facts about the situation in Colorado. I believe him to be a just man who has done and is doing much good. I don't believe he is in sympathy with much that has been done and is now being done in Colorado. The present persecution of the miners is a grave mistake. There will be no lasting peace in Colorado until operators and miners get together."

Labor bodies in every section of the country voiced vigorous opposition to the Lawson trial and conviction. Mass meetings were held. Five thousand miners held a protest meeting in Scranton, Pa., and condemned Judge Hillyer. The Chicago Federation of Labor packed the Garrick Theater and filled the streets outside. Mother Jones, Chairman Walsh of the Industrial Relations Commission, and John Fitzpatrick, president of the Chicago federation, bitterly condemned injustice in Colorado.

At a mass meeting held in Philadelphia under the auspices of the
Federal Council of Churches of Christ, such labor leaders as
Samuel Gompers and Frank Morrison, president and secretary of
the American Federation of Labor, condemned the sentencing of
Lawson and the Colorado courts. At the same meeting, Gifford
Pinchot proposed that the United States government take over
Rockefeller's properties in Colorado.

"If Lawson is guilty, not of actual murder, but for leading
the striking miners, then Mr. Rockefeller, as the leader and
employer of the murderous gunmen, should be in the same cell
as Lawson," Pinchot declared. "If it is right for Lawson to go
to jail for life, then I want to see John D. Rockefeller, Jr., go to
jail for life."

A resolution was adopted urging the removal of Judge Hillyer
and the prosecution of mine guards and militiamen. It denounced the "coal companies for their flagrant dominance of
government and courts in various parts of Colorado."

Professor Brewster spoke in Ann Arbor and other educational
centers, calling for justice for a simple miner, John Lawson.
One of the most effective meetings was held in Mt. Carmel, Pa.,
Lawson's boyhood home.[1] Miners, business and professional
men, the clergy, public officials, and men and women in every
walk of life, joined hands to do what they could to obtain justice for the boy who had grown up among them and moved
West. Labor leaders from every section of the East, led by Vice
President Frank Hayes, went to Mt. Carmel for the meeting.
On the day of the demonstration, the Sayre colliery whistle
sounded at 7 a.m. and a well-organized parade moved out with
flags and the town band in the vanguard. Twenty-six automobiles carried visiting officials and dignitaries. The chief of
police, councilmen, borough officials and leading citizens followed on foot. A boys' band, a Lithuanian band and other
musical organizations led the many divisions of the parade. At
the town park, the Rev. Arthur Willis Spooner, pastor of the

[1] United Mine Workers Journal, Sept. 30, 1915. P. 13.

Presbyterian church, where Lawson had attended Sunday School as a boy, presided. Hayes and the other labor leaders spoke, reciting stories of the strike and the legal persecutions. Mrs. Theodore Puitz of Philadelphia, Lawson's sister, thanked the people of Mt. Carmel for their interest and friendliness.

One old man, who was devoted to Lawson, was unable to be present. Thomas Ramage, Lawson's uncle, was confined to his bed with miner's asthma in a humble little cottage in the extreme west end of the town. He could hear the roar of the crowd, but he could not lift his head from his pillow. On a table near the bed was a pile of magazines and newspapers containing articles about Lawson. The old man's son, Thomas, Jr., was at the meeting, but his wife sat by the bed. The old man listened to the crowd and the occasional strains of band music.

"Thank God they are doing something for John," he said feebly. "I have only a short time to live, Mother, but it is my prayer that before I go John will have won his freedom."[2]

The roar of protest brought a pause to No. 26 Broadway and to officials in Colorado. Brickbats were coming from every side. Scheduled trials of Ed Doyle and other miners charged with murder in connection with the Hecla Mine battle were again set over.

The first ray of hope for John Lawson came Aug. 17, 1915, when the Colorado Supreme Court issued a writ of supersedeas staying his sentence of life imprisonment.[3] The effect of the writ was to prevent his removal from the Trinidad jail to the state penitentiary in Canon City before the high court had time to act upon his application for a new trial. Even more important, the Supreme Court handed down a decision ousting Judge Hillyer from further hearing of strike cases.[4] The writ of prohibition applied specifically to only three cases, those of John Burke, Charles Haines and K. Uyada, who were held in Walsenburg, charged with the murder of Major Lester of the militia

[2] United Mine Workers Journal, Aug. 19, 1915.
[3] Denver Labor Bulletin, Aug. 17, 1915.
[4] Denver Labor Bulletin, Aug. 21, 1915.

during the battle between guardsmen and miners on the hogback near the town April 29, 1914, but it spelled the end for Judge Hillyer.

In issuing the two writs, the Supreme Court did not pass upon Hawkins' demand that Lawson be released on bail, but it ordered both prosecution and defense to file briefs before the opening of the Fall term, Sept. 13, 1915. Justice S. Harrison White, who delivered the orders of the court, emphasized that "the first ideal in the administration of justice is that the judge must be free from bias and partiality. Men are so agreed on this principle that any departure therefrom shocks their sense of justice."

The writ held that Judge Hillyer "has within the meaning of the law bias or prejudice that would in all probability prevent him from dealing fairly with the relators as defendants." Only two of the seven justices, Chief Justice William H. Gabbert and Associate Justice James E. Garrigues, both Republicans, dissented. Hawkins and his associate attorneys, the able Charles Mahoney of Denver, Mr. Costigan, John East of Walsenburg, and A. M. Belcher, United Mine Workers attorney who had won a reputation in West Virginia strike trials, had argued well. The two Supreme Court rulings were the first issued by the court in the strike cases, and labor saw in them a stinging indictment of Governor Carlson, Attorney General Farrar and the coal magnates.

John Lawson was eating a skimpy lunch from a tin plate when news of the decisions was carried to him in the Trinidad jail. His face lighted.

"This is the first step toward my vindication," he said enthusiastically. "There has never been a question of Judge Hillyer's prejudice. Now I am hopeful of a new trial and eventual vindication for all these men and for myself."

Judge Hillyer received the news in Walsenburg. He said he was surprised.

"There is nothing I care to say at this time," he said. "I may have a statement later."

Within the week, the coal companies suffered another severe blow. The Industrial Relations Commission issued its reports, confirming most of the charges made against gunmen and militiamen. One of the reports, prepared by George P. West, charged John D. Rockefeller, Jr., with having approved measures to coerce the Colorado state government and of having flouted the will of President Wilson. Responsibility for the strike was placed on the shoulders of the coal operators; the two Rockefellers, senior and junior, were accused of selecting incompetent and reactionary persons as executive officers in their corporations, and with giving heartiest indorsement and support to these same officials after they had taken actions which precipitated the worst of the strike troubles.

"During all the seven tragic and bitter months that preceded Ludlow, Mr. Rockefeller wrote letter after letter in enthusiastic praise of men whose acts during this period had precipitated a reign of terror and bloodshed," the report said. "It was only when the Ludlow massacre filled the press of the nation with editorial denunciation, when mourners in black silently paraded in front of his New York office, when cartoons in the conservative press pilloried him and his father before an angry public, that at last complacency gives way to concern in his telegrams and letters to Denver.

"Mr. Rockefeller's responsibility has a significance beyond even the sinister results of his policy in Colorado. The perversion of and contempt for government, the disregard of public welfare, and the defiance of public opinion during the Colorado strike must be considered as only one manifestation of the autocratic and anti-social spirit of a man whose enormous wealth gives him infinite opportunity to act in similar fashion in broader fields.

"The nation-wide significance and importance of the Colorado conflict and the company's ruthless policy of suppression are emphasized again and again. By June, 1914, Rockefeller has formulated something like a definite plan for a nationwide campaign. Yet it is important to remember that Rockefeller's character and policies are important only as showing the possibilities inherent in an economic and social situation that permits one man or group of men to wield such enormous economic power, and through that power not only to control the destinies and dictate the circumstances of life for millions of wage earners, but to subsidize and control to a large degree those agencies that mold the public opinion of a nation. Even should Rockefeller change over night, those possibilities of evil would remain inherent in our economic and industrial situation, as a menace to freedom and democracy."

In discussing the Colorado Fuel & Iron Company's rejection of President Wilson's strike settlement plan, the report said: "Rockefeller not only rebuffed the President by denying his earnest request, but if the letters of his agents may be relied upon, he apparently deceived the President and the public by means of the company's letter of rejection. This letter was written by President Welborn in collaboration with Mr. Ivy L. Lee, a member of Rockefeller's personal staff, whom he had sent to Colorado for the purpose."

Many of the letters written by Rockefeller to officials of the C. F. & I. Co. were reproduced in the report along with the comment:

"But Mr. Rockefeller's part in the Colorado conflict was not confined to these letters of praise and indorsement which so heartened and sustained the Colorado operators. Prior to the massacre at Ludlow on April 20, the letters proved quite sufficient for Mr. Rockefeller's purposes. But the storm of popular wrath that rose after Ludlow demanded more active participation. It was then that Mr. Rockefeller initiated the nation-wide publicity campaign by which he hoped to convince the country that the strikers, and not his company's mine guard-militiamen, were responsible for the deaths of thirteen women and children who perished at Ludlow, and that the strike itself, instead of a struggle for freedom, was a revolt by bloodthirsty and an-

archistic foreigners, led by men who obtained huge incomes
from organized agitation and lawlessness. Still hiding behind his
executive officials in Denver, Mr. Rockefeller employed a publicity expert and advanced him money from his personal funds
to begin the campaign. He chose for the purpose Mr. Ivy L.
Lee, publicity agent for the Pennsylvania railroad. The president of that railroad consented that Mr. Lee should devote a
part of his time to Mr. Rockefeller's service, and the pamphlets
and bulletins were to be dispatched in bulk from Mr. Lee's Philadelphia office to Denver, for distribution from the office of the
Colorado Fuel & Iron Company. They were to go forth under
the name of the operator's committee, as correct information
gathered and written on the scene by men familiar at first hand
with the facts.

"Early in the summer of 1914 there began that remarkable
publicity campaign by which Mr. Rockefeller flooded the nation
with bulletin after bulletin, defending the coal operators and
denouncing the strikers and their leaders. These bulletins contained false and deceptive statements. Salaries paid to officials
of the United Mine Workers in Colorado for the year ending
November, 1913, were conspicuously displayed as salaries for the
nine weeks ending in that month. This gross and palpable
slander was mailed to thousands of congressmen, editors, ministers of the gospel, school teachers, public officials, business and
professional men whose names appear on Mr. Lee's carefully prepared mailing lists. No correction was made until it had been
exposed by the Commission during the hearing in Denver in
December, 1914. The preparation and distribution of these
bulletins was carried on with the greatest secrecy as to the
authorship of Mr. Lee and as to his employment by Mr. Rockefeller. When the Commission demanded the name of the writer
of the bulletins of Mr. Welborn, during the hearing in December, Mr. Welborn refused to answer until he had consulted his
attorney. Even then he carefully refrained from revealing the

fact that the publicity campaign had been initiated and paid for by Mr. Rockefeller."

The report found fault with the so-called Rockefeller Plan which the capitalist was planning to put in effect as a substitute for unionism.

"Even if we grant that the concession has substantial value," the report said, "it must still be characterized not as a concession to democratic principles, but as an instance of that handing down of favors in which autocrats have always delighted. It embodies none of the principles of effectual collective bargaining and instead is a hypocritical pretense of granting what is in reality withheld. The testimony and correspondence not only proved this, but they contain indisputable evidence that the plan was conceived and carried out, not for the purpose of aiding the company's employees in Colorado, but for the purpose of ameliorating or removing unfavorable criticism of Mr. Rockefeller which had arisen throughout the country following his rejection of President Wilson's plan of settlement, and which had found utterance even in those conservative circles and newspapers in Eastern cities where Mr. Rockefeller's self esteem could not escape injury by such criticism."

The report referred to John Lawson as "a man of exceptionally high character and a good citizen in every sense of the term."

"The killing of John Nimmo, a mine guard, by the strikers during one of the many skirmishes between them and the deputies was the crime for which Mr. Lawson was convicted," West's report said. "No effort was made to prove that he fired the fatal shot. He was held responsible for the death of Nimmo because he was leading the strike and was at the Ludlow colony on the day of the battle. Nimmo was one of a small army of deputy sheriffs employed and paid by the coal companies and deputized by subservient sheriffs who made little or no effort to investigate their records. This Sheriff Jefferson Farr of Huerfano County testified before this Commission that the men to whom he gave deputies' commissions might have been, so far as he knew, red-handed murderers fresh from the scene of their crimes. That many guards deputized in this illegal fashion and paid by the Colorado Fuel & Iron Company were men of the lowest and most vicious character has been clearly established. That their function was to intimidate and harass the strikers had been demonstrated in the strike of 1903-1904, and had been made apparent early in the present strike by the shooting to death of Gerald Lippiatt, a union organizer, in the streets of Trinidad immediately after the calling of the strike, by a Baldwin-Felts detective employed by the Colorado Fuel & Iron Company and its associates and deputized by the sheriff of Las Animas County. In fact it was to these deputies, then masquerading as national guardsmen, that national guard officers attempted to attribute the murder, looting and pillage that accompanied the destruction of the Ludlow tent colony of strikers later in the strike.

"The prosecution and conviction of Mr. Lawson under these circumstances, and his sentence to life imprisonment at hard labor, marked the lowest depths of the prostitution of Colorado's government to the will of the Colorado Fuel & Iron Company and its associates. It is the crowning infamy of all the infamous record in Colorado of American institutions perverted and debauched by selfish private interests. It is anarchism stripped of every pretense of even that chimerical idealism that fires the unbalanced mind of the bomb thrower. It is anarchism for profits and revenge, and it menaces the security and integrity of American institutions as they seldom have been menaced before."

The Industrial Relations Commission reports, lengthy and full of detail, were issued in four sections. The report of the employes' representatives on the commission, which was drawn up by Basil Manly, director of research and investigation for the commission, was signed by Reps. Frank Walsh, John B. Lennon, James O'Connell and A. B. Garretson. Each of these commissioners issued what were termed "supplemental opinions and suggestions."

A dissenting report was issued by Commissioner Weinstock. Regarding the work of the commission's field agents, he wrote:

"We find that the alleged findings of fact, and, in a general way, the comments made thereon in the report of the staff of this commission, under the direction of Mr. Basil M. Manly, which has been made a part of the records of this commission, without the indorsement, however, of the commission, are so manifestly partisan and unfair that we cannot give them our indorsement."

The Weinstock dissenting report, which was signed by Reps. Ashton and Ballard, who also represented the employers, admitted corporation control of courts and legislatures, exploitation of women, children and unorganized workers; employment of disreputable characters as gunmen, low wages, long hours, the suppression of free speech and the right of peaceful assembly, and bribery, but upheld the general position of the employers.

"There is, therefore, no gainsaying the fact that labor has had many grievances and that it is thoroughly justified in organizing and in spreading organization in order to protect itself against exploitation and oppression," the dissenting report said. It then went on to criticise labor union politics, the closed shop, alleged contract breaking on the part of labor groups, restriction of output, prohibition of use of non-union made tools and materials, and acts of violence against non-union workers and the properties of employers.

All of the reports agreed that Congress should enact laws to correct industrial evils. A number of recommendations, including a proposal that laws be enacted to insure minimum wages and hours, and the unrestricted right to organize, were made. All members of the commission approved collective bargaining through the medium of unions.

A two-year investigation was brought to an end through issuance of the reports.

CHAPTER XXIV

CROESUS IN OVERALLS

Attorneys Hawkins and Costigan went to the Colorado Supreme Court with a petition for release of John Lawson from the Trinidad jail on bond until such time as the court could hand down a decision in his case.

"His is not a capital case, but one which this court has authority under the constitution and laws in which to allow bail," the petition contended. "His personal record for keeping the terms of his bail bonds has been at all times perfect. There is no possible question about his compliance with any bond he may give. His personal character and high standing were testified to during his trial and never challenged by the prosecution. If this court in its discretion denies bail, however guarded it may put its reasons, its action will be construed as a prejudgment of the case against Lawson without the case having been fully heard and argued in the Supreme Court. Finally, Lawson, at this time, contrary to what the courts hold should be done, in advance of full hearing of his case, after Judge Hillyer's prohibition foreshadows a reversal, is being needlessly punished by confinement in a place publicly condemned by the State Board of Charities and Corrections as 'unfit and unsafe, a menace to the administration of the law and a reproach to the community and the State of Colorado.' "

Attorney General Farrar opposed the bail in a lengthy brief, and then struck at Hawkins and his associate, Fred W. Clark of Trinidad, by filing an information in Las Animas County District Court charging them with subornation of perjury in connection with the affidavit of Grover Hall, the Lawson juror, who had sworn that a bailiff told the jury it could not have food or water until it returned a verdict. Clark was arrested in Trinidad and released a short time later on bond of $1,500. Hawkins telephoned from Denver that he was ready to be served any time and would go to Trinidad when wanted.

"I have a few things I would like to attend to before I surrender," Hawkins told Sheriff Kane.

"Go ahead," Kane said. "I guess there isn't any awful hurry."

Clark charged the action was another frame-up on the part of the state and asserted he had been warned some legal action might be taken against him. Horace P. Clark of Denver, a former clerk of the State Supreme Court and an uncle of the attorney, blamed the charges on Governor Carlson in a public statement.

"In this dirty, under-handed work, the governor has given his sanction," Clark said. "Representatives of the attorney general's staff have repeatedly approached my nephew with mysterious hints of a knowledge of criminal acts on his part in connection with the defense of the striking miners and made offers of immunity if he would 'confess' and throw himself on their mercy, and incidentally assist them in breaking down the defense."

Four days later, the long promised visit of John D. Rockefeller, Jr., materialized. He arrived unheralded in Trinidad with his private secretary, Charles O. Heydt; W. L. Mackenzie King, and Mr. King's secretary, F. A. MacGregor.[1] President Jesse Welborn and Manager E. H. Weitzel of the Colorado Fuel & Iron Co. greeted the party and conducted it to a hotel. The man in whose name corporation officials had long ruled the Kingdoms of Las Animas and Huerfano was on the ground at last. Fresh

---

[1] Denver Labor Bulletin, Sept. 25, 1915.

from his offices in New York, Rockefeller did not waste a minute. He went directly from the hotel to the coal camps.[2] He went first to Berwind, above Ludlow, with a retinue of mine company officials, reporters and photographers. Opposite the site of the Ludlow tent colony, the car bearing Rockefeller came to a brief halt, and the reporters scribbled hasty notes while Weitzel pointed out where the 13 women and children had died.

Rockefeller's eyes swept the desolate prairie and the charred ruins of the colony. His face was grave. He made no comment when his guides showed him the place where Lieutenant Linderfelt had clubbed the unfortunate Tikas with a Springfield rifle. The party moved on up the crooked road to Berwind. It was noon when they reached the camp. Rockefeller was taken directly to the company boarding house. He put his coat on a nail and took his turn at the single tin wash basin. Begrimed miners filed into the dining room, awed by the presence of the capitalist. Welborn did the honors.

"Mr. Borovich—Mr. Rockefeller. Mr. Morelli—Mr. Rockefeller."

The miners were shy and timid. Rockefeller smilingly clasped each hand firmly.

"You'll sit at the head of the table, Mr. Rockefeller," Welborn said.

"No, I'll sit with the men," Rockefeller replied. The reporters scribbled away again as he took his seat between his superintendent, Thomas P. Davis, and Tony Sardakowski. Ranged across from him and on either side were other coal miners—Dan Morelli, Pat McGahan, Andrew Marinoff, Venezelos Paschopulous, Jake Ryan and Eddie Smith.

The young millionaire helped himself from a dish of steaming baked beans.

"These look bully," he said. "I'll start them around this way."

Reporters for newspapers friendly to the Colorado Fuel & Iron Co. watched Rockefeller eat and carefully listed each article

[2] The Denver Post, Sept. 21, 1915.

of food. Their accounts, with full pages of pictures, were glowing. The boarding house fare was described with adjectives
calculated to increase the flow of digestive juices. It was recorded that Rockefeller asked questions during the meal, shrewd
questions designed to bring him more information than he
could get from his executive subordinates. The answers were
guarded. This was the Mr. Big of the Colorado Coal Industry,
all in capitals, and a miner could not very well climb to his
feet and make a speech on injustices under the circumstances,
especially with Welborn and Weitzel looking on.

"Go ahead," Rockefeller said. "Talk straight from the shoulder. I've had to take the word of company officers for a long
time. Now I want to see what has been done and hear what you
men have to say."

Several said conditions had been improved somewhat since
the strike. Old frame houses were being replaced in Berwind
by modern cottages. A clubhouse was under construction.
From the boarding house, after the miners had gone back to
work, Mr. Rockefeller climbed the hill to the school house. He
talked with the teacher, Miss Edna Campbell, and with the children.

"You remind me tremendously of my own children," he told
the class. From the school, he went to the office of the company
doctor, then to the company store, and finally into the homes
of more than 30 families.

For two days Rockefeller made the rounds of his properties.
He went to Segundo, Frederick, Primero and other camps. The
number of newspaper reporters grew with each passing hour.
They came from everywhere, New York, Boston, Chicago and
other large cities. Rockefeller was photographed in overalls and
miner's cap, coming in and going out of mines. Harmony and
peace were the themes of every outgoing press dispatch. The
only jarring note came in a telegram from Mrs. Champion and
Mrs. Sarah L. Scanland, officers of the Justice League in Denver.

"It is understood you have come to Colorado to learn the truth," the telegram said. "It has been stated that the deplorable conditions which have existed in Southern Colorado were unknown to you, and many persons have disclaimed your personal responsibility for the atrocious crimes which were committed at Ludlow on the pretext that you were ignorant of their perpetration. Believing that two contending organizations can be neither all right nor all wrong, the Justice League asks that you give audience to the officers of the United Mine Workers as well as the officers of your company. It also asks that you visit John R. Lawson, now in jail for the murder of a man he never saw. It asks that you confer with the United Mine Workers' attorneys, who have had ignominy brought upon them through the medium of the legal machinery of the State of Colorado manipulated by officials friendly to your companies and unfriendly to the miners."

Rockefeller did not go to the Trinidad jail to see Lawson, nor did he meet with the United Mine Workers, but he did talk to Hawkins who had gone to Trinidad and posted bond in the subornation of perjury charge. Hawkins was standing in a hotel lobby when President Welborn approached him. Hawkins was taken off his guard as Welborn walked up with a friendly smile.

"Mr. Rockefeller is over here," Welborn said. "He wants to see you."

The meeting was brief, but friendly. Rockefeller shook hands warmly.

"I will be in Denver in a day or two and I would like to have a chat with you there," Rockefeller said.

"Fine," Hawkins replied. "I will be glad to talk with you any time."

Later in the day, Hawkins went to see John Lawson.

"Rockefeller doesn't seem like a bad sort," he said. "He seems friendly."

"That is what I thought when I met him in New York," Lawson replied bitterly. "I am reserving my opinion now until I see what is done with these men in the jails."

Hawkins nodded.

"You are right, John, as always. A handshake isn't compensation for persecution."

From Trinidad, Rockefeller went to Denver and to the nearby country home of President Welborn. He made daily visits to the C. F. & I. offices in the Boston Bldg. in Denver and held numerous conferences. While he was thus occupied, Southern Colorado was thrown into an uproar by another murder.

Robert Mitchell, editor of the Walsenburg Independent, who had long fought Sheriff Jeff Farr and his political machine, was assassinated at the door of his home as he returned from a picture show.[3] Mitchell had been gathering evidence to show that Farr had stolen the last election. Part of his evidence had been turned over to U. S. District Attorney Harry B. Tedrow in Denver.

Sheriff Farr obtained bloodhounds and set out on the trail of the assassins after announcing the killing was undoubtedly the work of burglars. The trail led to the C. F. & I. Company's nearby Walsen mine. Posses went through the miles of underground passages without finding the murderer.

"The murder looks like a political killing to me," U. S. Attorney Tedrow said in an angry statement. "Mitchell had led the fight against the notorious Farr gang and he had been a great help to me in my investigations of alleged corrupt election methods."

Tedrow refused to say whether he planned to use the evidence gathered by Mitchell or whether he had planned to call Mitchell to testify before a federal grand jury scheduled to meet in Pueblo within the week.

[3] The Denver Express, Sept. 27, 1915.

While Huerfano County officers made an apparent effort to solve the murder and the people of Southern Colorado put two and two together according to their political persuasions, Rockefeller was busy in Denver. He announced his labor plan, conceding practically every union demand with the exception of recognition. The plan was given the outline of a memorandum of agreement between the company and its employes, covering rent of houses, charges for electric light, water, coal, powder for the miners, a pledge by the company to build fences around houses as an encouragement to gardening; a promise to erect bathhouses and social centers, assurance that the men and their families could use their own discretion in selecting a privately-owned or a company store, and a stipulation regarding hours of work—eight hours for workers underground and nine for those employed on the outside. Latitude was granted for arbitration of disputes and the company promised to keep its wage scales up to the levels of competitive mining districts.

Rockefeller presented the plan himself to a group of men brought into Denver from the coal camps as representatives of the miners.

"In one of my earlier statements to the Walsh committee, I went on record as being opposed to the recognition of the union," Rockefeller told the coal camp delegates. "That merely expressed my view at that time. Conditions since have altered, and undoubtedly will continue to change. I want you to know that I am always willing to do what is for the common interest. I will not now make a flat statement that I will not recognize the union, but there is nothing in my present plan that forever closes the door to recognition of the union. If, in a few years, the personnel of the officers of the United Mine Workers changes, and the greater part of my employes want the union recognized, it is possible recognition might be given. I simply never cross a bridge until I get to it."[4]

[4] This statement assumed great importance in view of the attitude of the United Mine Workers of America in their dealings with John Lawson during 1916.

It was agreed the Rockefeller plan should go to the directors of the Colorado Fuel & Iron Co. and to the mining camps for approval by both executives and workers. In this fashion was the company union system—with President Welborn as its head, Mackenzie King as its guiding spirit, and Rockefeller as its godfather—brought into the world.

Rockefeller went to Hawkins' offices in Denver to discuss the strike and the prosecutions.[5] He sat in a comfortable chair, a tired man who had seen many things and heard many strange stories in the last few days.

"Give me your opinions, Mr. Hawkins," he said wearily. "You've been in the thick of this thing for many months."

Hawkins was not a man to miss an opportunity. He talked frankly and avidly.

"You are to blame, Mr. Rockefeller," he replied. "You have thousands of men working for you in this state, and you should not have stayed away so long."

Rockefeller looked out of the window toward Denver's packing house district where black smoke billowed lazily upward toward a bright, blue sky. "Tell me more," he said.

"I have a number of reports on your visit to Southern Colorado and they have come, in part, from men and women who hate your name," Hawkins said. "You made a good impression down there. I believe you could be elected sheriff of Las Animas County."

Rockefeller laughed.

"Perhaps," he said. "I know I have been accused of being sheriff of Huerfano County. What about these trials?"

The attorney leaned across his big desk and outlined a plan, a bold, daring plan. He spoke swiftly and to the point. Rockefeller nodded.

"I think you are right, Mr. Hawkins," he said. "I'll do what I can."

[5] Source: Horace Hawkins.

They shook hands and parted friends. Each man understood the other thoroughly.

"Not a bad fellow," Hawkins murmured when the capitalist had gone. "Hmmmm. Not a bad fellow at all."

Hawkins was filled with foreboding the next day. He feared vigorous attacks on the Rockefeller Industrial Plan might interfere with his own scheme. He was afraid the assaults would drive Rockefeller back into his shell. Lawson had dressed the Rockefeller Plan down in a statement issued from the Trinidad jail; Samuel Gompers, president of the American Federation of Labor, had ridiculed it as "the Rockefeller pseudo-union, an organization of miners formed by the richest man in the world who employs its members."

However, Attorney Hawkins' fears were forgotten when he learned that Rockefeller had gone to the State Capitol and conferred with Governor Carlson. Hawkins could scarcely contain himself when it was reported in the press, and not denied by either Governor Carlson or Rockefeller, that the latter had asked for dismissal of the strike cases. Two nights later, an oddly assorted group gathered in Governor Carlson's home. The visitors included Hawkins, John McLennan, president of the United Mine Workers' District 15; Verner Z. Reed, wealthy Denver capitalist and metal mine operator, who had repeatedly called for dismissal of the strike cases and a clean slate; Juvenile Judge Ben B. Lindsey, and Eugene Millikin[6], Judge Carlson's secretary.

This meeting, Hawkins believed, would clinch his plan to have the strike cases wiped from the records. Governor Carlson had already received hundreds of telegrams, letters, telephone calls, and personal visits from the prominent of the nation and the state. "Let there be peace in Colorado," had been the theme of each plea. "There can be no peace as long as the coal miners are persecuted in the courts."

[6] Eugene Millikin (R) was appointed to the U. S. Senate in December. 1941, by Gov. Ralph L. Carr to fill a vacancy caused by the death of U. S. Senator Alva B. Adams (D) of Colorado.

For once, Governor Carlson listened patiently. Hawkins and the members of the committee argued eloquently. At 2 a.m., Governor Carlson rose stiffly from his chair in a sign of dismissal.

"I don't know, gentlemen," he said. "I don't know. There are several people I must talk to before I say or do anything. It may be that your requests can be granted. I don't want to say yes or no at this time."

Later in the morning, the committee gathered in Hawkins' law office to await the governor's decision. Much hinged upon it. When it came, Hawkins waved a bony hand despairingly.

"We've failed," he said in a low voice.

Governor Carlson had decided the prosecutions must be continued. General Chase and a few coal company barons had objected to the plan. Hawkins' spirits rose again later in the day, however, when he was summoned to the Supreme Court. The justices, in an unprecedented action in a murder case in Colorado, ordered Lawson released on bond. Bail was fixed at $35,000. Former U. S. Senator Thomas M. Patterson said he would sign the entire bond, but Verner Z. Reed insisted he, too, be allowed to sign. Edward P. Costigan immediately put through a telephone call to the Trinidad jail. The sheriff brought Lawson from his cell to the telephone.

"The Supreme Court has ordered you released on bond, John," Costigan said. "Everything is fixed up. You should be home by Sunday. I telephoned your home first and told Fern. I could hear her shout to Mrs. Lawson."

"I'm glad you called them first," Lawson said weakly. "I never doubted that such word would come from you, and I'll be glad to get out, though it won't be easy to leave these other boys here."

"Typically Lawson," Costigan told Hawkins when he had replaced the receiver. "He is worrying about the other men."

"He is always worrying about someone else," Hawkins replied with a shake of his head.

John McLennan went to Trinidad with the bond. The sheriff readily accepted it and sent a turnkey for Lawson. Thin and pale from his long confinement, Lawson walked into the sheriff's office with his shoulders back and his head up. He shook hands with McLennan and asked to use the telephone. His call was put through to Olive, and the sheriff and McLennan stepped into an adjoining room. John Lawson had not seen Olive and Fern for many weeks. He talked to both of them for several minutes, and then called to McLennan.

"When does the next train leave for Denver? I want to get there as fast as I can."

Before they left the jail, Lawson insisted upon making the rounds to tell his miners goodbye.

"So long, John," they called. "We're sorry to see you go but we hope to hell you never come back to this hole."

He managed a grin.

"Don't worry boys, you'll be out of here before very long."

Lawson and McLennan caught the night train for Denver. The district president promptly fell asleep, but Lawson sat up. He had many things to think about. . . . Olive . . . Fern . . . his job. He was now free to aid in the fight against persecutions and tyranny. He might yet go to the penitentiary for life, but in his heart he felt the Supreme Court action admitting him to bond presaged a new trial and acquittal. He was still turning his many problems over in his mind when the train pulled into the Union Station in Denver. As on another occasion, a crowd awaited him. This time Olive was among the greeters. When he stepped to the platform, she ran forward, trying bravely to fight back the tears that filled her eyes. She looked tiny and childlike in the arms of her big husband.

"Olive, Olive," he said. He held her tightly and looked around for Fern.

"She's waiting at home," Olive said. Her mother, Mrs. Hood, came up and embraced them both.

"I'm the happiest woman in the world," Olive said when newspaper reporters insisted she say something.

"And you, Mr. Lawson, what have you to say?" the reporters asked. Olive was anxious to be gone, but she knew that his fight was not over. He must talk, talk, talk.

"I am sure I will get a new trial," Lawson told the newsmen. "Colorado miners did not lose the strike. It has been a victory for the things for which we contended. It has awakened the nation to the need of granting labor just compensation and decent working conditions. The Rockefeller Plan will not work as well with Rockefeller back in New York as it would if he remained here. What will the same old bunch of C. F. & I. officials do when he goes away?"

Lawson did not know that the day before, in a speech before the Denver Chamber of Commerce, Rockefeller had admitted that the policy of the C. F. & I. had been in error, or that he had promised that a strike would never happen again.[7] Rockefeller had done even more. He had urged cooperation between capital and labor, and had rebuked Governor Carlson for his failure to declare an amnesty in the strike cases. Seven hundred business and professional men had given John D. Rockefeller a five-minute ovation.

Lawson and Olive walked arm in arm through the station. Admirers and reporters followed, calling greetings and questions.

"What about recognition of the union?" a reporter asked.

Lawson laughed.

"The Rockefeller Plan is recognition in part in that it recognizes many of our demands," he said. "I know they are going to recognize the union some time and this plan will prepare the way. Because of it, there will be less of a shock when union recognition does come."

The reporter started to ask another question, but John and Olive were gone.

[7] The Denver Express, Oct. 9, 1915.

Attorneys and businessmen called Mrs. Hood's home later in the same day. They wanted him at this conference, that meeting, or some other gathering as a speaker.

"Not today, boys," he said good-naturedly. "It is wife and daughter and mother-in-law for me today. I may be out tomorrow if Mrs. Lawson will let me—but I doubt it."

John Lawson had come home. The other John, the man of many millions, left the same day for New York.

CHAPTER XXV
CZAR FARR LEAVES THRONE

Henry Ford asked Lawson to be his guest on the Oscar II, the capitalist's peace ship, which was ready to leave for war-ridden Europe on an idealistic if futile mission. More than 100 representative Americans, imbued with the idea that their pleas might bring peace to Europe, would be aboard. Lawson could have used the invitation to focus attention upon himself and his cause. Many union leaders in Colorado urged him to do so, but he refused to take advantage of Ford or the possibilities involved in the peace trip. His telegraphed reply contained union propaganda, it is true, but it was propaganda that came straight from the heart.

"Your message inviting me to be your guest on a mission of peace received," Lawson wired Ford. "Permit me to express my appreciation and the sincere hope that your generous efforts will be successful in hastening, not only peace, but justice and happiness among the millions involved in this needless and ruthless war. Unfortunately, I am prevented from accepting your invitation by the fact that industrial peace has not yet been returned to this state. Here, due to causes commercial, political and personal, similar in some respects, although, of course, relatively less conspicuous, to those operating abroad, many members of organized labor are being subjected to bitter, one-sided persecution, placing life, liberty and happiness in jeopardy. My first

duty under the circumstances is by the side of these men and
their families, yet those of us endeavoring to secure industrial
peace and reasonable justice would be shortsighted indeed not to
wish you all good fortune and speed in your practical contribution to world-wide brotherhood."[1]

Lawson did not dare leave Colorado and his jailed miners for
long at a time. They needed such counsel and advice as he
could give for the state was pushing plans for additional trials.
The corporation-dictated prosecutions thus far had not been
particularly successful. A further effort must be made to save
face and justify the Lawson and Zancanelli cases. Scores had
been tried in the different coal counties yet none had been convicted except Lawson and Zancanelli in Las Animas County,
and David Robb and Ben Richardson in Fremont County. The
Supreme Court, which had these four cases before it, had undoubtedly stopped wholesale convictions when it issued its writ
of prohibition against Judge Hillyer. Several of the counties had
protested against further prosecutions on the ground their treas-
uries were bankrupt and they would be plunged into debt if
400 more men were tried.

As the days and weeks passed, the attorney general began to
drop cases here and there. The bitterness engendered by the
strike did not seem to abate, however. In Huerfano County,
where the Democrats contended they had won the election of
1914 and had been deprived of the fruits of victory by the Farr
machine, the election contests dragged slowly. The murderer of
Editor Mitchell had not been found.[2] The smallest spark might
again ignite Southern Colorado. The fight for political control
was being waged as relentlessly as before the great strike despite
Rockefeller's fine words. Sheriff Farr, who contended he had
won the 1914 election by a majority of 329 votes, was still sitting in the court house in Walsenburg in June, 1916, when the
Colorado Supreme Court gave the coal companies of Colorado

[1] Nov. 29, 1915.
[2] The murder case never was solved.

their first major setback in a ruling that threw out the entire vote of a number of closed precincts in which the company had controlled both the polling place and the votes that were cast.[3] The court found that the companies had throttled public opinion, denied to foreign-born electors the right of free choice, stifled public discussion, designated what citizens could or could not enter upon public property, and prostituted the ballot. It was a long opinion, more than 10,000 words, and it provided final confirmation by the highest authority in the state to charges that had been circulated in the coal districts and the state since before the turn of the century. It said in part:

"The federal troops entered the district in May of 1914, and the testimony is in agreement that no serious acts of violence occurred thereafter, and that order was preserved up to and subsequent to the election and to the time of this trial.

"It was under this condition that in July, 1914, the board of county commissioners changed certain of the election precincts so as to constitute each of such camps an election precinct, and with but one exception where a few ranches were included, these precincts were made to conform to the fences and lines around each camp, protected by fences in some instances and with armed guards in all cases. Thus each election precinct by this unparalleled act of the commissioners was placed exclusively within and upon the private grounds and under the private control of a coal corporation, which autocratically declared who should and who should not enter upon the territory of this political entity of the state, so purposely bounded by the commissioners.

"With but one exception all the lands and buildings within each of these election precincts as so created, were owned or controlled by the coal corporations; every person resident within such precincts was an employe of these private corporations or their allied companies, with the single exception; every judge,

[3] Colorado Supreme Court, June 21, 1916.

clerk, or officer of election with the exception of a saloon keeper, and partner of Farr, was an employe of the coal companies.

"The polling places were upon the grounds, and in the buildings of these companies; the registration lists were kept within the private offices or buildings of such companies, and used and treated as their private property.

"Thus were the public election districts and the public machinery turned over to the absolute domination and imperial control of private coal corporations, and used by them as absolutely and as privately as were their mines, to and for their own private purposes, and upon which public territory no man might enter for either public or private purposes, save and except by the express permission of these private corporations.

"This right to determine who should enter such so-called election precincts, appears from the record to have been exercised against all classes, merchants, tradesmen or what not, and whether the business of such person was public or private. Indeed, it appears that in one instance the governor and adjutant general of the state while on official business were denied admission to one of these closed camps. And that on the day of election, the Democratic watchers and challengers for Walsen Mine precinct, one of which was Neelley, the Democratic candidate for sheriff, were forced to seek and secure a detail of federal soldiers to escort them into the precinct and to the polls, and that such soldiers remained as such guard during the day and a part of the night. . . .

"But if there was any doubt concerning the condition of the closed camps and precincts, and the exclusion of representatives of the Democratic Party from discussing the issues of the campaign within the precincts comprising the closed camps, it was entirely removed by the testimony of the witness Weitzel for contestee Farr. He testified that he was a resident of Pueblo, and was manager of the Colorado Fuel & Iron Company; that Rouse, Lester, Ideal, Cameron, Walsen, Pictou and McNally are camps under his jurisdiction. That he had general charge of the camps

OUT OF THE DEPTHS

to him in this respect except the president; that the superintendent and other employes are under his supervision; that the
federal troops came about the 1st of May, 1914, and continued
until January, 1915. That in all those camps he tried to keep
out the people who were antagonistic to the company's interest;
that it was private property and so treated by his company; that
through him the company and its officials assumed to exercise
authority as to who might or might not enter; that if persons
could assure or satisfy the man at the gate that they were not
connected with the United Mine Workers, or in their employ
as agitators, they were let into the camp. That 'no one we were
fighting against got in for social intercourse or any other'; that
he and officials under him assumed to pass upon the question of
whether or not any person coming there came for the purpose
of agitation. That Mr. Mitchell, the chairman of the Democratic
committee, as he recalled it, was identified with the agitators,
ran a newspaper and was connected either directly or indirectly
with the United Mine Workers; that Mr. Neelley, Democratic
candidate for sheriff, was identified with the strikers, and he
would be considered as an objectionable character. That when
the federal troops came they restored peace and normal conditions; there was no rioting after that, there was no fear on the
part of the company when the federal soldiers were here, except
fear of agitation. Asked if he guarded the camp against discussion, against the espousal of the cause of the company, he
replied, 'We didn't encourage it.' The company would not encourage organizers to come into the camp, no matter how
peacefully they conducted themselves; that the company did not
permit men to come into the camp and discuss with the employes certain principles, or to carry on arguments with them
or to appeal to their reason, or to discuss with them things along
reasonable lines because it was known from experience that
if they were allowed to come in they would resort to threats
of violence. They might not resort to any violence at the time,

but it might result in the people becoming frightened and leaving, and they were anxious to hold their employes. He was
asked whether or not one had business there depended upon the
decision of the official in charge; he replied that the superintendent probably would inquire of him what his business was.
That any one that Farr asked for a permit to enter the camp
would likely get it.

"It appears that the number of registered voters in the closed
precincts was very largely in excess of the number of votes cast,
and this of itself was sufficient to demand an open and fair investigation as to the qualifications of alleged voters.

"It appears from the testimony that in these closed precincts
many of those who voted were unable to speak or read the
English language, and that in numerous instances, the election
judges assisted such, by marking the ballots for them in violation of law. . . . Thus such voters were not choosing candidates,
but, under the direction of the companies, were simply placing
the cross where they found the particular letter R on the ballot,
so that the ballot was not an expression of opinion or judgment,
not an intelligent exercise of suffrage, but plainly a dictated coal
company vote, as much so as if the agents of these companies
had marked the ballots without the intervention of the voter.
No more fraudulent and infamous prostitution of the ballot is
conceivable. . . .

"Counsel contended that the closed precincts were an 'industrial necessity' and for such reason the conduct of the coal companies during the campaign was justified. However such conduct may be viewed when confined to private property of such
corporations in their private operations, the fact remains that
there is no justification when they are dealing with such territory
after it had been dedicated to the public use, and particularly
involving the right of the people to exercise their duties and
powers as electors in a popular government.

"The fact appears that the members of the board of county
commissioners and all other county officers were Republicans,

and as stated by counsel for the contestees, the success of the Republican candidates was considered by the coal companies vital to their interest. The close relationship of the coal companies and the Republican officials and candidates appears to have been so marked both before and during the campaign, as to justify the conclusion that such officers regarded their duty to the coal companies as paramount to their duty to the public service. To say that the closed precincts were not so created as to suit the convenience and interests of these corporations, or that they were not so formed with the advice and consent of these corporations, is to discredit human intelligence, and to deny human experience. The plain purpose of the formation of the new precincts was that the coal companies might have opportunity to conduct and control the elections therein, just as such elections were conducted. The irresistible conclusion is that these closed precincts were so formed by the county commissioners with the connivance of the representatives of the coal companies, if not by their express command.

"There can be no free, open and fair election as contemplated by the constitution, where private industrial corporations so throttle public opinion, deny the free exercise of choice by sovereign electors, dictate and control all election officers, prohibit public discussion of public questions, and imperially command what citizens may and what citizens may not, peacefully and for lawful purposes, enter upon election or public territory. . . .

"We have heard much in this state in recent years as to the denial of inherent and constitutional rights of citizens being justified by 'military necessity' but this we believe is the first time in our experience when the violation of the fundamental rights of freemen has been attempted to be justified by the plea of 'industrial necessity.' Even if we were to concede that there may be some palliation in the plea of military necessity on the theory that such acts purport to be acts of the government itself, through its military arm and with the purpose of preserving the public peace and safety; yet that a private corporation with its privately armed forces, may violate the most sacred right of citizenship of the state and find lawful excuse in the plea of private 'industrial necessity' savours too much of anarchy to find approval by courts of justice. . . ."

The Supreme Court then annulled the votes cast in the coal company precincts and ordered Farr to turn the office of Huerfano County sheriff over to E. L. Neelley.

Sheriff Farr and his henchmen had ruled over the Kingdom of Huerfano for 20 years. They represented the power of the coal barons and No. 26 Broadway. Jeff and his heavily-armed lieutenants held on to the Walsenburg court house for another week while corporation attorneys sought to carry their case to the U. S. Supreme Court. That tribunal would have none of it, and Jeff Farr abdicated.[4]

He marched out of the court house early in the morning, long before most of the residents of Walsenburg were up and about, with three satellites at his heels—Col. William H. Freeland, county clerk; Jose Sanchez, county assessor, and Antonio Valdez. Jeff paused a moment on the stone steps. The new sheriff, Neelley, who had been elected 18 months before, stood on the sidewalk with J. G. Archuleta, C. H. Sanchez and Robert Young, waiting to take office. Jeff looked at the new officials and then up and down Walsenburg's main street. A train was just easing into the little depot across the way. Jeff threw out his chest and stuck his thumbs in the armpits of his vest.

"When I die everyone will come to my funeral," Jeff said in a loud voice.

Joe Sanchez was the only one of the dispirited group to ask why.

"Because they'll all want to make sure that old son-of-a-bitch is dead."

[4] Trinidad Free Press, July 20, 1916.

With that, Jeff stepped down and walked briskly to the
street without so much as a nod to the incoming officials. The
Czar was through.

The passing of Jeff Farr did not escape national notice for
Frank Walsh wrote Rockefeller about it.

"The Committee on Industrial Relations has just received
from the Supreme Court of Colorado, which is the court of last
resort of that state, its opinion and judgment in the Colorado
election cases, in which your conduct and that of your associates is branded as anarchistic, fraudulent and destructive of free
institutions. Thus far you seem to have paid no attention to
that judicial condemnation. The court in its judgment found
the notorious Jeff Farr was your agent.

"The court placed the direct responsibility for the most re-
volting political and industrial corruption directly at the door
of the company. It is declared that the public machinery 'had
been turned over to the absolute domination and imperial control' of your company and was 'used by them as absolutely and
privately as were their mines, and to and for their own private
purposes.' The findings of the court were based upon the sworn
testimony of the general manager in charge of all the Rockefeller mining properties in Colorado, who still retains control
and thereby your authority, and thereby has autocratic control
over the lives of your workers and their dependents."

Walsh asked Rockefeller what he was going to do about it.
He wanted all of the guilty officials discharged at once. Rockefeller replied from Seal Harbor, Me., where he was vacationing,
that he had not heard of the decision or of the ousting of Jeff
Farr.

"I can only say that any offenses, no matter by whom committed, which could have been justly characterized in such
language as you have quoted would be quite as abhorrent to me
as to you, and I am confident that no such conditions as you
describe could exist in the camps of the Colorado Fuel & Iron
Co. under the plan of representation which was adopted by the

joint action of the company and its employees at the time of my
visit to Colorado last fall."

By early August, most of the court dockets in the state had
been cleared of strike cases. Attorney General Farrar had quietly
dismissed them. No step was taken, however, to rectify the
wrong done to Lawson. The Denver Express, noting that Governor Carlson and Farrar were cognizant that an election was
approaching, gave them credit for quashing the strike cases and
then demanded that Lawson be freed.[5]

In a boxed editorial on its front page, the Express said, "The
charge against John R. Lawson is almost the only one to be
retained. Without doubt there is hardly a person in this state,
with the exception of a very few whose eyes are blinded by
hatred that the passage of time should have dispelled, who believes Lawson guilty of any crime. Farrar has frankly stated
that the strike cases were dismissed because there was no hope
of conviction. Does he believe that Lawson is more guilty than
the men released, or does he hope to save his face by convicting
him? To argue that Lawson's alleged crime is more heinous than
those for which hundreds of strikers were excused and exonerated is an affront to common sense. Finally, the continuance
of the Lawson charge is either an attempt of the administration
to save a little from the wreckage of strike prosecutions, or it is
outright persecution. It is high time that the wounds of the
strike were healed. Public welfare, not private prejudice, should
guide their acts."

Despite the constant appeals, Governor Carlson and Attorney
General Farrar took no action to clear Lawson. There was no
way of knowing when the Supreme Court would act. Lawson
did not worry a great deal about it as he had Hawkins' assurance that everything would come out all right, and he was
working too hard to do much worrying. Two elections were
approaching, that of District 15 of the United Mine Workers

[5] The Denver Express, Aug. 5, 1916.

and the state election. There were ominous clouds on the union horizon. Lawson had grown into a powerful national figure, a symbol of persecuted unionism. Many leaders in the organization were not pleased with his prominence. Intimations of petty jealousy and backbiting came to him. Privately, Lawson told his confidants that he had no ambitions where the national organization was concerned.

"My work is here," he said simply. "I have no desire to do anything more."

Ed Doyle and a number of other stalwarts stood fast with Lawson as the storm within the organization gathered. The miners of the state were with him. Lawson was their hero, their ideal of a fair, honest labor leader who could not be corrupted by any influence. As far as the state election was concerned, Lawson and his aides were determined to strike another blow at corporation domination. Governor Carlson and Attorney General Farrar must be relegated to the same political oblivion that had engulfed Governors Peabody and Ammons at the close of their first terms.

Woodrow Wilson was again the standard-bearer of the Democratic Party which was confident of success. The Republicans, however, had most of the progressives back in the fold and, with Charles Evans Hughes as their presidential candidate, were apparently as vigorous and formidable as ever. Governor Carlson, as a candidate for re-election, was opposed by Julius C. Gunter, a soft-spoken courtly Southern Democrat who had served on the district bench in Trinidad and in the Supreme Court. Attorney General Farrar was opposed by Leslie E. Hubbard, a young Denver attorney. As was the case in the nation, war was an important issue, but it was not more important in Colorado than those raised by the strike. Both Carlson and Farrar were repudiated at the polls.

Before the new state officers took their oaths, the United Mine Workers held their election.[6] John Lawson was elected

---

[6] Denver Labor Bulletin, Dec. 30, 1916.

president of District 15, and Ed Doyle was named to Lawson's old post on the international board. Both men won by large majorities, but the result was displeasing to several international officers who had quietly opposed their candidacies. They had contended that Lawson had not carried on organization work in Colorado with proper diligence. He countered with statistics to show a substantial growth within the state, and with a statement that the international organization could place as many organizers in the field as it saw fit.

Attorney Hawkins took no part in the fight. He was a lawyer, not a union official, and he still had plenty of legal work for the union to keep him busy. He freed himself and Clark of the subornation of perjury charges, and pressed to clear Lawson and other convicted miners. Lawson consulted him frequently in regard to the court cases, but he walked alone in the intra-union battle.

In the background of the dispute was the refusal of John Lawson and Ed Doyle to approve the so-called Woodrow Wilson settlement plan in June, 1914, a plan approved at the time by Vice President Frank J. Hayes. President Wilson's mediators, William R. Fairley and Hymel Davis, had proposed the settlement to Lawson, Doyle and Hayes at a meeting in Denver June 22, 1914. At that meeting Fairley had argued that the strike was lost and that someone had to be "the goat" in the closing of the strike.

Both Lawson and Doyle turned the proposal down because of a clause that provided no one should get work "who may be indicted." This was later changed to read "who are indicted." A copy was made of the proposal and given to Lawson, Doyle and Hayes. They rewrote the proposition to include clauses Lawson and Doyle could accept as the basis for a settlement.

On June 26, 1914, Hayes gave the rewritten proposal to Fairley, saying: "We have considered your proposition thoroughly and have suggested changes that we believe the operators can agree to in view of their announcements ever since the strike to the effect that they have granted all except recognition of the union."

Fairley read the proposal and said he would have to discuss it with his colleagues. Three days later, Fairley again met with Lawson, Hayes, Doyle and John McLennan. Fairley told them he felt the mediation commission had outlived its usefulness and that he felt he should return to Washington with a recommendation that President Wilson appoint a commission to give an award after hearing both sides of the controversy.

Oddly enough, Fairley said he wanted the original proposal destroyed and he did not want a record of it. He asked Doyle how many copies had been made.

"Four," Doyle replied.

"Let's burn them then," Fairley said.

"Why burn them?" Doyle asked suspiciously. "Why not just cut off the letterhead and the signatures? We'd like to keep it in that shape."

"It would look suspicious if it ever got out," Fairley replied. At Hayes' insistence, Doyle produced the copies. Fairley put the original in his pocket and then burned the four copies in a cuspidor, saying it would be considered as if never written, and that he would go back to Washington with a recommendation that a commission be named.

The matter rested there until Aug. 30, 1914, when Mother Jones called Ed Doyle and asked him to request President Wilson by telegram to do something to end the strike with the understanding the miners would accept any proposition he offered. Doyle refused to send such a telegram though Mother Jones used all of her persuasive powers to get him to do so. Fairley returned to Denver Sept. 5, 1914, and talked several times to Hayes. The next night, Sept. 6, 1914, Doyle read in the Rocky Mountain News that President Wilson had offered a proposition to settle the strike. The canny Doyle hurried to his office and secured an extra copy of Fairley's original proposal, which he had had made before the cuspidor burning, and compared it with the new Wilson proposal. They were identical.

"What do you think of double-crossers who would secure the President's signature on a proposition which was burned right here in this office and in that very cuspidor?" Doyle asked Hayes when they met in the union headquarters the next morning.

"I know it is away out of line, but what can you do about it?" Hayes asked. "We will have to accept it since the President offered it."

Hayes was impatient to secure ratification from the miners of the state and insisted on calling a meeting for Sept. 15, 1914, though the policy committee was to meet in Omaha Sept. 12. At the Omaha meeting, attended by Lawson, Hayes, Doyle, John McLennan, James Lord, William Diamond, Percy Tetlow, President White and Secretary William Green, Doyle proposed that the committee go to Washington and explain the situation to the President and ask for modification of the objectionable clauses.

"Why, you would insult the dignity of the President of the United States," Green said.

The committee refused to accept suggestions from either Doyle or Lawson. It sent a letter to President Wilson accepting the settlement proposal. Three days later, when the Colorado miners met in Trinidad to consider it, Hayes and Fairley urged approval. The delegates to the convention, led by promises that never were kept and by subtle threats of withdrawal of national support, finally gave their approval.

Subsequently President White and Green asked President Wilson to modify the proposal along the exact lines suggested earlier by Lawson and Doyle. The latter interpreted the maneuvering as an attempt by the national officers of the UMWA to trade off the strike for a commission, and to thus get rid of the strike while protecting their own positions. Doyle attempted to expose the entire plot at the international conven-

tion of the United Mine Workers in Indianapolis Jan. 27, 1916.
John L. Lewis was presiding and Green was serving as secretary.
When Doyle spoke, Green instructed the reporter, Mrs. Mark
Burk, not to take Doyle's speech for the record. Lewis refused
to allow Doyle to speak later in the meeting in rebuttal to talks
made by White, Hayes, Green and Fairley though their speeches
were made part of the record of the convention.

CHAPTER XXVI

LAWSON IS FREED

The internal strife in the union came to a head in February, 1917, when the executive board, at a special meeting in Indianapolis, gave a sub-committee of five authority to suspend the charter of District 15.[1] Lawson asked that a five-man investigating committee be named to make a thorough study in the state and report back to their international body before any action was taken. He offered to step aside voluntarily if it could be shown he had retarded the growth of the union movement in any way. Although the sub-committee of the executive board had until April to act, it did not waste a minute. James F. Moran of Iowa and Warren Pippin of Kansas were sent to Denver to take charge of Colorado. The charter of District 15 was suspended and all official positions connected with the district union were abolished. The central offices were moved from Denver to Pueblo.[2] Lawson and Doyle were out. Their dream of a strong, united labor movement, motivated by principles of brotherhood and common good, seemed to be vanishing before their eyes after years of heart-breaking struggle and danger. A spirit of compromise with the coal operators had seized the international officers in the hope of getting rid of a costly strike without losing face or their lucrative positions. The Colorado miners were

[1] Denver Labor Bulletin, Feb. 10, 1917.
[2] Denver Labor Bulletin, Feb. 24, 1917.

threatened with loss of all that had been accomplished in the years since Governor Peabody and Adjutant General Sherman Bell had ruthlessly suppressed the workers. Lawson and Doyle had refused to compromise principle so they must go. Lawson was bitter at first as expressions of loyalty poured in from every section of the state, but he soon resigned himself as he knew he was helpless against the machinations of the international officers. They controlled the machinery of the organization and there was nothing he could do. The sentence of life imprisonment for murder still was hanging over his head. With his job gone, he was faced with the necessity of finding work immediately to support Olive and Fern.

Once again John Lawson returned to the coal mines. He found work in the Ideal Mine in Northern Colorado. An expert miner, he was welcomed by the Ideal superintendent. Good miners such as John Lawson were hard to find. The hard labor eased his mind and toughened him. It seemed perfectly natural to go into the shaft each morning with his lunch bucket and his lamp; to walk home to Olive and Fern each night, tired and dirty. His years as an organizer had not taken his skill from him, and his muscles soon hardened. He had his mighty physique and his knowledge of mining to carry on.

The movement to which he had given such impetus and strength did not falter despite the internal dissension. The Victor-American Fuel Co., long one of the bitterest foes of the United Mine Workers, signed a three-year contract in March, 1917, unionizing its 12 big mines in Colorado and two properties in New Mexico. Recognition was granted. The new contract gave rise to predictions that every coal operator in the state soon would sign with the United Mine Workers. The miners were headed toward better days.

John Lawson, too, began to see light ahead. A few days after the Victor-American signed a contract, Attorney General Hubbard went into the Supreme Court and filed a brief, confessing error in the Lawson conviction.[3]

"This case was tried in a community which had been directly affected by the disturbed conditions growing out of the strike," Hubbard told the high court. "It was well known that public feeling in that region had been profoundly disturbed. Strong sympathies and prejudices had been aroused and popular opinion was sharply divided in its support and opposition to the respective interests. Violence and bloodshed became matters of frequent occurrence, and the intervention of the military power of the state and nation finally became necessary. The animosities engendered by this industrial conflict had by no means subsided when this trial took place. The defendant, as an officer of the union, had taken a conspicuous part in the strike and, of many charged in the same information, had been singled out for separate trial.

"Under the circumstances it was particularly unfortunate that he was tried before a judge against whom there rested the imputation of interest, bias or prejudice. If the judicial enforcement of law is to command universal respect, it must deserve that respect. And too great care can never be exercised to see that it does deserve that respect. We believe that when a strong showing of bias or prejudice is presented in good faith against a trial judge he should step down after calling to his place some other against whom the objection does not exist.

"We confess the prejudicial character of the above-noted, manifest errors the more readily because a thorough examination of this record has left in our minds the most serious doubts of the defendant's guilt of the offense charged."

Attorney General Hubbard analyzed the testimony of the state's chief witnesses against Lawson, saying, "Their avowed and brazenly admitted indifference to the results of their alleged activities in supplying the strikers with weapons and ammunition to be used, as they contended, for aggressive pur-

[3] Denver Labor Bulletin, April 14, 1917.

poses, destroys every vestige of respect for, or confidence in, them as witnesses in a cause where life and liberty are at stake. Without further discussion, we recommend that the judgment and sentence of the trial court be set aside not only because of the invalidity of the entire proceeding, but because of the prejudicial errors above commented upon."

Hawkins was jubilant. He called John Lawson on the telephone.

"You're out of the woods, John," he said enthusiastically. "It is only a matter of time until the court acts in your favor."

Lawson turned to Olive, who was standing by the telephone.

"Hubbard has confessed error," he said, a catch in his voice. "I'll soon be free."

Olive held him tightly as he thanked Hawkins and replaced the receiver.

It was April 20, 1917.

Special trains carried gay crowds from Trinidad and other Southern Colorado towns toward Ludlow. The roads to the site of the former colony were lined with automobiles and rigs. The United Mine Workers had purchased 40 acres around the Black Hole where 13 women and children had died.

A dozen bands greeted the incoming trains at Ludlow station. Old acquaintanceships were renewed in the dialects of a score of races. Ten thousand men, women and children gathered on the field where their comrades had yielded their lives in a fight for decent wages, hours and living conditions. A parade was formed in Tollerburg before noon. Five thousand marched in the line. Every man and every woman wore a red bandanna, the strikers' emblem, and carried a tiny American flag. The battle scarred flag of Ludlow rode the breeze at the head of the line. Beside it was a new flag of justice. The march down the canon to the prairie was a march of triumph. Thousands lined the road to greet the parade. Two of the humblest miners in line were John R. Lawson and Ed Doyle. They trudged along the dirt road with their fellow miners. The crowd spotted them and cheered as they marched by.

"There goes John Lawson and Ed Doyle."

They were no longer officials of the United Mine Workers or men of authority in the organization, but the miners and their families loved these two big men. They had stood fast when many of their critics were afraid to cross the state line into Colorado.

Both Lawson and Doyle spoke from the gaily decorated platform. They talked of the colony, of the strike, and of hope for the future. Other speakers followed them, delivering essentially the same messages in Italian, Slavic, Spanish and Greek. At the conclusion of the speaking program, big John Lawson dropped flowers into the hole that had proven a death trap for innocent women and children. The band played and the crowd sang, "Nearer My God to Thee."

Long shadows crept across the field as the crowd drifted homeward.

"See those shadows, Ed," Lawson said. "Those same shadows were here three years ago today. They stabbed at the colony. They foretold the tragedy of that day."

Doyle nodded soberly.

"It was a tragedy the like of which we won't see again," Doyle said. "Death is gone from these hills now."

Lawson let his eyes wander along the ragged line of foothills where the mines were located before he replied:

"Death is always present in the coal districts, Ed. It will strike many times, perhaps in a different way and in different circumstances, but it will always be present."

"I know what you mean," Doyle said. "A rock fall and a man dead."

"Yes," Lawson replied. "Hundreds, perhaps thousands, will die here yet for King Coal."

Doyle thought of Lawson's words seven days later when the Victor-American's Hastings Mine, a few short miles from Ludlow, blew up with a roar and a flash of flame. Mine rescue crews were summoned from other properties. Women and children gathered about the entrance of the mine and started the death chant. They seemed to know their men, fathers, husbands and sweethearts, were dead. Somewhere in the miles of underground entries 121 men were sealed away. Lawson, filled with horror, rushed south again to lend assistance. His offer of aid was welcomed and he was placed in charge of a rescue party. With Lawson leading the way, the men penetrated the mine to a depth of 7,000 feet. They found bodies, twisted and burned until they did not appear to be human.

"There isn't a man left alive in there," Lawson told James Dalrymple, chief mine inspector, when he came to the surface. "Some are mutilated and some were just blown over like stems of wheat."

Other crews brought bodies out and a carload of coffins was shipped from Denver. Lawson made the rounds of the camp, offering consolation to the survivors. There was the pretty, dark-eyed Austrian girl who stood forlornly by the side of a shack. She was to have been married to Steve Rockich within the week. Steve was dead. Jesus Herrera sobbed brokenly on Lawson's shoulder. He had helped lift his 17-year-old brother, Fillipe, from under a half-ton rock.

All that day and all that night Lawson worked tirelessly, giving aid wherever he could. In the small hours of the morning, when the charred body of Tony Galavich was carried from the mine, screams came from the Galavich home. Mrs. Galavich, a widow now with eight children to support, was giving birth to a baby.

At dawn, Lawson went to the machine shop where 117 bodies were laid out and covered with tarpaulins. This was to have been May Day, a gala occasion for the Austrians, Italians and Greeks. Little white dresses had been laundered and ironed days in advance, a dance had been planned, a Mass was to have been said in the little Catholic church on the hill. A Mass would be offered, but it would be a requiem for the dead.

The mine explosion had apparently started in the sixth entry about 6,500 feet from the surface. There was one great flash of fire and that was all, investigators decided. The blast had worked upward, killing every man in its path. Lawson stayed on for the funerals. The dead were taken to Trinidad. Services were held in a dozen churches at once and the bodies were taken, eight on a dray, to the cemetery.

The work of exploring the wrecked mine continued unabated. One victim was found on his knees, in an attitude of prayer, with a piece of canvas over his head. John Lawson worked eight-hour shifts with the crews. A company official, who had learned to despise the name of Lawson during the strike days, told a group that "no matter what else might be said of Lawson, he has a heart as big as a ham."

A Denver newspaper reporter, who was covering the story, wrote, "The biggest figure in Hastings today is John Lawson, the well-known labor leader and international character. Lawson has made the rounds of the little camp daily since coming here, offering what consolation he can to the stricken people in their hour of sorrow. Lawson is a man who, once met, can never be forgotten. His name is on every tongue in Hastings. To those who witnessed the frightful scenes in Ludlow, just three miles from here, and then can see the present attitude of the mine owners and labor leaders toward each other, the contrast is striking. It means but one thing—everlasting industrial peace in the southern coal camps."

When the Hastings tragedy had become merely another black mark on Colorado's coal mining records and the mine had been cleaned up, Lawson went back to his Northern Colorado job. As he left Hastings, after 15 days of hard work, a Victor-American official thanked him for what he had done.

"We don't see eye to eye on a lot of things, but we know a

good miner when we see one and we appreciate what you have done."

Not long after he had returned to Denver, Lawson's name was cleared by the Supreme Court which reversed his district court conviction. The case was not remanded for trial. John Lawson was a free man. At the same time the court granted a new trial to Louis Zancanelli. Attorney General Hubbard immediately announced that a new trial would not be held. The strike slate was wiped clean.

Lawson's fight with the United Mine Workers was settled a few weeks later when the Colorado State Federation of Labor met in Boulder for its twenty-second annual convention. Lawson and Doyle were in attendance as were the international officers who had taken charge of District 15. For two days the differences were discussed, at times heatedly, and then a statement, signed by Lawson, Doyle, James P. Moran, Robert Uhlich, and John M. O'Neil, was issued. It read:

"The labor movement of Colorado is bigger and greater than any individual in the membership of organized labor and bigger and greater than any elements that may be identified with its membership, and believing that every member whose union is affiliated with the Colorado State Federation of Labor should stand united in the strength of a labor movement that should be one and inseparable, we, the undersigned, appeal in the name of organized labor, that dissension among officials and members shall be no more, but that each and everyone among whom personal differences or prejudices may have arisen, shall sink such personal differences or prejudices, and unite in that great army of labor that will be invincible in its unity, with every promise of marching onward and upward to the goal of industrial liberty."

By unanimous vote, the convention adopted the statement in resolution form. John R. Lawson, as had been the case many times before, had made another sacrifice, a sacrifice of self, for the union and for the principle that had motivated his every act in the struggle to unionize the Colorado coal fields.

CHAPTER XXVII

OUT OF THE DEPTHS

In the years since John R. Lawson went up and down Colorado risking the bludgeon, the assassin's bullet and the dungeon to preach unionism in the camps of a relentless enemy, the objective he sought has been achieved by the working men and women of the state. On the foundation he laid at little meetings in hotel rooms, barns, miners' shanties and on windswept hillsides, far from the prying eyes of brutal gunmen, a strong superstructure has been raised. Today, Colorado mines are union mines. The men carry United Mine Workers cards without fear of intimidation or reprisal from coal company officials. They trade where they please, vote as they please, and are, in short, free men. It is true there are still conflicts between employers and employes in the mountain states, but Ludlow is ever present, a grim reminder that the conference table is more in keeping with American civilization than the torch and the machine gun.

Unionization of the Colorado mines was not achieved completely, however, without extreme difficulty. After the 1913-1914 strike, the Rockefeller Plan was put into effect in all C. F. & I. Co. mines. Known as the Industrial Representation Plan,[1] it gave the workers some recognition as men and attempt-

---

[1] The details of this plan are touched upon only briefly here as it has been the subject of a thorough study and report by Ben M. Selekman and Mary Van Kleeck in "Employes Representation in Coal Mines," Russell Sage Foundation, N. Y., 1924.

ed to establish a personal relationship between management and wage earners. For purposes of administration, the C. F. & I. divided its territory into four districts. Each district and each mine had its own representation. The privilege of voting in an election of representatives was limited to wage earners who had been on the payroll for at least three months prior to the date of the election. One representative was elected for each 150 employes in a mine, but no mine had less than two. The representatives, who served for one year, were elected at annual meetings of employes on the second Saturday in January. Secret ballots were used for both nomination and election. Immediately after the election and each four months thereafter, the president of the coal company called a conference in each administrative district. The miners' representatives met with an equal number of representatives of the management, who were appointed by the company president, to discuss working and living conditions, discipline and promotion of mutual interests.

In addition, each district had four committees known as joint committees on industrial relations. They dealt with safety and accidents; sanitation, health and housing; recreation and education, and industrial cooperation and conciliation. Each committee consisted of six members, three elected by the miners and three appointed by the company. Each committee, on matters within its jurisdiction, reported its findings to the president of the company or any other designated company official for his consideration.

Although the company reserved the right to hire and fire "with fairness of the action subject to review," it was agreed union membership was not a reason for refusing a miner employment or discharging him. There were many complaints against the plan, some justified and some not. Coal company officials made every effort, for the most part, to carry out its objectives. That it ultimately failed was due to its fundamental weaknesses and the persistent opposition of workers who believed an independent union, free from any company participation or connection, was the only proper bargaining agency for the coal miners.

Although the Industrial Representation Plan continued in effect until 1934, when the National Recovery Act brought about its demise and the complete organization of C. F. & I. mines by the United Mine Workers, it did not prevent strikes in the intervening years. The miners walked out Nov. 1, 1918, when a nationwide strike was called by the UMWA as a result of conditions in Indiana, Ohio, Illinois and Western Pennsylvania. The Colorado miners went back to work Nov. 12 and 13 on instructions from UMWA leaders. On Nov. 30, 1919, they received a 14 per cent wage increase in conformity with increases granted in other districts of the nation.

In 1921, the Colorado Fuel & Iron Co. wiped out the wage increases of Nov. 1, 1917, and Nov. 30, 1919. The order was effective Sept. 1, 1921, and the miners struck on that day. The State Industrial Commission intervened, however, and restored the original scale pending an investigation. The miners went back to work. On Nov. 4, 1921, the Industrial Commission found for the coal company and on Nov. 16, 1921, the company posted a notice to the effect the wage decrease would take effect Nov. 17, the following day. Oddly enough, Governor Oliver H. Shoup, a Republican, declared martial law the day the notice was posted (though none of the miners had yet walked out) and Adjutant General Patrick Hamrock, the officer who had been in charge at the Ludlow Massacre, was sent to Walsenburg with militia and state police units. These troops remained in the field until Jan. 28, 1922. When they were withdrawn, two companies of rangers were left behind, remaining in the coal fields until November, 1922.

Throughout the long coal strike of 1922, the rangers industriously prevented picketing and broke up union meetings. Arms and ammunition were seized in Walsenburg, and union officials were denied admittance to the mining camps. There was no violence, however, and at the conclusion of the strike the C. F. & I. restored wages of its miners to the 1920 level, a scale which had been maintained by the unionized mines throughout the difficulty.

The last noteworthy strike was the Sacco-Vanzetti strike of 1927. Organized and directed by the Industrial Workers of the World, the strike broke in the Fall of 1927 (Nicola Sacco and Bartolomeo Vanzetti, Italians, were executed Aug. 23, 1927, for the murder of Frederick A. Parmenter, South Braintree, Mass., shoe factory paymaster in 1921). Few members of the United Mine Workers were in sympathy with the strike, but many refused to pass through picket lines. Governor William H. Adams, a Democrat, sent state police to the Columbine Mine of the Rocky Mountain Fuel Co. near Lafayette in the northern fields. The gates of the mine property were kept open, but the state police objected to I.W.W. pickets entering on the property. During one demonstration, guns of the police were turned on the pickets. Five were killed and 24 persons were wounded.[2] During this strike, John Lawson, as a mine inspector employed by the State Compensation Insurance Fund, helped settle the strike in the southern field.

Lawson himself suffered a great deal after the 1913-1914 strike as did his comrade, the genial Ed Doyle. Lawson's troubles did not end when his name was cleared of the ugly charge of murder, nor with the peace resolution signed at the Boulder convention. His job at the Ideal Mine played out, and he was without financial means or prospects of employment. Most avenues of work were closed to him. The big coal operators wanted none of him, and the UMWA had frozen him out. Doyle was in an equally bad plight, without money and without work to support his wife and children.

During part of 1918, Lawson occupied himself as a volunteer war worker. At the request of Governor Julius C. Gunter, who had made the appointment over the protest of the coal operators, Lawson served on a special Americanization committee

[2] Nov. 21, 1927.

which worked among the aliens of the state, bringing hundreds into the fold of citizenship. When the task was done, Lawson was in even more desperate financial circumstances. It appeared for a time as though he and Doyle must either starve or be driven from the state they loved so well. They went to Kansas and worked for a time in the land leasing department of the Argus Oil Co. When they returned to Colorado, Doyle went to work for the railroad brotherhoods. He is with a brotherhood today, as a traveling auditor.

Lawson went to Durango in Southwestern Colorado to manage a coal mine, the Morning Star. He stayed there two years, long years in exile and isolation, and then returned to Denver to be an inspector of mines for the State Compensation Insurance Division, a modest post with an equally modest salary attached. Lawson was well fitted for this work as during his earlier years he had worked with James Dalrymple on a state coal mining law which had decreased fatal and non-fatal accidents in Colorado mines. Before this law was adopted, Colorado had the blackest accident record in the nation.

A year after Lawson became a state employe, his fortunes took a strange turn. John J. Roche, owner of a majority of stock in the Rocky Mountain Fuel Co., died. His daughter, Miss Josephine Roche, a nationally known advocate of social and industrial reforms, became head of the firm. Miss Roche had worked in Denver Juvenile Court with Judge Ben. B. Lindsey and had long been associated with Edward P. Costigan in reform and progressive movements. When she took over the reins of the company, she looked about for an able, practical man to help her. She picked John Lawson. The man who had had to steal into coal camps at night, the man the coal moguls had called a dangerous agitator, became vice president of the Rocky Mountain Fuel Co. and a member of its board of directors. During the 11 years he served as vice president of the firm, in active contact with the operations in its big mines, his relationships with the United Mine Workers were warm and cordial. On one occasion, when a proposed union contract was under discussion, Lawson handled the negotiations for the coal company. At the end of the first meeting, a miner in the rear of the room called out:

"Let John Lawson write the contract and we'll accept it."

The other miners nodded their heads in affirmation and the vice president of a Colorado coal company wrote a union contract. It was immediately accepted.

Lawson improved conditions in Rocky Mountain Fuel Co. mines with Miss Roche's enthusiastic backing. The company paid the second highest wage scale in the United States and treated its employes with the utmost consideration and fairness. In one instance, when the life of the company was jeopardized by a price war, which was led by the Colorado Fuel & Iron Co., the miners voluntarily loaned part of their wages to the firm. Other union groups also came to the rescue. They appointed special coal committees and scoured the state to obtain new business for the firm.

As vice president of the Rocky Mountain Fuel Co., John Lawson was a director of the Employers Mutual Insurance Co., a firm owned by 45 independent coal operators. Frank West, the former deputy attorney general who had prosecuted Lawson in Las Animas County, was attorney for the insurance company at a salary of $5,000 a year. The directors of the firm were anti-union coal barons of strike days. At first they looked upon Lawson with suspicion. Soon, they learned to love him for his warm heart and to respect him for his ability.

Mr. West regretfully resigned as attorney for the firm and Horace Hawkins, the man who had sat across the table from West in the Las Animas County court room, was employed at a salary 50 per cent greater than that which had been paid to West.

John Lawson served as vice president and director of the Rocky Mountain Fuel Co. until June, 1939, when he resigned to devote his time to an invention of his own, a coal mining machine. Had he been with the Rocky Mountain Fuel Co. in 1927, the Columbine Mine killings would not have occurred.

What of the others who played roles in the great Colorado strikes, particularly the strike of 1913-1914?

Perry C. Coryell, the New Castle mine owner, who shot Lawson down with a shotgun, left Colorado and went to the Pacific Northwest. There he again resorted to guns, murdered two men during an argument over a real estate deal, and went to prison for life.

Attorney General Fred Farrar, after leaving office, became, as might have been expected, chief counsel for the Colorado Fuel & Iron Co. in Colorado, a post he has since held. Needless to say, his political days are ended. Jesse F. Welborn, president of the C. F. & I., retained his position until retirement. The former governor, Elias Ammons, disappeared from the political scene after his defeat, but, strangely enough, his son, Teller Ammons, became governor in 1937. He did everything possible to compensate the laboring men of Colorado for old wrongs, and his relationships with unions were friendly. His lieutenant governor was none other than Frank Hayes who is still an organizer for the United Mine Workers of America.

Horace Hawkins never entered political life, but has remained through the years a successful and respected member of the Colorado bar. His aide in the strike days, Edward P. Costigan, had a colorful and useful political career. He was appointed to the U. S. Tariff Commission by President Wilson and served on that body with distinction for many years. When President Coolidge took office, he offered to reappoint a number of officials, including Mr. Costigan, if they would sign undated resignations and place them in his hands. Mr. Costigan spurned the offer and handed in a dated resignation. He returned to Colorado and for many years was chief counsel for the Rocky Mountain Fuel Co. In 1930, he bested two strong Democratic opponents to win the Democratic nomination for the U. S. Senate. His platform was progressive and liberal. The laboring men of

Colorado gave him their wholehearted support and he was victorious in the general election by an overwhelming majority.

Senator Costigan made an enviable record in Washington. His
outlook was national and he played a conspicuous part in the
early days of the New Deal as a warm and ardent supporter of
President Franklin D. Roosevelt. Senator Costigan's political
opponents never dared hurl the charge of rubber-stamp at him
for he was a New Dealer long years before the term was originated. Illness forced Senator Costigan's retirement from public
life and he subsequently died in his home in Denver, honored
and respected by all who knew him.

Major Boughton's name still is a by-word in Colorado. He
went to France during the World War and became General
Pershing's authority on international law. After the war, he
returned to Colorado, but not to stay. His Colorado days ended
with the 1913-1914 strike and he now practices law in the East.
His two assistants in the troublous strike days, Captain W. C.
Danks and Philip S. Van Cise, have retained the respect of all
groups in Colorado. Both saw World War service and both are
active in Colorado affairs today. Danks has been a member of
the Colorado Public Utilities Commission and has held a number
of other public posts, while Van Cise is a successful lawyer in
Denver. In addition, Van Cise has to his credit a brilliant record
as district attorney in Denver.

A. C. Felts, the Baldwin-Felts gunman, went back to West
Virginia and pursued his vocation of breaking strikes. He died
in action while attending to business. His boon companion,
Walter Belk, stayed on with the agency in Colorado until the
Fall of 1931 when his health failed. He went to Bluefield, West
Virginia, the headquarters of the agency, and a short time later
retired. He purchased a farm at Monroe, North Carolina, his
birthplace, and turned it into a resort.

Lieut. K. E. Linderfelt still is anathema to the union men of
Colorado. He too, went to France with the rank of colonel.
When the cavalry was broken up, he was assigned to the 159th

Infantry with which he served throughout the conflict. After the Armistice, he returned to the West and lived for a time in Oklahoma. Always the soldier of fortune, he was chronically broke. In recent years he has made his home in San Diego, Calif. Colonel Patrick Hamrock was another militia officer who served in France. He died in Denver in 1939. General Chase, too, is dead. Of the militia officers who were active in strikes prior to 1913-1914 few remain. The swaggering Sherman Bell, the adjutant general who wore the $1,000 uniform, passed away in January, 1942, in Fitzsimons General Hospital, a federal institution on the outskirts of Denver.

Frank Gove, the operators' spokesman and attorney, is dead. Judge Greeley Whitford, Ed Doyle's "old injunction Whitford," served a term on the Colorado Supreme bench, a single term from 1921 to 1931. The people of Colorado relegated him to private life in 1932 after he had injudiciously referred to a popular governor, W. H. Adams, as "an old buzzard." Judge Whitford died in May, 1940.

That other judge of strike days was less fortunate. Granby Hillyer, the man selected by the coal operators to preside in strike cases, served for a time as U. S. Attorney in Denver and then retired to a cubbyhole office. Long after strike days, he was disbarred by the Colorado Supreme Court for his handling of a private case. He was reinstated later with Attorney Hawkins' aid, but he lived in political and legal obscurity until his death in January, 1942.

Judge Northcutt retired as C. F. & I. Co. counsel years ago and alternated his declining years between California and Colorado. His marked abilities might have been at the disposal of the coal miners instead of the companies in 1913-1914, but the union decided his corporation ties were too close. Filled with nostalgia, he went to Trinidad early in 1942, spent his days on the streets shaking hands with old friends—and old foes—a kindly old gentleman who was forgiven much. He died April 10, 1942.

One of Northcutt's newspaper friends of strike days, Ned

Cowdrick, who was sent by the Associated Press from Denver to Trinidad to cover the 1913-1914 conflict, enjoyed the same type of promotion as that received by Attorney General Farrar after the strike. The Associated Press made an investigation of charges that its strike reports were biased, and that all dispatches sent out of Trinidad were first submitted to Judge Northcutt for his approval. On completion of the investigation, the Associated Press cleaned out its Denver bureau, discharging the manager, Clyde O. Hoober, and Cowdrick among others. Cowdrick then became executive assistant to the Colorado Fuel & Iron Company's president, Welborn, and subsequently was advanced to a position with the Standard Oil Co., another Rockefeller enterprise.

Louis Zancanelli lives in Wyoming, a stalwart coal miner as he was in the bloody days in Colorado.

Mother Jones went often to the labor wars after her Colorado experiences and in the end, before she died and was laid to rest in Mt. Olivet, Ill., she shook hands again with John D. Rockefeller, Jr. The newspapers made a great fuss about it, and moralized at great length.

Peace reigns in the coal fields of Colorado. Thousands of begrimed men still tramp along the narrow canons late each afternoon to their little homes. And below the canons, out on the wind-blown prairie, an imposing monument of granite, erected by the United Mine Workers of America, gleams in the last rays of the setting sun, a mute reminder of those who died at Ludlow that others might lift themselves out of the depths of poverty, industrial servitude and despair.

THE END

BIBLIOGRAPHY

MAJOR SOURCES:

An Answer to the Commanding General, United Mine Workers of America, Labor Journal Publishing Co., Cheyenne, Wyo.

Bureau of Labor Statistics, Colorado, 1903-1904, 1907-1908, 1909-1910, 1911-1912, and 1913-1914.

Conditions in the Coal Mines of Colorado, Hearings of the Subcommittee of the Committee on Mines and Mining, U. S. House of Representatives, Government Printing Office, 1914. Vols. I to XI.

Facts Concerning the Struggle in Colorado for Industrial Freedom, series issued by the coal mine managers.

Fink, Walter J., The Ludlow Massacre, 1914.

Military Occupation of the Coal Strike Zone by the Colorado National Guard During 1913-1914, Report of the Commanding General.

Report of Colorado Labor Investigating Committee to Gov. Elias M. Ammons.

State of Colorado, County of Las Animas, In the District Court, No. 6949, Memorandum Brief of John Lawson, et al.

United States Commission on Industrial Relations, Vols. VII, VIII and IX, and Report on the Colorado Strike by George P. West, Washington, D.C., 1915.

MINOR SOURCES:

Jones, Mary., Autobiography of Mother Jones; Charles H. Kerr & Co., Chicago, Ill.

Langdon, Emma., The Cripple Creek Strike.

Lawson, John, Abstract of Record in the Colorado Supreme Court, No. 8730.

Militarism in Colorado, Colorado Federation of Labor Report, 1914.

Selekman and Van Kleeck, Employes' Representation in Coal Mines, Russell Sage Foundation, New York, 1924.

Sinclair, Upton, King Coal.

Van Kleeck, Mary, Miners and Mine Management.

MAJOR INTERVIEWS:

    Casey, Lee Taylor, Denver, Colorado.
    Doyle, Edward, Denver, Colorado.
    Hawkins, Horace N., Denver, Colorado.
    Keating, Edward, Washington, D. C.
    Lawson, John R., Denver, Colorado.
    Van Cise, Col. Philip, Denver, Colorado.

PERIODICALS:

    Coal Mining Review, Columbus, Ohio.
    Colliers, 1915.
    Harper's Weekly, 1914 and 1915.
    International Socialist Review, Aug., 1915.
    Masses, 1915.
    Metropolitan, 1914, 1916, and 1917.
    The FRA, A Journal of Affirmation, Aug., 1914.
    The Miners Magazine, Western Federation of Miners, June, 1913.
    United Mine Workers Journal, 1914 and 1915.

NEWSPAPERS:

    Advertiser, Trinidad, Colo., 1915.
    Boulder County Miner, Boulder, Colo., 1915.
    Boulder Daily Camera, Boulder, Colo., 1914.
    Chronicle-News, Trinidad, Colo., 1913, 1914, 1915, and 1916.
    Colorado Labor Advocate, Denver, Colo., July 15, 1926.
    Daily Free Press, Trinidad, Colo., 1914, 1915, 1916, and 1917.
    Denver Express, Denver, Colo., 1913, 1914, and 1915.
    Denver Post, Denver, Colo., 1911, 1912, 1913, 1914, and 1915.
    Denver Republican, Denver, Colo., 1912 and 1913.
    Denver Times, Denver, Colo., 1913, 1914 and 1915.
    Headlight, Pittsburgh, Kan., 1918.
    Herald-Democrat, Leadville, Colo., 1917.
    Independent, Walsenburg, Colo., 1918.
    Labor Press, Pueblo, Colo., 1914.
    Milwaukee Leader, Milwaukee, Wis., July, 1915.
    Minnesota Union Advocate, July, 1915.
    Mount Carmel Item, Mount Carmel, Pa., September, 1915.
    New York Call, New York City, 1915.
    Non-Pariel, New Castle, Colo., 1904.
    Rocky Mountain News, Denver, Colo., 1911, 1912, 1913, 1914, 1915, 1916.
    Rocky Mountain Sentinel, Denver, Colo., 1914.
    Sun, Pittsburgh, Kan., 1918.